A ZEN ROMANCE

A ZEN ROMANCE

One Woman's Adventures in a Monastery

DEBORAH BOLIVER BOEHM

KODANSHA INTERNATIONAL
Tokyo • New York • London

NOTE TO THE READER:

Japanese names are written in the Western style: given name first, family name last. Macrons on Japanese words and proper names (e.g., Sōdō, Totsuō) are omitted.

This is a true story, but the names of all characters except the narrator have been changed to protect their privacy. The featured temple, too, has been given a fictitious name, although the book contains abundant clues to its identity and location.

To avoid confusion, the term "*sanzen*" is used to indicate any audience with a Zen master, although in many cases it would be more precise to use "*dokusan*."

Distributed in the United States by Kodansha America, Inc.,
114 Fifth Avenue, New York, N.Y. 10011,
and in the United Kingdom and continental
Europe by Kodansha Europe Ltd.,
95 Aldwych, London WC2B 4JF.
Published by Kodansha International Ltd.,
17-14 Otowa 1-chome, Bunkyo-ku Tokyo 112,
and Kodansha America, Inc.

97 98 99   10 9 8 7 6 5 4 3 2 1

Library of Congress CIP data available

ISBN 4-7700-2177-1

TABLE OF CONTENTS

Let us dream of evanescence, and linger
in the beautiful foolishness of things.

Okakura Kakuzo
The Book of Tea

PROLOGUE

✛

MY DEVADASI DREAM
(A Flash-Forward)

I t was half past the Hour of the Tiger when I knocked on the door of the monastery of Zenzenji Temple in Kyoto. After a few moments the door slid open and there stood Zan-san, one of the senior monks, wearing a gray wraparound jacket, matching calf-length trousers, and his usual sardonic smile.

"Good morning," he said, as I stepped from the darkness of the rock garden into the *shoji*-screened entry hall, which was illuminated, dimly, by a Noguchi-shaded oil lamp in one corner. "Ohayo gozaimasu," I mumbled, looking down at my feet. I couldn't bring myself to meet the monk's radiant sepia gaze, for only twenty minutes earlier I had reluctantly awakened from a wonderfully tender erotic dream about him, and I still felt flushed, embarrassed, and tainted by worldly desire.

I had gone, in the dream, to Zan-san's narrow, austere room to ask some mundane procedural questions about O-Zesshin, a week-long session of manual labor, sleep deprivation, and intensive *zazen* meditation. I was the first foreigner ever to be permitted to participate in an O-Zesshin at Zenzenji, and I was determined to do everything in accordance with archaic Zen punctilios. As I was rambling on about self-doubt and mealtime etiquette, the monk suddenly took a step toward me and placed two warm fingers across my lips.

It was the first physical contact I had ever had with him, and I froze in surprise; I could have sworn that my heart stopped beating, my cells stopped dying, my lungs stopped processing air. I just stood there, mouth agape, staring into Zan-san's bottomless brown eyes as he grabbed me by the shoulders and kissed me strongly on the lips. My knees buckled under me, making us approximately the same height, and then, swept away by a *tsunami* of desire, I began to respond to the kiss like a temple harlot, or a woman of the world.

Within a few seconds we had left our feet and were lying intertwined on the bare *tatami* mat with its vague sweet smell of sun-warmed hay. Conveniently, if uncharacteristically, I was wearing no underwear, and Zan-san's trousers had magically dematerialized, although he still wore his kimono-style jacket. The rough homespun cloth rubbed against my skin, sanding me smooth; he never took his mouth from mine, and we fed on each other like cannibals in love. As I breathed the monk's intoxicating aura (incense, sweat, impossibility), I could feel myself becoming languid and glutinous, like some passionate sea creature stripped of its shell. "Ah," I sighed. "Ahhh," echoed Zan-san, and I thought that was the most profound conversation I had ever had with another human being.

At the end we lay slack-limbed on the floor, our bodies stuck together like caramel apples, our eyes closed with shyness and bliss, and I knew that I had never felt so miraculously whole, so ridiculously happy, or so completely filled with love.

Suddenly the euphoric tranquility was shattered by a noisy beep-beep-beep, like a smoke alarm or a truck backing up in a narrow alley. I opened one eye and saw that the sound was coming from a large, black, complicated-looking diver's watch on Zan-san's wrist. That's odd, I thought, he wasn't wearing a watch before, and then I woke up.

Of course it wasn't Zan-san's watch that was beeping; it was my raucous green alarm clock. The clock was set for three a.m., and its clangorous eruption brought me abruptly back to consciousness, to a world in which my dream-lover was an aloof, intimidating, and presumably celibate monk, and I was, to the best of my recollection, still a virgin. My first thought upon awakening was, Oh no, it was just a dream, but the initial disappointment was soon overshadowed by relief that I hadn't actually committed such a flagrant indiscretion in the halls of perfect holiness.

As I recalled the steamy, acrobatic details, though, I began to feel increasingly guilty and sinful. I couldn't help wondering, also, how a supposedly virginal mind could produce such a vividly-textured sex scene. Had I tapped into the adults-only section of the collective unconscious, or was it the subliminal legacy of reading too many racy novels too close to bedtime?

I dressed quickly in the cool early-summer dark, in my chosen uniform of that week: a long blue antique silk skirt, a boat-necked rayon jersey in a darker blue, and a black satin kimono jacket hand-painted more than fifty years before with violet, mauve, and indigo flowers that looked as if they had just bloomed that morning. As an afterthought, for symbolic insulation, or penance, I put on an extra pair of underpants.

It was still the black of night rather than the darkness before the dawn as I walked through the silent temple grounds to the monastery; I was living in a tiny room in a small sub-temple next door, so it was a journey of perhaps a hundred steps. I felt even more nervous than usual about entering the Sodo (monastery) that morning, but I took a deep breath and ducked through the low Alice-in-Wonderland door next to the massive main gate.

Many times in my travels I had wandered through the grounds of exquisite, inscrutable temples, and had fantasized about what might lie beyond a weathered wooden gate or a crumbling saffron-colored wall. The Sodo was enclosed by just such a wall, and I always entered the monastery with a feeling of amazement that this time-warp oasis was really a part of my life. It seemed astonishing that the monks behind the ancient gate were expecting me; that my purple *zabuton* cushion was waiting in the great meditation hall; that a place was laid for me at breakfast; and that I was, if not universally welcome, at least cheerfully tolerated here in the all-male abbey of one of the oldest Zen temples in Kyoto. For in that euphoric, excruciating summer of 1970, the Zenzenji Sodo seemed to me to be the most intriguing, the most mysterious, and the most desirable place in the world.

FOUR ON THE FLOOR

The perversions of pop-Zen . . .

Arthur Koestler
The Ghost in the Machine

—VERMONT/MASSACHUSETTS

When I got on a Tokyo-bound plane at Logan Airport in the spring of 1968, I took with me a vaguely negative impression of Zen Buddhism. My initial introduction to Zen had been felicitous enough; a fellow student at Goddard College in Vermont lent me a book called *Zen Flesh, Zen Bones* by Paul Reps. I enjoyed the paradoxical parables, and I especially liked the anecdotes about Eisai, who was, according to legend, the monk who first brought green tea to Japan from China. Little did I dream that within two years I would be living in the very temple of which Eisai, in his lively caffeine-fueled dotage, had been the head priest.

It was obvious to me that *Zen Flesh, Zen Bones* contained some profound existential insights, but I couldn't figure out how to integrate them into my skewed, unfocused existence at Goddard. I had been similarly confused by reading the *Tao Te Ching*; it seemed to prescribe a serene vacuum of inactivity bordering on catatonia, and I was surprised to learn later that Lao-Tzu, the author, had been a nine-to-five Chinese bureaucrat. I sometimes mused, during those vertiginous times, that the covers of certain books should have been emblazoned with a cautionary cerebellum-and-crossbones and the warning: DANGER! NOT TO BE TAKEN LITERALLY!

There were a number of self-styled "Zen freaks" floating around the campus clutching the obligatory copy of *Earth House Hold* and reeking of what I've since come to think of as Eau de Sixties Crash Pad: a fetid compound of neglected laundry, patchouli, hash oil, and long, fermenting hair. Although Zen—both the curiously euphonic word and the enigmatic concept—seemed rather engaging, I couldn't help noticing that most of its disciples at Goddard were smug, humorless, and often incoherent.

The person who lent me the Reps book was not an official Zen Freak at all, just a tall, dark, laconic ex-Marine who was an omnivorous reader and secret writer. He once came to my dormitory room, uninvited but not unwelcomed, and stared at me in silence for over an hour while I worked on a Rapidograph drawing of a beatific blue-scaled dragon. I didn't notice that my visitor had stood up to leave until he paused at the door, and spoke at last. "You have brown hair," he said, and then he was gone. Was *that* Zen? I wasn't sure, but that breathless, mystifying moment has remained frozen in my mind, fossilized forever in the amber of romantic memory.

My second encounter with Zen, American-style, came one chilly fall evening in Cambridge, Massachusetts. I had hitchhiked down for the weekend with two friends from Goddard. One was a woman named Ursula whom I considered my spiritual Doppelgänger, for we both had wild, voluminous hair and opinions to match, and we shared a passion for soul music, metaphysical fiction, and wit in any form. (Some of our cultural icons that year were Edith Piaf, Jorge Luis Borges, Edward Gorey, Cyril Connolly, Nigel Molesworth, and James and Bobby Purify.) My other fellow-traveler was Corin, a London-born painter of possums and roses who looked uncannily like Oscar Wilde, talked like Terry-Thomas with tonsillitis, and was a fey and hilarious companion.

In classic sixties style, we had invited ourselves to sleep on the floor of the apartment of an old friend of mine named Henry who lived on Bigelow Street, near Central Square. We arrived late on Friday afternoon, and that evening the usual Fugs, John Fahey, and Archie Shepp records were played; the usual illicit substances went up in smoke; the usual Hostess Cupcakes and Morton's frozen pies were consumed, for this was long before the advent of health-food consciousness raising; and the usual long smoky silences were punctuated by elliptical dialogues and sudden eruptions of solipsistic laughter.

Among the guests sitting around on the floor by candlelight was a short-haired, clean-shaven, spiffily-dressed Harvard freshman (by counterculture standards, a total weirdo) who declared, repeatedly and without being asked, that he was very much "into Zen." I remember arguing with him about every abstruse philosophical point he tried to make—not so much because I disagreed, but because I couldn't bear his pompous, egotistical, hipper-than-thou attitude. Around one a.m. the conversation, such as it was, finally faded out; the candles flickered low in rainbow puddles of wax; Henry and his fleshy consort went into their bedroom and closed the door; and those guests who were too tired, too stoned, or too gauche to go home curled up on the several moldy pallets that were the living room's major furnishings, wrapped themselves in the omnipresent India-print bedspreads, and fell into restless, intoxicated dreams.

My two Goddard friends and I were quickly outshuffled in this game of musical mattresses, and since the kitchen was overrun with hyperkinetic, un-housebroken kittens, we had no choice but to sleep in the bathroom. That wasn't as bad as it sounds, for the lavatory was actually the coziest and most attractive room in the apartment, if you could ignore the incessant rumble of the ancient plumbing. Henry, who was an artist (Boston Museum School via RISD), had lacquered the walls with glossy black enamel and then adorned them with twenty or thirty small oddly-shaped antique mirrors with silver-painted frames. The room was illuminated with the official light of the sixties, a bare red bulb: sixty (what else) watts of pure transcendent grooviness. "Oh, far out," everyone said, and there *was* something extra-spatial about the luminous black walls and the red bordello-light reflected in and out of all the strange old mirrors with their lumpy quicksilver frames.

Corin and Ursula and I curled up under a composite blanket made up of two raccoon coats and one Navy pea jacket (this was before the advent of animal-rights awareness, too), and eventually my two companions fell asleep. Three companions, actually, if you include Thelonius, the little wheat-colored dog who burrowed in with us after being dispossessed from his usual bed in the kitchen by the frenetic kittens. As a child of the sixties, I was quite accustomed to camping out on cold, unyielding floors, but for some reason I couldn't get to sleep. It must have been around three a.m.—the Hour of the Tiger again—when I heard the door open, and saw the red light go on. Obviously someone wanted to use the bathroom for its intended purpose, and we were in the way.

I was struggling to extricate myself from the tangle of coats that covered us completely, heads and all, when I heard a shriek from the direction of the bathroom door. After another moment of thrashing, I managed to emerge from the musty pile of raccoon pelts, just in time to hear the door of the apartment slam. Henry's apartment was a third-floor walk-up, so I went to the living room window and peered down at the street. Seconds later, the glass-paned front door of the building rattled shut, and the Harvard know-it-all came charging out and ran screaming down the street. For some reason, this bizarre sight was very soothing to my soul; I went back to the red-lit bathroom, climbed into the humid nest of wool and fur, and slept like a baby raccoon.

The next morning I figured out that the drowsy, drug-dazed Zen scholar must have fled in genuine terror, thinking that the headless heap of fur he saw writhing on the bathroom floor was the larva of some rough unfriendly beast slouching toward the bathtub to be born. Soon after that encounter, I concluded that Zen Buddhism was an esoteric Eastern religion which seemed to appeal mainly to the more fatuous of my peers, and that I would be happy never to hear another word about it.

It was about a year later that I found myself on a Pan Am 707 headed for Japan, where I was planning to stay with relatives in Tokyo and attend a Japanese university. The plane stopped at Anchorage Airport to refuel, and while I was looking at a departure-lounge exhibit of paintings by Alaskan schoolchildren (frozen albino landscapes, moose-groupings, self-portraits with rosy nose and snowshoes), an unnaturally wholesome-looking fellow passenger came up to me. "Hi there," he said, in a flat, uninflected Midwest-cornfield voice.

"Hello," I said warily. With his crew cut, white shirt, and black tie, the young man looked suspiciously like one of those earnest door-to-door salesmen of salvation who pedal energetically around the major metropolises of the world on bicycles, their pale blue eyes agleam with ethnocentric missionary fervor. He looked me up and down with a knowing smirk on his pudgy choirboy's face.

Although I hadn't smoked pot since that surreal night on Bigelow Street, the image I projected was still more Red Lightbulb than Young Republican. My hair had grown past my waist, and I was wearing a black turtleneck sweater, a short black wool skirt, purple tights, the long thundercloud-gray suede boots I had bought in Florence, a purple beret (crocheted by my mother), and extra-large, extra-dark sunglasses.

"Hmm," said the missionary clone, with an air of self-satisfied omni-science. "I'll bet you're going to Japan to study Zen."

"On the contrary," I replied triumphantly. "I'm going to Japan to get away from Zen!"

WILD WOMEN
DON'T GET THE BLUES

Evening of fugitive spring
How lively the sutra
Chanted by that insane girl
Under the wisteria

Yosano Akiko
Tangled Hair

—KYOTO

"I think you'll like Toozie," Karen McKie was saying as we walked through the grounds of an ancient temple in one of the traditional geisha-districts of Kyoto, on our way to a late-afternoon tea party. "She's kind of slovenly, and kind of fat, and kind of foulmouthed, but she's also very funny and talented, and she has a really good heart." Karen had told me that Toozie Zane, a fellow potter's apprentice from San Francisco, rented a small room in a Zen temple. That struck me as terribly romantic, and I was eager to meet this "fat, funny, foul-mouthed" person.

I had arrived in Kyoto two days before from the so-called dark side of Japan, Shimane Prefecture, where my summer pilgrimage to Lafcadio Hearn's old hangouts had been cut short by a bizarre free-diving accident: a sea urchin had stung me in the eye. The discomfort was almost unendurable and, nursing fears of permanent blindness, I rushed back to the relative familiarity of Kyoto, where an elderly Japanese ophthalmologist kindly opened his office on a Sunday afternoon to remove the stinger from my retina. I would not otherwise have ended up in Kyoto that summer, and I realized in retrospect that once again the hand of

Fate had chosen to communicate through a code of pain.

I was staying at the student dormitory where Karen lived with her boyfriend Tatsuya, a Japanese law student, but the person whose room I had borrowed was expected to return the following day, so I was in imminent need of another place to stay. "We'll ask Toozie," Karen said. "She always has lots of ideas about everything." Karen was a good friend, if not an old one. I had met her at an expatriate party in Tokyo about a year before, and by the time she went off to Kyoto to study ceramics with a famous traditional potter, we had shared so many side-street adventures and late-night confessionals that it seemed as if we had known each other since nursery school.

"*Gomen kudasai*," Karen called out as we slid open the tall wood-and-paper door and stepped into the *genkan* (entry hall) of the vaguely shabby temple-within-a-temple. "Is anybody home?" Ahead of us was a wide tatami-matted hall. Along the right side were several sliding doors; across the back was a large screen painted with a flock of iridescent peacocks in full plume; and on the left side, closest to us, was a single sliding door with a diagonal overlay of slightly tattered paper patterned with maple leaves. To the right of this door was a recessed altar filled with an assortment of fascinating and unfamiliar objects. I only had time to register a few fleeting impressions—a black lacquer chest with gilded hinges, a little pyramid of mandarin oranges, a wooden bell in the shape of a fish, the slightly dizzying smell of recently-burned incense—before my sensory inventory was interrupted by the sound of the door to our left sliding open.

"Welcome to Hotel Satori!" said a raucous voice, and there stood Zabriskie Zane, better known as Toozie. She was wearing an oversized blue chambray workshirt with purple paint stains on the front, button-fly blue jeans spattered with dried clay, and a red "Janis Joplin Fan Club" baseball cap. Her long, stringy hair, which didn't appear to have been recently washed or combed, straggled out from beneath the cap. She was 5'7" and she weighed at least 160 pounds, but she seemed to be completely and unapologetically at ease with her large body. What struck me most about Toozie Zane, that first day, was her remarkably clear, opalescent gray eyes. There was nothing slovenly about those eyes.

"Glad you could come along; the more the merrier!" Toozie said after Karen had introduced us. "Come on in—it may be tiny, but at least it's messy!" Toozie's room consisted of three and a half tatami mats, which translates roughly into dimensions of six by eight feet—the size of a walk-in closet, or of some sybaritic bachelor's custom-made waterbed. "Tiny" was putting it mildly, and "messy" may have been the understatement of the decade. There was a low table covered with an assortment of plates and dishes, encrusted with the colorful remains of what appeared to have been a seven or eight-course lunch, or the previous night's dinner. A well-worn futon, which had not yet been folded and placed on its shelf in the built-in closet, took up almost half the floor space, and there were clothes, books, magazines, folded matchbook covers, ashtrays, dirty clothes, candy wrappers, and pottery tools strewn all over the place.

"I'm sorry," Toozie was saying. "I've been so goddamn busy this week that I haven't had time to clean up this fucking rathole." (Aha, I thought, there's 'foul-mouthed'!)

"Let us help," Karen said, and she began to stack the dirty dishes on a bamboo tray, while I folded the futon and put it on the shelf. It seemed a bit like instant intimacy to be handling the grungy bedding of someone I had just met three minutes earlier, but Toozie seemed grateful for the help.

"Thanks, guys," she said, picking up armfuls of books, clothes, and papers, and tossing them in the closet. "Just let me move some of this shit so we can sit down." Within five minutes most of the debris had been cleared away, and the room that emerged from the chaos, while still undeniably diminutive, began to look quite pleasant.

We sat on indigo zabuton around the little low table, which was covered with a piece of hand-woven blue-and-white *kasuri* cloth. Toozie brewed some fragrant tea in a bamboo-handled pot and served it in pretty little white-glazed cups she had made herself.

Karen and I had stopped on the way at a Japanese-style sweet shop next to Minami-za, the Kyoto Kabuki Theater, to buy their famous specialty, sticky rice-flour cakes shaped like bow ties, in three soft colors: green, (flavored with powdered green tea); brown (cinnamon); and white (pure *mochi* flavor, for which there exists no gastronomic analogy, although some would argue that "Oriental library paste" or "orthodontic-mold plaster" come close). We arranged these treats on an oblong black-glazed plate, along with some remarkable confections which Toozie produced from a package wrapped in pink paper: hollowed-out sections of golden bamboo, filled with mashed, sweetened adzuki beans. "This all looks too artistic to eat," remarked Karen, whereupon we proceeded to devour everything on the plate.

Several cups of jasmine tea later, Toozie was telling a long story about the "far-out dude" she had picked up on her motorcycle (a rakish black BMW 1000) one rainy afternoon the week before. He was a studio drummer from Los Angeles, and apparently it was a case of love (or more probably, as Toozie cheerfully admitted, of lust) at first sight, for after a quick cup of coffee they had gone back to the small inn where he was staying and made experimental music together—all day, as the Kinks used to sing, and into the night.

Toozie shared the most graphic details in a droll, matter-of-fact way. "This guy was a totally magnificent specimen," she said at one point. "I mean, the next day I thought I was coming down with strep and then I realized that my throat was just sore. Now I know why they call it 'horsing around'!" I tried not to look too shocked, and Karen said, "Hey, Tooz, don't you know love means never having to say you're sore?" Toozie hooted with delight at this uncharacteristically risqué comment from Karen, who, in spite of her extensive experience with men, always managed to project an image of innocence and naïveté.

Toozie's story of rainy-day instant gratification sent my mind fishtailing off into a familiar romantic reverie, which ran along the wistful lines of "I wonder what I'm missing, besides risk of disease and unwanted pregnancy, by not being sexually active?" True, I had spent several decidedly un-Platonic nights with assorted "soulmates" in recent years, but I had waited so long, and had struggled so hard to resist the desperate pleas and Greco-Roman wrestling moves of so many would-be first lovers, that the idea of relinquishing my virginity had become a major issue in my mind. Although I was raised in a liberal Unitarian/Adlai-Stevenson-Democrat household, somewhere along the way I had decided that birth control was unnatural, and that you should not have sex with anyone unless you would be happy to bear his child if a pregnancy were to result from the union. This atavistic (some said priggish) attitude pretty much ruled out a sporting approach to physical relationships, but it didn't keep me from engaging in passionate romances, or from spending a great deal of time pondering the mysteries of sexual conjugation.

Since that particular daydream always caused my eyes to glaze over, I must have levitated several inches when Toozie suddenly turned to me and said in her hearty voice, "You've been awfully quiet, Deborah. Come on, it's your turn—show and tell!"

"Okay," I said reluctantly, racking my brain for a suitably romantic anecdote. "Well, three or four years ago I was riding on the London subway."

"The Tube," Toozie interpolated knowingly.

"Anyway," I continued, "it was very crowded, and I had to stand. At one stop—I think it was Bayswater—a young man got on and grabbed the strap next to mine. He had long blond hair and a pale feline face and he wore a suit of rose-colored silk over a black leotard, and he had on sunglasses, and a necklace of cloisonné dragon-beads, and ten thin ivory bangle bracelets—five on each arm.

"This man struck up a conversation about the book I was holding—I think it was *The Crock of Gold*—and I wasn't surprised to learn that he was a ballet dancer, because he moved with such extraordinary grace and fluidity. 'Do you like the ballet?' he asked. 'Oh, yes!' I said. 'And I absolutely love Nureyev.' The blond man took off his sunglasses and looked at me with his amazing golden owl-eyes. 'Of course you do,' he said slowly. 'But would you love him if he wasn't beautiful?' Just then the pneumatic doors whooshed open and the dancer was gone, with a sibylline smile and an ivory wave. But the question he asked will echo in my mind, forever."

"Wow," said Karen.

"Far out," said Toozie. (In the late sixties, that was the equivalent of a standing ovation.) Later, as Toozie was enthusing about a phallic-cult shrine festival she wanted to take us to later in the week, I mentioned my housing problem. "You're welcome to crash here," she said.

"In this room?" said Karen, looking around with a dubious frown.

"Sure, why not?" said Toozie. "I've had guests before and it was no problem. I have extra futon, and I enjoy having company."

"But you hardly know me!" I said.

"That's okay; any friend of Karen's, and all that jazz. Besides, I'm a great judge of character, and I'm sure we'll get along. You don't snore, do you?"

"Not as far as I know," I said. Oh my God, I thought, what if I have bagpipe sinuses, and no one ever told me?

"Okay, then, it's settled," said Toozie. "You can bring your stuff over anytime tomorrow—if I'm not here just rent a bulldozer and make yourself at home."

"This really is unbelievably kind of you," I said. "You'll have to come stay with me in Tokyo sometime, as soon as I find a place." I had been staying with my older sister and her Slovenian husband, but they had returned to Europe in June. Thanks to my policy of non-acquisition, I was able to stuff all my belongings into two suitcases, out of which I had been living, in low-rent inns in picturesque places, while I traveled around Japan on my summer break from school in Tokyo.

"It's a deal," said Toozie. "I'll bring the grass and the Snickers bars." It didn't seem like an appropriate time to mention that my drug-experimentation phase was long behind me, so I just smiled. "By the way," I said, "what's the name of this temple in case I get lost tomorrow?

"It's called Zenzenji." "Zenzenji," I repeated. "I think I can remember that." Karen and I finally left around seven o'clock; we would gladly have stayed longer, but Toozie had to get cleaned up for a "hot date" with a French merchant seaman whose ship was sailing from Kobe the next morning. The temple grounds were eerily beautiful in the bruised light of early evening, and I marveled at the subtle gardens, the effulgent white buildings with bell-shaped windows, the great tiled roofs with the sweep of a Hokusai wave. The stone paths were lit by pole-lamps with the soft phosphorescence of bottled moonlight, and as we strolled along I couldn't help feeling that the travel gods had been very kind to me this time around.

I was certain that getting to know Toozie would be an adventure, a vicarious spin through the exotic realms of loose talk, casual sex, and no regrets. Beyond that, I was completely captivated by the Zenzenji compound, with its air of recondite serenity, and as I trod those ancient paths I felt like a very small tadpole tossed into the deep well of the unknown.

It was a bit of a shock to emerge from the tranquil grounds of the temple directly onto a slanting street of purple neon and medieval-turreted love hotels, but Karen and I managed to convince ourselves that this odd juxtaposition of architectures and moral philosophies was just another facet of the ever-surprising paradox of Japan. There seemed to be a theatrical floating-world aura about the street, and about the entire city, on that hazy summer night. *Wild contrasts*, I wrote in my journal, *but no disharmony.*

We stopped to eat rice-and-seaweed soup at a small restaurant whose round-cheeked proprietress—perhaps sensing that we, too, would for-

24

ever be aliens in this most insular and bloodline-conscious of countries—sighed with nostalgia for her childhood on the sere and windy steppes of Mongolia. Her lovely solemn daughter stood behind the counter in a Chinese singing-girl dress of turquoise satin, silent the entire time, folding squares of silver paper into perfect origami cranes.

THE DECADENT SONG
OF CICADAS

The West moistens everything with meaning.

Roland Barthes
The Empire of Signs

—KYOTO

It was the day after the mad potter's tea party; I had just moved my things into Toozie's tiny room, and I was walking alone down the broad cobblestone slope that ran alongside the crumbling tile-topped wall of the Zenzenji Sodo. The sky was a pale, faded-denim blue, the sun was hot overhead, the stones were hot underfoot, and the temple grounds seemed to have been gilded with shades of buff and sand and saffron. Suddenly, a cool flash of polar-bear white shot across the monochromatic landscape and came rushing toward me.

It was a little hybrid-husky dog with amber eyes and fluffy fur, and as I bent down to stroke its fine, soft coat a shadow fell over us. I looked up and saw a monk looking down at me. He was very short and very stocky, and he was wearing wooden *geta* clogs and a calf-length, full-skirted *koromo*, or monk's robe, of patched blue cotton. There was a wry, speculative smile on his rather old-fashioned–looking face with its high pale brows, elongated eyes, full cheeks, a nose so small and well-crafted that it reminded me of a *netsuke*, and tiny shallow ears like fava beans.

"Konnichi wa," said the monk, in a gruff but not unfriendly voice.

"Good afternoon," I replied. We introduced ourselves, and he said that his name was Toku. Toku-san nodded knowingly when I explained who I was, as if he had heard that yet another *hen na gaijin* (strange foreigner) had come to disrupt the serenity of the temple. I couldn't imagine a group of monks discussing anything so mundane, for I was certain that their conversation must consist exclusively of significant silences punctuated by deeply metaphysical dialogues and the occasional therapeutic kick in the teeth.

"Is that 'Toku' as in 'Tokuto' [baldness]?" I asked, and immediately wished I could retract my silly, reckless joke.

"No," the monk replied in a neutral tone of voice, evidently neither amused nor annoyed. "It's 'Toku' as in 'Tokudo' [Buddhist salvation]." In Japanese, there can be many readings for the same word or syllable, due to the proliferation of homonymic (or, more often, heteronymic) sounds ascribed to the *kanji* characters originally borrowed from the Chinese language. This makes the study of Japanese confusing, frustrating, and infinitely beguiling.

"Naruhodo," I said, using the versatile Japanese word which can mean "Oh, I see," or "That makes sense," or "Now I get it"—a sort of miniature *satori*. "And your dog? What's his name?"

"Shiro," replied the monk. *Shiro* means white in Japanese.

"Naruhodo," I said again. I suddenly remembered a line I had read somewhere: "To the prosaic, everything is prosaic; but to the truly enlightened, everything is profound." It occurred to me that if an American cleric bought a black dog and named it Blackie, people might suspect him of having an impoverished imagination. But when a Zen monk names a white dog White, it is likely to be perceived as a manifestation of the subtle art of seeing things as they appear, and appreciating them for what they are.

After issuing a cordial invitation to come and visit the monastery anytime, Toku-san took his leave. I stood watching as he and the frisky Shiro continued up the stone walk to the Sodo gate, then vanished through the low door beside it. The gate was flanked by two antique wooden plaques; the rain-blurred calligraphy on one read "Professional Training Center" (Senmon Dojo) while the other proclaimed "The Gateless Barrier" (Mumonkan).

A monk named Salvation out walking his dog on a sun-bleached afternoon; clatter of wooden geta on ancient stones, slight smell of incense in the air, doves crooning languorously in the trees. It was an ordinary temple tableau, no doubt, but to me it was an exquisite epiphany: a perfect midsummer moment suspended like a spider on the web of time.

* * *

Journal entry, Kyoto, August 1969: *Wandering in and out of tiny shops filled with gourd flasks and tea-whisks, sachets and lanterns, wooden combs and handmade paper, I ran into a classmate from Tokyo whom I knew as Gerald Greenberg. "Hi, Gerald," I said. "Fancy meeting you here!" Gerald peered at me through an uncombed curtain of Yiddish dreadlocks.*

"I don't go by Gerald anymore," he said. "I've changed my name to Gwyddno." I suddenly remembered a whispered conversation we had had in the university library stacks, in which Gerald had told me that he thought he had a Welsh soul.

"So now you're Gwyddno Greenberg?" I asked.

"God, no," Gerald said (a bit patronizingly, I thought). "Gwyddno Garanhair. Haven't you read The White Goddess?*" I hadn't, then.*

"Anyway," I said brightly, "it certainly is a coincidence to see you here!" "There are no coincidences," Gwyddno intoned, and this time the condescension was unmistakable. "No accidents, no random acts, no chance encounters. So, shall we grab some coffee, or what?"

"I have to run," I said, and I ran.

No chance encounters: the perfect leitmotif phrase for this day. First, Toku-san, who strikes me as someone I would like to know forever. Then as I came charging around a corner I almost bumped into a tall, ectomorphic priest with elongated earlobes like the Buddha's, dressed in a splendid robe of royal purple satin trimmed with gold brocade. (As my cosmic classmate might say, "There are no collisions, only congruences.") The priest stopped and gave me an odd look of incredulity mixed with alarm, as if I were a ghost with a machine gun. Then a gardening monk with a kindly face and immense, statuesque ears (shaped like a pair of question marks, or two halves of a Valentine heart) paused, holding his rake like a trident, and bowed to me. Why am I noticing everyone's ears today? I think it's because when the head is shaved, the ears have nowhere to hide.

Finally, a no-accident encounter with a vision of the sort of woman I would like to become, someday. I was walking very slowly past the monastery gate, eavesdropping on the galvanizing sea-rhythms of indecipherable sutra chants, when I turned and saw a woman strolling by, face hidden behind a peony-patterned bamboo umbrella, slender body clad in plummy silk kimono (faint scent of cryptomeria sachet), tiny bare feet in wooden geta with black velvet straps. Slowly, the umbrella was lowered, and a lovely, intelligent, ageless Tale-of-Genji face looked at me, smiled a smile full of encouragement and wisdom, and vanished behind the peony parasol.

I wonder who she is, what she does, where she lives; and most of all, I wonder whether she attained her exquisite, angelic aura through the study of Zen. How could I ever have jeered at my fellow Americans for being smitten with Zen Buddhism? It strikes me now as the source of the most aesthetic, intriguing atmosphere I have ever seen, or heard, or breathed.

* * *

"Let's go check out the guys next door," Toozie said early one afternoon, several days after my initial encounter with Toku-san. She had come back to the temple for lunch, which was unusual since she usually ate with the other apprentices at the home of the potter, Kusabuka-sensei ("sensei" means teacher or master). Even more rare, she had the rest of the day off, for the potter had taken his wife and children to visit the graves of his parents at a temple up in the mountains.

"Seems like sort of a morbid picnic," Toozie had remarked as she plopped down at the table and peeled off her blue workshirt, revealing a tight, bulging, clay-spattered magenta T-shirt underneath. "But whatever—at least it means I have an afternoon free for once! I just have one errand to do around 2:30."

I cleared away my papers and pens and bottles of ink—I had been writing kanji in a gridded notebook—and went out into the alfresco hall, which overlooked a garden abloom with hollyhocks and morning glories, to fill the teakettle with fresh cold water. Meanwhile, Toozie began unwrapping the various packages she had brought. There was *kappa-maki* sushi (crisp cucumber and toasted sesame seeds on rice, wrapped in dark green *nori* seaweed) from the little sushi shop just outside the east gate of Zenzenji; there were two rectangular paper boxes of *yaki-soba*, buckwheat noodles sautéed with onions and carrots and cabbage, tossed with a thick sweetened sauce, and garnished with flamingo-pink pickled ginger and powdered seaweed; there were little English-garden-party sandwiches, thin-sliced tomato and cucumber on crustless white bread impastoed with mayonnaise; there were plump round *mikan* tangerines; and finally there were our favorite sweets, the green tea and cinnamon bowtie *mochi* from the shop beside the Minami-za Kabuki Theater.

"This really isn't fair," I said. "All I'm providing is the tea." At that moment the teapot, as if to emphasize the triviality of my contribution, began to shrill and spew steam toward the ceiling. I removed it from the single-burner hot plate and poured the boiling water into a large brass teapot which I had filled with a combination of green tea leaves and roasted barley. "No problem," said Toozie, popping an entire roll of kappa-maki into her mouth. "You're responsible for dinner!"

An hour later, after we had eaten everything in sight and (at my insistence) had cleaned up the mess, Toozie put on a fresh workshirt, and I forced my uncooperative hair into a braid. Then we walked around the corner and crept through the small door next to the wide gate of the monastery, which was almost always barricaded with a vertical shaft of bamboo. I had peeked through that gate every time I passed by, marveling at the perfectly-groomed white gravel garden, the shapely trees, and the graceful buildings that lay beyond, and I was thrilled to be entering the mysterious world of a Zen monastery for the first time.

The genkan was cool and shadowy, and there wasn't a soul in sight. "Gomen kudasai," Toozie called out, in her confident, American-accented Japanese.

"Hai!" came the response: a reverberant male voice from deep in the maze of dark wood and pristine shoji screens. There was the sound of footsteps, bare feet slapping against polished wood, and then a monk appeared on the landing above us. For a moment I thought someone had turned on a light, but then I realized that the glow was purely human: an incandescent combination of golden skin, a shining shaved head, an aura of joyful repose, and a hugely amused smile of welcome.

I smiled back—there was nothing else to do—and out of the corner of my eye I could see that Toozie, too, was grinning uncontrollably. The monk listened patiently as Toozie tried to explain that we were living next door and had stopped by at Toku-san's invitation. Occasionally, when her syntax became particularly tortuous, the monk's smile would fade for a moment, and his beautiful, luminous face would take on a puzzled expression, but then he would decipher the meaning ("Ah! You have come to visit Toku-san!") and once again that supernatural smile would light up the entryway.

I stood by in silence, not wanting to cause Toozie to lose face by interrupting or by correcting her atrocious grammar. I didn't feel superior in the least; on the contrary, I sometimes envied the anarchic, unself-conscious abandon with which she spoke the language. "I should have let you do the talking," Toozie said later. "My Japanese really sucks duck eggs."

"No, no," I protested, and I meant it. "You do amazingly well for someone with no formal training."

The radiant monk told us that his name was Zo and said that he had seen both of us from a distance, and was happy to meet us at last. Then he motioned for us to remove our shoes and follow him down the hall. Toozie was wearing motorcycle boots and I was wearing hand-made gladiator sandals from the Harvard Square leather shop; we took them off and left them with the toes pointing toward the gate, ready to hop into for a quick getaway. Then we stepped up onto a platform of cool stone, and from there onto the polished worn-wood floor of the hallway. Silently, Zo-san led the zigzag way down an open-air hall; always keeping the increasingly verdant garden on our right, while a succession of screened-off rooms slid by on our left.

Finally, five or six sharp turns and what seemed like about a thousand yards later, Zo-san stopped in front of a closed door and said in a low voice, "Excuse me, you have some visitors." He did not use the word "gaijin" (foreigners), which I thought was very tactful, but he must have indicated it somehow by his tone, for there was no surprise at all, only undisguised pleasure, on Toku-san's broad face when he slid open the door.

"Welcome, welcome," he said, beckoning us into the room. He had been sitting at a low wooden table with two other monks, but they quickly bowed and took their leave, exiting through the sliding doors on the other side of the room. As the monks left, I caught a glimpse of a terra-cotta courtyard and a bright green stand of iris shoots beyond the railings of the outdoor corridor.

Zo-san excused himself, too, saying that he had some business to take care of. "Zo-san speaks English fluently, you know," Toku-san said. He was dressed in a V-necked white undershirt and knee-length white cotton trousers, and he looked even sturdier than he had in his gorgeous blue koromo.

We all sat down at the table, and after a few minutes a moon-faced young monk with several livid clots of blueberry-colored bruises on his calves appeared at the door. He was carrying a tray with three covered teacups containing fine-leafed *sencha* tea, and three little bamboo dishes, each with a single slice of delicately translucent *aoyanagi yokan* ("Blue Willow" bean jelly), and a tiny bamboo fork to eat it with. Toku-san ate his *yokan* in one manly, gargantuan gulp, while Toozie and I politely dissected our servings into microscopic bites.

As we sipped the fragrant tea Toozie chattered on, in her wildly imaginative Japanese, about all sorts of things: the incredulous response of pedestrians when she flew by on her big black motorcycle; the saintly kindness of Mrs. Maeda, the wife of the priest at Kaiko-in, the sub-temple where we were staying; and the way people gawked at us in the public bath (I shot her a warning look at this point, but she blundered blithely on with her story of the shameless old man who had been caught hanging over the partition leering toothlessly at the two buxom Westerners). I was embarrassed by this intimate revelation, but Toku-san laughed loudly and then said, with mock solemnity, "Please allow me to apologize on behalf of all Japanese males."

Determined to steer the conversation away from the topic of naked breasts, I inquired after the health of Shiro, the adorable white dog. "Oh, Shiro's fine," said Toku-san. "I'll show you his mansion a little later." By then we had finished our tea and sweets, and Toku-san stood up, said "Excuse me," took his blue indigo-dyed koromo down from a bamboo-pole hanger, put it on, wrapped a matching quilted sash around his hips, and then led us through the door we had come in.

Toozie and I both thought that he was going to show us out, but to our surprise he turned left instead of right. "This way," he said, and we followed him along the walkway of smooth gray-brown wood. It wasn't exactly a guided tour—no one, not even the voluble Toozie, spoke a word. The summer afternoon stillness was broken only by the occasional plop of a frog jumping into an old pond, and by the sound of half-seen carp breaking the gray-green surface of the water and, in apparent violation of everything we had learned in Basic Biology about lungs versus gills, appearing to gasp for air.

The corridor finally ended at a large whitewashed building with bell-shaped windows trimmed with wood the color of bittersweet chocolate. Toku-san led us through a sort of anteroom, a long stone-floored rectangle with a high, wide tatami-matted shelf along one wall, and a stack of reddish-purple *zabuton* cushions in the corner. An open door led to a well-tended graveyard, where clumps of tiny yellow wildflowers grew among the dark-granite obelisks of the headstones. I was hoping that this would be our destination, for I suspected that Eisai might be buried there, perhaps with a bonsai tea bush planted on his grave.

Instead, we turned right and entered a cool, airy room, about half the size of a high school gym. "This is the Zendo," said Toku-san. "This is where we meditate, and where the young monks sleep—if they're lucky!" He explained that the Zen phrase meaning monk, *unsui no ryokyaku* (*unsui* for short) could be translated, literally, as "cloud-and-water guest."

There were two wide tatami-matted platforms, one on each side of the room; Toku-san explained that each mat was the sleeping area of an individual monk, who kept his bedding and personal supplies bundled up at the rear of the mat. At the far end of the hall was an elaborate altar, and beyond it was a door framing a manicured green-and-yellow garden. Toku-san led us outside and showed us the cast-brass bell, and the block of wood, suspended from a rope, that was used to strike it every evening at twilight.

"This is the bell you hear every day," he said. "You probably find it very annoying."

"Oh, not at all," I said. "I love all the sounds of the Sodo—the bells and the wooden clappers and the chanting and the raking of leaves—" Suddenly aware that I was gushing like a wide-eyed Zen groupie, I stopped my litany in mid-sentence.

Just then Toozie glanced at her watch and said, "Uh-oh! I forgot, I'm supposed to go check the kiln!" After a quick "Gochisosama" ("Thanks for the feast") she was gone.

"Toozie-san is a very *omoshiroi* (interesting) person, isn't she?" said Toku-san. It is also possible that he meant "a very amusing person," for one of the ambiguities of Japanese is that the word "omoshiroi" can mean either interesting or amusing, and it is sometimes difficult to ascertain which is meant from the context. In Toozie's antic case, it could well have been both.

We walked back to the Zendo, and Toku-san explained that the long perpendicular anteroom was where guests sat during meditation. Hmm, I thought, eyeing the pile of burgundy zabuton, but I didn't have the nerve to ask whether the guest list ever included foreigners. Instead, I asked the sturdy monk if he thought it was morally wrong to wear shoes made from leather.

"According to the rules of Buddhism, you shouldn't consume meat or dairy products, nor should you wear garments made of animal hide," he said. Then a mischievous smile spread over his face. "But I feel that if you get too hung up on superficial details and rigid prehistoric rules, you can lose sight of the really important things in life. Besides," he added cryptically, "women can never become Buddhas, anyway."

Later I found myself wishing that I had asked the simple, obvious questions: What are those important things, and why can't women become Buddhas? But at the moment I was more interested in finding out how I might be perceived by a Zen monk, so I said, "Then you don't automatically assume that someone who is wearing leather shoes—or, let's say, sandals—is hopelessly worldly and unenlightened?"

Toku-san smiled. "I don't automatically assume anything," he said, and I felt even more foolish and unenlightened than before. Everything I said seemed to be a perfect Zen straight line, setting up the wise, flexible response. "Oh, Toku-san," I blurted out. "Please teach me something—anything!"

"I don't know anything," came the inevitable reply.

"Naruhodo," I said. "I see." And in a very limited, myopic way, perhaps I did. We walked back to the main building of the Sodo, once again in pleasant silence. There were several young monks working in the garden; they were dressed in gray trousers and matching wraparound jackets with the sleeves bound out of the way by long white cords that went around the neck and were tied behind the back, and they wore white kerchiefs over their shaved heads, pirate-style. All the unsui (I loved that word, and the thought behind it) nodded respectfully as Toku-san and I passed by, without missing a stroke of the rake or a slash of the scythe.

I had expected to slip into my animal-hide sandals and say goodbye when we reached the genkan, but to my surprise Toku-san led me past it, through a long room with a low, U-shaped table—"This is where we eat," he said—and into the dim, cavernous kitchen. There were several wood stoves with great black pots on them, and racks of bamboo utensils, and, as in the rest of the Sodo, there was an aura of cleanliness, purposeful tranquillity, and order. The monk we had met earlier, Zo-san, was standing at a wooden counter, chopping a large bunch of green onions while the round-faced blueberry-bruised monk peeled carrots into a stainless steel sink.

I wondered what the daily menus were like at the Sodo; I imagined that they must eat a lot of brown rice and vegetables and buckwheat noodles, like my old macrobiotic friends in Cambridge, Massachusetts and Westport, Maine. "You must come for dinner one night," said Zo-san, as if reading my mind.

"I'd love to; it would be an honor," I said, thinking even as I spoke that my response was probably overly effusive and utterly un-Zen-like. Until I figured out what a proper Zen response would be, though, I decided to stick with my own super-polite, overstated, forehead-to-the-mat style.

"Let's go see Shiro," said Toku-san. Zo-san grinned and waved good-bye with his gleaming knife and his assistant made a grave little bow as Toku-san led me out of the kitchen and into a sunny courtyard. "That's the bath house over there," Toku-san said, gesturing toward an out-building. "And that"—pointing at a freestanding bungalow with a shallow verandah—"that's the guest house."

Seeing the hopeful gleam in my eye, he added, "Only men and married couples are permitted to stay there. No single women—unfortunately!"

As Toku-san was speaking, one of the shoji doors of the guest house slid open and a remarkable-looking person stepped out onto the verandah. He had a shaved head, like a monk, but he was dressed in an opulent kimono of shimmering pale gold silk, the color of North Beach *zabaglione*, with a Dijon-mustard-colored *obi* sash. Aside from his unascetic costume, there was something about the way he held himself, a sensuous, intelligent arrogance, that told me this was no ordinary monk. Or, for that matter, no ordinary man.

The un-monk stepped off the verandah into a pair of wooden geta almost as high as those worn by noodle-delivery boys on the back streets of the Ginza. Toku-san himself was wearing three-inch clogs, while I had slipped into a pair of sturdy gray rubber guest *zori* outside the kitchen door. I was petting Shiro, who was lying half-asleep in a rather luxurious doghouse with a pitched roof and a tatami floor, and when I stood up I felt, as I always did in Japan, discourteously tall. Thank God I'm not wearing geta, I thought.

"This is Fuji Mugen; everyone calls him Mugen," said Toku-san, indicating the striking-looking man with the shaved head, who had joined us. At close range Mugen's face seemed startlingly saurian (thick-lidded eyes, wide nostrils, slightly protuberant mouth), but then he turned his head a fraction of a degree and he was suddenly beautiful, with the poignant, precarious kind of beauty that's always teetering on the edge of ugliness. The post-noon light seemed to illuminate his tea-colored eyes from behind, and his distinctive features and haughty, bemused demeanor reminded me of a portrait (colored ink on silk) I had once seen of a fifteenth-century warlord-poet. For the first time in several months I felt the symptoms of romantic affinity (not dissimilar from the sensations that herald hyperventilation, or dyspepsia), and I found myself wishing I had tied my braid with a proper ribbon instead of a piece of green-and-white striped string from a package of takeout sushi.

"This is Deborah; she's staying next door at Kaiko-in with Toozie," Toku-san said. He mimed a wrist-twisting motion and made the "vroom-vroom" sound of a big motorcycle starting up. "You know," he added, "the potter who rides a BMW." He pronounced Toozie "Tsuji," which is the closest Japanese approximation. (My name is easily transposed into the Japanese syllabary, although they pronounce it "Day-bow-rah.")

"I know," said Fuji Mugen, "I've seen them both around." He held out his hand, Western-style, and we shook hands for what seemed like several minutes. "I'm glad to meet you," he said, staring up into my eyes with such intensity that I had to swallow, and blink. (Even in his four-inch geta, he was an inch or two shorter than I.) "I'm the Sodo's *isoro*— I'm living here while studying the tea ceremony."

Isoro? I wasn't familiar with the word, but I made a mental note to look it up in my well-worn Kenkyusha dictionary as soon as I got back to my room. I should probably have been thinking of it as "our room," or more accurately as Toozie's room, but after only three days within the charismatic walls of Zenzenji I was beginning to feel, irrationally, that it was I (not Toozie) who lived there, and that it was Toozie (not I) who was the cloud-and-water guest.

SILVER STOCKINGS
(SEE HOW THEY RUN)

*According to the esoteric scripture
known as the Conquest of Hell,
the heart likes bitter foods.*

Zen Master Eisai

—TOKYO

*T*o *be anywhere is a miracle, but to be in Tokyo in autumn, living
in a funky Japanese-style bungalow, is a particular delight. Framed
in my sitting-room window, like an antique ink painting on a
parchment scroll, is a leafless persimmon tree with one lustrous orange
fruit suspended from an otherwise barren branch. The background is an
unusually blue and cloudless sky—almost artificial-looking in its flawless-
ness, like one of the bright paper backdrops in the dissolute photographer's
studio in* Blow-Up. *Sound effects: wooden clogs clopping by on the cobblestone street outside, the splash of water as the landlord gives his prize bonsai plants a drink, the sudden shrill ring of a telephone in the house of the
anarchist next door.*

My appreciation of my picturesque new dwelling was heightened by
the memory of what a struggle it had been to persuade the landlord and
his wife to rent the house to me. My friend Barrie, an Australian painter
who also taught art at a nearby elementary school, was living next door
with an aikido black-belt journalist named Dai. One day in early September, just after my return from Kyoto, I came to visit Barrie and Dai
for the first time. Their cottage lay at the end of a marvelous garden full
of pale-plumed birds in bamboo cages and tiny, tortured trees set in
miniature fiefdoms of mountains and meadows and medieval castles,

and as I walked through I noticed a shabby, deserted-looking structure on the left.

"Oh, that's just an old guest house that got too run-down to use," Barrie explained. "Dr. Dobashi, the landlord, uses it as a gardening shed." On my way out, I boldly slid open one of the rickety doors and peered in. The interior was musty and mildewed, but I could see that it was spacious and potentially charming. The wood was mellow cryptomeria, vaguely luminous and fragrant even under the dust, and the shoji screens, although in dire need of cleaning and repapering, opened on one side onto the fairyland forest of birds and bonsai, while the other offered a view of high-walled estates, a filigree park, and, far below, a lively shopping street decorated with paraffin-colored paper lanterns and garlands of plastic maple leaves, orange and russet and gold.

"I have to live there," I told Barrie later. "I could be ecstatically happy in that house, I just know it."

Barrie laughed. Her own rented house was a relatively new faux chalet with indoor plumbing, glass windows, and a dishwasher. "Well," she said, "I can introduce you to the landlord and give you a terrific character reference, but after that you're on your own. I wouldn't get my hopes up if I were you—I heard that another foreigner wanted to rent the house last year and Dr. Dobashi said absolutely no way."

My first meeting with the landlord couldn't have gotten off to a worse start. Barrie had promised to come along but she had to rush off unexpectedly to meet Dai after one of his secret Anarchists' Association meetings ("You have to live busily and dangerously," she said on the phone, by way of explanation). I was left alone with the landlord and his silent wife, sitting awkwardly on artichoke-green cushions around a dark-red lacquer table. We sipped weak yellow tea and nibbled on crisp *senbei* (rice crackers) flecked with red-violet seaweed, and after a few moments of stilted conversation I screwed up my courage and said, "Perhaps Barrie has told you that I am very interested in living in the old house in your garden."

"Oh, that's impossible," said Dr. Dobashi, while his wife nodded in mute agreement. "That building is not fit for human habitation; it's just an old shack. There is no hot water, the bath is unusable, and the plumbing is not—modern."

Unwilling to take "impossible" for an answer, I explained that none of those things mattered to me. I could make my own hot water (for there was, at least, electricity); I was in any case a devotee of the public bath, and I had noticed a particularly inviting-looking one only two blocks away; and as for the plumbing, I was not one of those hyper-civilized gaijin who believed that a flush toilet was a prerequisite to happiness. "Besides," I said, attempting a little latrine humor, "I plan to burn a lot of incense."

If the doctor and his wife were amused, they didn't show it. "I'm sorry, it's simply out of the question," said Doctor Dobashi brusquely. "That house is not fit to live in. In fact, I only agreed to talk to you as a favor to Barrie."

I decided to try a new tactic: the feigned retreat. "Your garden is really exquisite," I said casually. "How did you become interested in bonsai?"

Two hours later I had been treated to a lengthy tour of the enormous bonsai garden, and had agreed to have a selection of plants of the Southwest (Mormon Tea, juniper, assorted cacti) mailed from Sedona, Arizona by my mother, who was a dedicated gardener and cultivator of succulents. (I knew she wouldn't mind.) Fortuitously, it turned out that Dr. Dobashi had once driven through the Arizona desert when the wildflowers were in bloom, and had found it a deeply moving experience.

"About the house—" I said as we were exchanging forehead-to-knee bows and elaborate farewell greetings at the front gate. It was a sun-streaked, rain-furrowed wooden gate, with a roof of slate-colored tiles which were almost completely obscured by the vivid creep of moss in shades of chartreuse and forest-primeval green, punctuated with random outbursts of putty-colored lichen that looked uncannily like peeling paint.

"Oh," said Dr. Dobashi with a preoccupied wave, "if you insist, you can try living there for a while. I'll pay for electricity and water, and the rent will be—let's see, how about 7,500 yen a month?"

I had come prepared to negotiate the rent, and had even spent some time rehearsing a line ("I'm sorry, but I can't possibly afford to pay more than ten thousand yen a month") in front of the mirror the night before. Given the classiness of the neighborhood and the convenience of the location, I had expected the asking price for the hovel of my dreams to be around fifteen thousand yen, and I was hoping to compromise on 12,500, which I could just afford.

So when Dr. Dobashi said "7,500 yen," I was so surprised that I responded, automatically and with well-rehearsed fluency, "Oh, I'm sorry, I can't possibly afford to pay more than ten thousand yen a month."

The doctor's mouth fell open, but he quickly said, "All right, ten thousand yen will be just fine."

"Wait a minute," I said in dismay, hastily switching off my automatic pilot. "You said 7,500."

"Yes, I did," he agreed pleasantly. "But then you said ten thousand." The dialogue continued in that intransigent vein for a few minutes, and we eventually "compromised" on 8,500 yen a month. A thousand yen was not an insignificant sum in those days, and I kicked myself every time the rent came due and I had to fork over the extra thousand-yen note. I did learn a priceless lesson from that farcical negotiation: it's fine to rehearse your lines if you are an actor, but real life is best dealt with spontaneously.

It took four days of hard scrubbing to remove the grimy patina of neglect from the old house in the bonsai garden, but it was worth it, for the restored wood was a rich butterscotch color. Next I removed all the filthy, tattered paper from the shoji screens and replaced it with hand-made "rice" paper (actually made from mulberry pulp) in a deep dusty rose. When the sunlight, or the lamplight, or the candlelight shone through the newly-papered screens, the rooms were filled with a lambent rosy glow; it was like being afloat in a glass of mulled wine.

After the house was cleaned up I was ready to go looking for furniture. I waited until very late at night when everyone (including all the yappy little upper-class watchdogs) would presumably be asleep, and then I ventured out into my new neighborhood and began to sort through the tasteful trash which my affluent neighbors had placed on the curb to be collected the next day. I found some extraordinary things: an enormous round black lacquer table; a swan-necked brass lamp in perfect condition; a set of like-new futon featuring a pastel-satin patchwork quilt with a border of lavender velvet, fit for a fairy princess; several unused zabuton cushions in deep-sea shades of blue and green; a tall rush-seated stool for my rustic kitchen; and an oval mirror with a braided-bamboo frame. There was more—enough to furnish a modest mansion or two—but I had been impressed by the airy minimalism of the interiors at the Zenzenji Sodo, so I stifled my natural Western desire to cram my new home full of every appealing object I saw. "You take what you need/And leave the rest," I sang happily as I carted my exotic plunder through the silent streets.

That lovely, decaying house in Moto-Azabu was the first dwelling I had ever had to myself, without family or roommates. It was a long rectangle, with a number of rooms (including a non-functional bath room made entirely of aromatic cedar) which were in such disrepair that they were simply unusable, but there was a large tatami-matted room with windows on both sides where I ate, slept, and studied. The kitchen had a stone floor and a big persimmon-and-moon-viewing window above the deep metal sink, and there was a wooden counter on which I placed a double hot plate and a picnic-style cooler filled with ice. Since I was a vegetarian I didn't really need a refrigerator, but I liked to keep my grapefruit juice and *natto* (fermented soybeans) cold.

Because of my odd schedule, I was seldom home at dinnertime, so I usually grabbed a bite on the run: great peppery bowls of Korean vegetable soup, or lacy vegetable tempura, or noodles and *oden* eaten under the candlelit canopy of a street-vendor's stand. When I did have time to cook, shopping was absurdly easy. A well-stocked vegetable truck used to park outside the gate everyday around five p.m., and at 5:30 a discordant fanfare from a miniature brass horn would herald the arrival of the tofu seller, with the perfectly square blocks of pure, potent protein sloshing around in a water-filled wooden box mounted on the back of his ancient bicycle. He would scoop a smooth-textured ivory cube of tofu out of the tank with a brass dipper, wrap it in newspaper, accept a few yen in payment, and then ride off down the hill, cheerfully tooting his horn.

In those days the streets of Azabu were still full of mobile (or itinerant) vendors, and their quasi-operatic cries echoed through the labyrinthine back streets and stone-walled alleys. "Kin-gyoooo!" called the seller of gauzy-tailed goldfish as he pulled his glass-sided barrow behind him; "Yakiii-mooooo!" yodeled the purveyor of sweet potatoes roasted on hot stones (still the best treat I know of on a winter day); "Tooo-fuuu!" caroled the bean-curd man, between blasts on his seraphic horn. Add to these the assorted bell-ringing collectors of rags and old paper, and the ubiquitous political campaigners whose streams of obsequious platitudes were amplified by loudspeakers mounted on minivans, and the ambient urban murmur was sometimes more like an untuned-orchestra cacophany.

Looking back on that persimmon fall, I think the days must have been longer, somehow; or perhaps I had developed a Napoleonic metabolism, and was able to thrive on three hours of sleep a night. Some evenings, after I had come home from one of my assorted art-and-culture lessons, or from my English teaching, or from pursuing a promising friendship or a doomed romance, or, one memorable stormy evening, from guest-tending an arty little bar called Musasabi (Flying Squirrel) when my friend Mitsuko, who owned it, suddenly fell ill; after I had finished my homework and had filled the requisite number of windowpane-gridded pages with kanji practice and inadvertent inkblots (I used to write with a temperamental quill-style pen, dipped in black or violet or sepia ink); on those nights, after everything was taken care of, I would brew a pot of tea, light a stick of incense, and embark on my extracurricular studies.

Since my return from Kyoto, those investigations had begun to revolve almost entirely around my growing curiosity about Zen. I bought some books, and borrowed others, in the hopes that written words might somehow bring me closer to understanding the tantalizing mysteries I had glimpsed in the supernal serenity of the Sodo, and in the wise, lively faces of the monks. Slowly, like a midnight prospector panning for gold, I began to cull a few sparkling quotes from the sometimes murky prose that surrounded them.

Both singing and dancing are voices of the Way.
—Zen Master Hakuin

If all is void, where can the dust alight? ("Far out," said Barrie, leafing through my notebook one evening. "Sounds like a divine mandate for sloppy housekeeping!")

Never let the idea of a long life seize upon you, for then you are apt to indulge in all kinds of dissipation, and end your days in dire disgrace.
—General Uesugi Kenshin

When one is in poor spirits, one should drink tea.
—Zen Master Eisai, avatar of tannic enlightenment

Gradually, I became fascinated by the idea of the riddle-like *koan* (defined by D. T. Suzuki as "a problem given by the master for solution" and further characterized as "the unreason of reason"). The examples that kept cropping up were "Does the dog have Buddha-nature?" "What was your face before your parents were born?" and of course that cosmic chestnut "What is the sound of one hand clapping?" which, I was excited to learn, had originated at Zenzenji. These koan were, I gathered, questions without answers, or rather with an infinite number of acceptable answers (including silence, violence, and rude gestures), as long as the answer sprang from pan-somatic enlightenment, and not from conscious thought. The circular paradoxes of Zen affected me like extra-dry champagne: I found them tasty and intoxicating, but they ultimately left me with a dizzy headache and a sense of deep confusion.

I read about the role of *zazen*, or meditation, in koan-solving, and I was particularly intrigued by the occasional mention of *sanzen*: individual audiences with the Zen master, in which the struggling acolyte offers his latest tentative take on his koan, and the *roshi* (Zen master) responds, according to ancient tradition, with jeers and slaps and blows with a stick, or with some profoundly absurd remark. However, if the acolyte has finally attained satori—catalyzed, perhaps, by the splash of a frog in a pond, or a glimpse of the moon reflected in a bucket of well-water—the roshi, suddenly gentle and respectful, might say something like: "Well, then, you have passed beyond the Gateless Barrier. There is nothing more I can teach you."

My romantic daydreams, which had previously focused on fantasy-liaisons with Apollinaire and Keats and Modigliani, now began to take place exclusively at Zenzenji. "You are very wise, my child," a shadowy Zen master would say after I had demonstrated a deep nonverbal understanding of my koan by turning a perfect cartwheel with a single white rose in my mouth. "There is nothing more you can learn from me ..."

* * *

My friends Shoko and Koji were avant-garde artists (she was a sculptor, he a composer-and-deliverer of interminable existential monologues in crusty gangster-slang), so it was not surprising that they chose to have an unconventional wedding reception. The actual wedding, I was told, had been very private—just the two immediate families. No one seemed to know any details about the ceremony, so I assumed that it had been embarrassingly traditional, as a concession to parental pressure.

The reception, however, was anything but traditional; it was held in a raffish Kabukicho bar with the charming English name of Troglodyte. There was something undeniably cave-like, if not claustrophobic, about the ambience of the place; all the corners had been filled in with fluffy plaster, then painted a dark khaki, giving a sort of blighted-cumulus effect. (I later learned that this had been Shoko's first paying "environmental sculpture" job.) The rough-hewn tables and chairs and the pebbly, round-edged, camouflage-painted walls contributed further to the illusion of being inside an interplanetary war zone, or the womb of some mutant monster.

The lighting was evocative, and probably illegal; aside from a single flickering fluorescent work-light above the black Plexiglas bar, the only source of illumination was the thick stumpy green hand-made candles, one on each table, which gave off a faint, refreshing aroma of faraway forests and Arcadian dells. Troglodyte was a quirky, artistic sort of place, and it was the perfect setting for the wedding reception of an offbeat, poetic couple. The newlyweds' conservative prosodic parents evidently didn't think so, though, for they were nowhere to be seen. In fact, there was no one older than thirty in attendance.

The celebration consisted of the standard social activities of drinking *mizuwari* (cheap whiskey with lots of water); eating savory skewered morsels of *kushiyaki* (the specialty of Troglodyte's goateed proprietor); and singing to the accompaniment of an imperfectly-tuned piano. It was a boisterous, hard-drinking crowd of students, artists, actors, writers, and musicians, some on the brink of success, some on the verge of starvation, and some (like Koji, the groom) on the eve of abandoning their beaux-arts dreams and going to work for a relative's real-estate company, or for some chilly, heartless corporation.

In spite of being the center of attention, Shoko, who was wearing a short dress made entirely of interfastened safety pins worn over a red body stocking, high-heeled red pumps, and a silver chain-mail cloche hat, found time to introduce me to several people. One was a giggly, cherubic classical guitar player, who was supporting himself by working at a filling station ("Classical Gas?" I asked in English, and he laughed uproariously, though whether from amusement or incomprehension I couldn't tell); another was a frail, sad-eyed woman from Hokkaido who was still, at age twenty-six, trying to gain admittance to the oil-painting division of Geidai, the most prestigious art school in Japan. There was a petite, childlike young couple, both aspiring songwriters, who were working in the lost letter department—a poignantly lyrical concept in itself, we all agreed—of the Shinjuku post office. And then there was Kuri.

"Oh, Deborah-chan, I want you to meet my friend Kuri. We've known each other since elementary school," said Shoko, as she dragged me away from a convivial group of fledgling jazz musicians (who were "sunlighting," variously, as a Chiba-ken construction worker, a Tsukiji fish-gutter, and a necktie salesman at a Ginza boutique) and propelled me toward a tall man who was standing alone in the shadows, holding a bottle of Kirin beer.

"Hello," I said, "I'm happy to meet you."

"Ah, but I'm more happy to meet you," said the tall man—a curiously nonformulaic response. After completing the introductions, Shoko rushed off to check on the cheap-whiskey supply, and Kuri and I sat down at an empty table and began to talk. He was definitely the best-looking Japanese man I had ever seen; he was almost too handsome, but I was willing to overlook that.

He had the lofty cheekbones, curvilinear jaw, luxuriant mouth, and aquiline nose of a typical male model, but I thought I saw something in his eyes, a glint of character and a glimmer of humor, that made his face more than a collage of flawless features. Kuri's hair was straight, fine, and shoulder length, and he was dressed in classic decadent-intellectual style: a black turtleneck sweater, pleated trousers of soft amber corduroy, and a velvet jacket that was the dark bluish-purple of a summer plum, or a serious bruise.

As it happened, purple was my favorite color, and I was wearing a cowl-collared dress of aubergine jersey with long narrow sleeves, a circular skirt, buttons down the back, and a wide, tight belt. I wore silver squash-blossom earrings and a twisted-silver Navajo bracelet, and my hair was caught up in a silver barrette. The barrette had been made for me as a going-away-to-Japan present by Ursula, my former roommate at Goddard; it was a simple circle of hammered silver with a silver pin that slid under the hair and was held in place by the circle. The pin had a moonstone on one end, because I had been told by an elderly, benevolent witch in Boston that I should always wear a moonstone. That silver barrette was one of my most treasured possessions; I considered it a magical icon, and since the pin had a way of slipping, I was constantly adjusting it to be sure that the barrette wouldn't fall off.

I was wearing shimmery silver stockings, too, and my favorite shoes: they were like leprechaun boots, except that they didn't have a buckle, and instead of green leather they were made of rose-colored suede, trimmed around the edges in matching patent leather. I had bought them at Filene's Basement in Boston for six dollars, and, like the barrette, they seemed to have a sort of enchanted luminescence.

"This party is beginning to bore me," Kuri said, after we had talked for a while about life, and art, and the mysteries of marriage. Kuri was a composer of music in the Baroque style, he told me, and a part-time race car driver. How glamorous, and how well balanced, I thought, and then I braced myself for the inevitable coda: "—but right now I'm working as a toaster salesman to support my art." Instead, he said, "You probably expect me to say that I have some horribly mundane part-time job, too, but I don't. The truth is—and no one else knows this, so please keep it a secret—that all through my childhood I took care of my aunt, who was chronically ill, and when she died she left me a lot of money."

I nodded. I could imagine the comely young Kuri bringing flowers to the bedside of his languishing aunt, brewing her a cup of chamomile tea, and reading aloud from *I Am A Cat* or *A Thousand Cranes* in his melodic but very masculine voice. "Come on," he said suddenly, "I want to show you something." He pulled me to my feet and we ducked out the back door. I felt momentarily guilty about leaving without saying goodbye or thank you to the newlyweds, but they were standing by the piano, singing a soulful *enka* duet, and Kuri assured me that it would have been rude to interrupt. Besides, I had spent the entire morning making an elaborate illuminated scroll (Rapidograph, watercolors, gold-flake paint) to wish them a safe, happy journey on their honeymoon to Paris and in their lives together, and I had stuck it in Shoko's Moroccan bag.

Kuri hailed a turquoise taxi and we rode for a long time, in a silence which I mistook for the communion of soulmates, through the manic neon boulevards of Shinjuku and then through miles of dark, leafy residential streets. Finally the taxi stopped in front of an elegant old mansion, hidden from the street by a high stone wall. Kuri fumbled with his wallet and then said, "I seem to be a little short on cash. I have plenty of money in the house, though, so could I borrow some from you to pay the cab driver?" I handed him my striped cotton wallet and he took all but a hundred yen. I was seriously smitten by this time, and I trusted him completely.

As it turned out, Kuri lived not in the mansion itself, but in a two-room cottage in the tangled garden behind it. There was an unmade futon spread out on the floor, books and magazines and clothes were strewn everywhere, and dirty cups and glasses covered the low table, but I found the squalor artistic and endearing. (If all is void, where can the dust alight?) Besides, I thought, it's what you choose to put on your wall, not what you happen to drop (or spill) on the floor, that reveals who you are.

On his walls, Kuri had chosen to put an assortment of exotic performance-car posters, portraits of Bach and Vivaldi, and several works of modern graphic art, including a hanging sculpture of a red-lacquer tarantula with a grotesque human face which I recognized as one of Shoko's recent "Entomological Nightmare" pieces. I especially liked the *tokonoma* alcove, which featured a scroll-painting of three ripe persimmons on a blue-and-white Imari dish, a single purple clematis in an empty Strega bottle, and a large, glossy model of a black bathtub Porsche. While I was admiring this eclectic composition, Kuri came up behind me and buried his face in my hair. "Are you ready to see my most precious possession?" he murmured.

"I'd love to," I said, thinking he was talking about a work of art, or some talismanic treasure.

Six hours later I was sitting on a cross-town bus, surrounded by curious strangers, trying not to cry. In another hour I would be home, and then I could weep in private, and mend my dress, and throw away my ruined silver stockings, and chronicle my shame and disappointment in my journal, and wait impatiently for the public bath house to open at two o'clock. And maybe, after that, I could begin to forget about the sad and sleepless night I had just spent. I would never have told Shoko this, but her fine-looking childhood friend had grown up to be a liar, and a phony, and a bit of a satyr to boot.

At first Kuri had courted me sweetly, with flattering words and subtle caresses. I found him very appealing, and since I had naïvely convinced myself that there was some special, fateful bond between us, I was soon wishing that I were as wildly uninhibited as some of my friends. But when I explained that I was still, by complex philosophical choice, a virgin, Kuri suddenly turned into a vitriolic fiend, calling me a tease (among other, fouler names) and accusing me of having deliberately sent misleading signals from the moment we met. "You said you'd love to see my most precious possession!" he shouted, and I almost laughed out loud when I realized what he had meant by that delicate euphemism.

Kuri was surprisingly strong, and I was frightened when he grabbed me and, after a brief, grotesque parody of an adversarial foxtrot, pushed me down onto the unmade futon. We grappled for a few moments like ill-matched high-school wrestlers, and then in desperation I held him at bay with the sharp moonstone-studded pin from my hair ornament. It occurred to me later that that melodramatic tableau was a curious variation on the archetypal wench-versus-werewolf confrontation: a seemingly-refined male transformed by the rabid bite of lust into a raging if relatively hairless beast, then vanquished by a silver … barrette.

"Okay," Kuri said, panting like a thirsty *loup-garou*. "You can put away your stupid weapon. I give up. I'm not so desperate that I have to force myself on women. But you're going to have to stay here until the buses start running, because I lied—I don't have any cash at all. I lied about the rich aunt, too, and about being a composer, and about driving race cars. Those are all just pick-up lines; the truth is, I rented this place through a real estate agent. Isn't that horribly dreary and mundane? Actually, since I lost my job in an advertising agency I've just been playing around, and letting my fiancée support me."

"Your fiancée?" I felt a sharp spasm of irrational jealousy, a sort of psychosomatic angina, at the thought of Kuri (my beautiful beast) with another woman.

"Yeah, she flies for JAL. Gorgeous girl, but she's away too much, and I get lonely." "Lonely" struck me as a rather mild euphemism for such an advanced state of randiness, but I didn't say so. Kuri poured himself a large unwashed tumbler full of Chivas Regal, gulped it down, and then stretched out diagonally across the chaotic futon. At one point, just before he dozed off, he opened one languid bloodshot eye, looked at me, and said, "Are you sure you don't want to 'do it'? No one has ever turned me down before."

"Oh, I'm quite certain, thank you," I said politely, as if refusing a watercress sandwich. "It's terribly kind of you to ask, though," I added sarcastically. Kuri slept then, while I sat in a cluttered corner with my arms wrapped around my knees, waiting for the first light of dawn so I could go out and buy a bus trip home with my last hundred yen.

Kuri woke up around five a.m. and insisted on making me a cup of tea; he was strangely kind, although he offered no apology of any sort. Ordinarily I would have dumped two heaping teaspoons of sugar and a small tsunami of milk into my Occidental tea, but I chose to drink this cup straight. I figured unsweetened Twining's Orange Pekoe was the next best thing to a draught of wormwood, the traditional potion of choice for penance and purification.

Later, after I got home, I realized that I had lost something far more significant than one night's sleep, a thousand yen, and my trust of spectacular-looking, well-spoken men. (Would I have followed him home if he hadn't been beautiful? Not bloody likely.) My precious silver-and-moonstone barrette had fallen off, either during the struggle with Kuri or on the dazed journey home, and I never saw it again. Feeling bereft on a number of levels, I took out my journal, dipped my pen in bitter brown ink, and wrote a mournful little song:

> I met someone
> I thought I loved him
> He took me home
> He didn't say a word
>
> In the streetlight
> He looked like an angel
> But he turned out to be
> A devil of emptiness
> Not even pretending
> It was fate or good fortune
> That brought us together
> Or kept us apart
> I wasn't very smart
> To follow him home
>
> Tea next morning
> Betrayed and sleepy
> I asked him why
> He didn't say a word
> And even if he had
> I wouldn't have heard

It wasn't Cole Porter, or Carole King, but I felt better for having versi-fied my despair. I fell asleep at my big round table, and when I woke up it was early afternoon. I changed into a fan-patterned cotton kimono and packed my towel, my Ivory soap, and my seaweed-shampoo in a lit-tle brass-bound wooden bucket. Then I tottered off to the public bath in my geta, hoping that a ritual ablution of my body would rinse some of the tawdry taint from my soul as well.

A DATE WITH A DEMON

Tea, although an Oriental,
Is a gentleman at least.
Cocoa is a cad and coward;
Cocoa is a vulgar beast.

G. K. Chesterton
The Song of Right and Wrong

—TOKYO

E ven before I entered the bright vermilion gate of the shrine I could hear it: that tormented yet harmonious twanging. The *biwa* master was sitting on a large, lily-pad green cushion in the center of a miniature open-air Noh stage, surrounded by phantasmagorically gnarled and twisted pine trees, a motif which was reflected in a weather-faded painting on the screen behind the stage. The audience was small but attentive: students in uniform, aproned housewives carrying shopping baskets, elderly men and women in autumn kimono, and the requisite "strange foreigners"—in this case, a pair of tall, blond, Teutonic-looking men in *lederhosen*, sandals, and red Alpine-dandy hats. I arrived just as the concert was ending, but I saw and heard enough to know that I wanted to learn to play the biwa (the cacophonous cousin of the softer, more modulated Western lute), and that I wanted this man to be my teacher.

I had read in the newspaper that the biwa player was eighty-one years old, but his unlined face and bald head gave him an ageless quality. He was dressed in an opulent robe of white satin trimmed in metallic gold, with sleeves that were full at the top in an Elizabethan pirate–style and then tapered down to fit tightly around the wrists. He wore white half-gloves which covered his hands but left his long, pale

fingers exposed, and on his feet were white *tabi* (split-toe socks) and polished dark-wood geta with white leather straps.

I had to wait my turn to talk to the biwa master, for the German
tourists insisted on having him pose for several carefully-choreographed
pictures with each of them. While I waited, I recalled my previous visit
to the shrine, less than a week before. It had been one of the stops on a
marathon walk with a rather difficult friend from the Ochanomizu Art
Institute named Totsuo (an unusual name written with the characters
for 'convex' and 'concave') Takatori. I described Totsuo in my journal as
a nihilist-child in search of his own absurdity, but I remember him now in
less cryptic terms, as a moody young man with fine, almost feminine
features half-hidden under a side-parted curtain of glossy blue-black
hair. Totsuo was medium-tall and very well-built (he worked off and on
at industrial construction) so it always seemed curious that his art consisted of delicate miniature drawings of abstract cityscapes, rendered in
colored-pencil tones of ruby and turquoise, stippled and rippled and
blurred with the artist's saké-spiked saliva.

I had always thought of Totsuo as "just a friend," and he had never
expressed any overt dissatisfaction with the non-corporeal nature of our
friendship, so I was shocked when he turned to me that day and said,
"Of all the women I have ever known, you are the most like a mother.
Will you come live with me?" I was so startled that I nearly made an
Oedipus-meets-Christopher-Marlowe joke ("Come live with me, and be
my mom"), but instead I stammered out, "I can barely live with myself,"
and added, ever polite, that I was very flattered by the unexpected proposal. Or was it a proposition? We were standing in the courtyard of the
deserted shrine, next to a large stone fox-sculpture (messenger of the
gods, guardian of the gates) and I remember thinking: If only I were in
love with this man, what a wonderfully romantic moment this would be!

Finally, the last of the biwa-concert crowd dispersed; I shook off my
rueful reverie and approached the man in white satin. "That was marvelous," I said. "Ever since I saw the film version of *Mimi Nashi Hoichi*
('Hoichi the Earless') I've wanted to play the biwa." I had recently seen
an extraordinary horror movie called "Kaidan" (Ghost Stories), based on
Lafcadio Hearn's book of the same name, although he spelled it the old-
fashioned way: *Kwaidan*. One of the more terrifying tales chronicled the
supernatural adventures of a blind biwa player named Hoichi, who had
his ears torn off by angry medieval ghosts.

"Ah, yes," the musician said, carefully putting his beautiful old instrument into a wooden case lined with quilted white silk, like a vampire's coffin. "But the biwa is very difficult to play. Perhaps you would rather study the *shamisen*—or the guitar?"

"No," I said stubbornly, "it has to be the biwa." The biwa master told me that he no longer gave lessons, but he took my phone number and said that he would try to find me a teacher.

His parting words, as he was ushered off to a waiting taxi in a flash of white and gold, were: "You really should think seriously about the guitar. I think it would be much more becoming to you. Well, *saraba!*" ("Saraba," as any *chanbara*-movie fan knows, is a raffish, feudal-flavored synonym for "sayonara.")

Obviously the biwa master didn't think I was suited for the Japanese lute—or maybe, like the *shakuhachi* flute, it was considered primarily a man's instrument. His attitude didn't surprise me, for as an independent female foreigner living in a culture which was blatantly sexist and subtly xenophobic, I was quite accustomed to dealing with obstacles of reluctance and stereotyping. Many years later I learned that the "unbecoming" biwa was the chosen instrument of Benten, the White Snake Goddess, notorious for her promiscuous coupling with everyone from carriage-drivers to mountain mystics to the Buddha himself.

Thinking about how I would fit yet another weekly lesson into my already jammed-up schedule of school, work, and the semi-serious pursuit of assorted arts, crafts, and cultural cul-de-sacs, I wandered through the shrine compound. It was a warm, dappled October day, and the grounds were teeming with exuberant people and picturesque activities. The biwa concert had been one of a number of offerings; according to the newspaper, demonstrations of the tea ceremony, calligraphy, flower arranging, fortunetelling, and dancing by *miko* (shrine maidens with scarlet culottes and long black hair) were also scheduled. I was halfway up a flight of stairs, searching for the calligraphy tent, when someone bumped into me.

"Oh, excuse me," I said. I glanced at the person with whom I had collided, and was amazed to see that the face was familiar.

The incredulity and the recognition were simultaneous, and mutual: "Why, it's you!" said the deep, husky voice of Fuji Mugen, Zenzenji's *isoro* (defined in my Kenkyusha dictionary, by the way, as "a freeloader").

"And it's you!" I echoed. We stood gaping at each other for a moment. The mock-monk was dressed in an elegant dark-gray silk kimono with a black-and-lavender tie-dyed obi, and natural wood geta with black leather straps. His shaved head was partially concealed under a snap-brim cap of black pigskin, and he wore black-framed aviator sunglasses, but I would have known him anywhere. He looked me up and down, nodding in unmonastic appreciation. I was glad that I had taken the time to dress up a bit, in a long-sleeved, drop-waisted, scoop-necked, full-skirted dress of dark blue jersey with tiny white polka dots, and a navy blue straw hat decorated with a single red rose which someone had left anonymously on my doorstep the night before.

After a long, fertile moment of silence, Fuji Mugen finally spoke, like a person emerging from a trance. "Oh, how rude of me," he said in his scintillating samurai voice. "Let me introduce my friend." His companion was a square-faced, husky young man, an inch or two taller than Mugen, with a crooked nose and thick, chaotic eyebrows above black-framed glasses, and I was impressed to learn that he was the scion of one of the leading "tea families" in Kyoto. His name was Genji Masamune, and he had just finished performing the tea ceremony in a pavilion at the top of the stairs; that was why he was wearing formal *hakama* and *montsuki*—the traditional Japanese special-occasion outfit consisting of a white-crested black *haori* jacket worn over a kimono tucked into pin-striped hakama, a long, pleated culottes-like garment. On his feet were white tabi and wooden geta with white straps, and his hair, while not shaved like Fuji Mugen's, was cropped very close. He had applied some sort of gleaming pomade to his stubbly scalp, which made it resemble a freshly-planted rice paddy.

"Where are you going?" Mugen asked, removing his dark glasses and staring at me with his hooded hazel eyes. (Pure, pellucid greenish-brown: the perfect iris-color for an apprentice master of the art of tea.) I explained about my biwa-mission and said that at the moment I was just wandering around hoping to stumble across the calligraphy demonstration.

"Oh, that's already over, long ago," said Fuji Mugen. "Why don't you come with us and have some tea?"

"I'd love to," I said, envisioning a refined Japanese-style tea ceremony in some bamboo-walled hideaway. After all, these were the artistic heirs of one of the leading tea masters in Japan.

To my surprise, they led me instead to a nearby Western-style coffee shop called Versailles, where we ended up sipping Earl Grey tea from gold-rimmed china cups and nibbling on dainty seashell-shaped almond wafers. In keeping with the grandeur of its name, the coffee shop was decorated with ornate antiques, pink-and-white striped satin upholstery, crystal chandeliers as rococo as a stripper's rhinestone earrings, and, in a pleasant anachronism, several gilt-framed prints of Monet's water lilies. The musical playlist included Couperin, Saint-Saëns, and Aznavour, and the conversation was almost as eclectic as the music.

With Mugen leading the lively way, we proceeded rapidly from quotidian small talk to allegorical semiotics. "Did you happened to notice those lion-dog statues we passed on the way?" Mugen asked. I nodded. "And do you know why one always has its mouth open, while the other's mouth is closed?" He obviously expected me to say "No, I don't have a clue," but as it happened, I had recently spent an entire afternoon at the library researching that very topic. All but rubbing my hands together, I leaned across the table.

"Um," I said with counterfeit diffidence, "is it by any chance because the vocalization 'a,' as indicated by the Sanskrit letter 'ah,' is the least differentiated of all sounds, while "un" is its phonic opposite? Is it because 'ah-un' is very close to 'a-u-m,' or 'om'? Is it because 'ah-un' represents the beginning and the end, the entire spectrum of aperture and occlusion, enclosing all that ever was, is, or will be: every nuance of Nature, and music, and life?"

"Well, yeah, something like that," Mugen said grudgingly, but I could tell he was impressed, or at least dazed, by my monologue. A bit later, I excused myself to make a phone call, and when I returned Genji and Mugen were laughing.

"What's so funny?" I asked.

"Oh, Mugen just says the most outrageous things," Genji said. "He's a demon, you know."

"Not a demon," Mugen said. "*The* demon."

"In any case," Genji said, "you should watch out for him." Even to an ideological virgin, danger is an irresistible aphrodisiac.

"I'll be careful," I said, but I was even more intrigued than before.

Between tea-ceremony anecdotes and esoteric epigrams, I learned that Mugen was the only son of wealthy parents from the coastal town of Tsuwano; that he had considered being an actor but had finally agreed to continue a four- hundred-year-old family tradition by becoming a teacher of the tea ceremony; and that he wasn't really a freeloader at the Sodo but was paying for his room and board. I also learned that Genji Masamune had been an amateur boxer in college (hence the idiosyncratic starboard list of his nose); that he loved Buddy Holly's music (hence the black-rimmed glasses); that he played the guitar ("Not the biwa," he said with a grin) in his spare time; and that his family lived in a house which was over three hundred years old. I was welcome to visit any time I was in Kyoto, he said.

"Speaking of visiting," said Mugen, "did you know that some monks from Zenzenji are coming to Tokyo on *takuhatsu* next week?"

"What's 'takuhatsu'?" I asked. Mugen explained that it was a traditional form of begging, in which the monks made the rounds of various temples and private homes, picking up donations of cash and food. They would be staying at a temple in Tokyo called Shotokuji, and (he said) they would surely be pleased to see me if I stopped by on the following Thursday evening.

Genji had excused himself for a moment, and as soon as he was out of earshot Mugen leaned forward and whispered, "What are you doing tonight? Could you go to a movie with me?"

"Yes," I said. "I could." By that time I was so completely spellbound by this witty, mysterious man that I would probably have said yes to any destination he had suggested, however exotic and far away—Madagascar, Majorca, Minneapolis. A midtown Tokyo movie theater seemed rather tame.

"Can you meet me in Shinjuku at seven o'clock?"

"Yes," I said. "I can." Mugen was staring so intently at me that I had to blink, and it occurred to me that the last person who had peered into my eyes with such concentration had been the kindly old ophthalmologist in Kyoto, the summer before. His interest, though, had been purely clinical.

"And after the movie will you shave your head and cover your body with syrup, and seaweed, and sequins?"

"Yes," I said. "I will." That is, I might have said yes, but of course he didn't ask anything so outlandish. I felt giddy and reckless, and I was oddly relieved to find that my appetite for romance hadn't been spoiled by the sordid debacle with Kuri.

* * *

The movie Mugen wanted to see was *Rosemary's Baby*, but the line was so long that we gave up. It was probably just as well, because when I finally saw the film a few months later, I went around for days afterward looking at everyone with extreme suspicion, as if they might be the agents— or the spawn—of the devil. There was something undeniably devilish (though not quite diabolical) about Fuji Mugen, which was at odds with his monk-like appearance. I could sense the strong currents of passion and sensuality roiling beneath his calm, elegant surface, but I felt that he was interested in me as a human being who happened to be female, not just as a long-legged, blue-eyed, relatively nubile foreign curiosity.

For my part, while I would have described our rapport as primarily intellectual, I never tired of staring at Mugen's large, smooth, hairless head, his shapely saurian features, his enigmatic eyes, his broad shoulders, his muscular arms, his strong graceful tea-making hands. Still, it was a bit of a shock every time we stood up, for Mugen projected such a substantial presence that I always forgot how short he was, even in his trademark four-inch geta.

We wandered around the neon jumble of Shinjuku for a while, snacking on fried noodles and little fish-shaped griddlecakes filled with sweet warm bean-paste. Eventually we found ourselves in Shinjuku Park. It was completely dark by then, but the park was gently illuminated by the rosy flickering pole-lamps along the paths, and by the full moon which had just risen, fat and tofu-colored, above the lacy trees.

Almost all the benches were occupied by shadowy couples; some were talking quietly with foreheads touching, but most were fused in such intimate embraces that they looked at first glance like Siamese twins, or two-headed snakes. I stole a glance at Mugen; his remarkable face seemed to glow in the combined moon-and-lamplight, and he radiated every quality that I valued. Even if we had not been surrounded by contagiously demonstrative lovers, I would still have wanted to kiss him, at that moment, more than anything in the world. At last, we came upon an empty bench. Mugen stretched, yawned, and otherwise pantomimed extreme exhaustion, and I had to smile at such obviousness from one who was so subtle in every other way. We sat down together and suddenly, with no negotiation or awkwardness or butting of heads, we began to kiss.

Most Japanese men seem to have learned their kissing techniques by watching an electric drain-unclogger in action, but Mugen was different. He appreciated the erotic value of nuance and restraint, and he understood that a butterfly-brush of lips or a brief transfusion of bated breath can be far more stimulating than a direct assault on the adenoids. I had been necking with boys (and men) since I was fourteen years old, but I had never experienced such metaphysical kisses, or such a dizzying synthesis of psyches.

Somehow we ended up lying on Mugen's beautiful silk kimono under a tree, alternating rapturous silences with ardent whispers. "I'm sorry," I said at one particularly intense juncture, "I'm still a virgin, and I'm just not quite ready—"

"That's all right," Mugen said. "I'll wait forever, if I have to." I was touched by his patience, but it amazed me, and frightened me a little, too, to realize that if I had been ready, Mugen wouldn't have hesitated to make love to me right there on the green grass, in a public park, under the full moon and the spying stars, in the middle of the largest city in the world.

* * *

Shotokuji, the temple where the monks from Zenzenji were staying, was in a posh, verdant residential section of Tokyo. I had the name and the address written down, but I walked past it two or three times because I just couldn't believe that such a starkly futuristic concrete structure could be a Zen temple. It was, though, and once inside the desolate steel gate, it began to look a bit more familiar.

There were the usual icons and accoutrements: a scroll-painting of the Buddha holding a flower (said to be the origin of Zen), a large wooden fish on a purple cushion, an altar piled with tangerines, a straw-matted meditation hall, and everywhere the pervasive, evocative smell of incense. I was met in the entry hall by a black-robed monk with penetrating eyes and a friendly square-toothed smile. He introduced himself as Izumo, the caretaker of the temple, and explained that he was a student of *kanpoyaku*: Chinese herbal medicine.

The monks from Zenzenji were sitting around a table in the austere, institutional kitchen, drinking tea from earthy-looking cups and crunching sesame-studded rice crackers. The pottery, and the monks themselves, seemed to be oases of texture in the smooth-surfaced, monochromatic kitchen. They all greeted me by name, but to my disappointment their faces were all new to me. In my visualization of that eagerly-awaited encounter, the delegation of monks had always included Toku-san and Zo-san, who were my only real acquaintances in the Sodo. That is, aside from Mugen, who was now (to my hybrid delight and embarrassment) considerably more than an acquaintance.

After a few awkward moments, the conversation began to flow, and I soon discovered that each of the four visiting monks had his own distinct personality and charm. There was Zan-san, who wore a permanent secret smile which, in a layperson, might have been mistaken for a smirk. He didn't talk much, but when he did he said something trenchant and pithy, while the overhead light glinted off his gold-capped canine teeth. There was Také-san, tall and lithe, who had majored in Russian literature in college and had read *War and Peace* in the original. When I addressed him in my rusty high-school Russian, he looked extremely alarmed. "Oh, no," he said in Japanese. "I don't *speak* Russian; I only read it."

The third monk, Jun-san, was the teen-aged, round-faced son of the priest of a small Zen temple outside of Kyoto. After a moment I recognized him as the badly-bruised unsui who had been Zo-san's assistant in the kitchen. Finally, there was Ryu-san, a young monk with inverted V-shaped eyebrows who engaged me in an enthusiastic conversation about Motown music. Conversation is perhaps not the proper word; it was more like oral cryptography, as Ryu-san would name a performer, using the phonetic Japanese transliteration ("Uiruson Pikctto," "Za Shupuriimusu," "Otishu Rcdengu," "Burenton Uddo," "Paasshii Surejji") and I would try to guess, amid general hilarity, to whom he was referring.

I had been reading a lot of books about Zen since returning from Kyoto in late August, and my mind was filled with questions: How do you know when you've found satori? How do you choose a koan? And (on a more down-to-earth note), was the diet at the Sodo strictly vegetarian? The monks patiently answered all my questions about customs and practices, while skillfully deflecting my ingenuous inquiries about wisdom, truth, and enlightenment.

I wanted only to talk about Zen, but they were more interested in hearing about life in the United States, and they asked endless questions about American cars, movies, salaries, and courtship customs. At one point, after I had managed to steer the conversation back to the topic of meditation, I said in despair, "I don't think I'll ever be enlightened; for one thing, I have so much trouble getting to sleep at night, and I've always heard that truly spiritual people can fall asleep immediately, because their minds are at peace."

"Perhaps you need some sort of relaxing ritual at bedtime," said Izumo gently.

"Oh, I have one," I assured him. "I always brew a pot of tea, and drink it by candlelight, and then I try to meditate on the light at the end of the void."

"And what sort of tea do you drink?"

"Oh, just regular green tea." There was a moment's silence, and then everyone began to laugh.

I must have looked bewildered, because Izumo said, in his kindly way, "Didn't you know that green tea contains more caffeine than coffee?"

"No," I said. "I didn't." Shaking my head at my own self-defeating ignorance, I joined in the continuing laughter. "It's all Eisai's fault," I said, and everyone seemed to find that very amusing. I suspected that they were laughing at me rather than with me, but I didn't mind a bit.

My feeling that Zenzenji was the most interesting place on the planet was reinforced by my evening with the traveling monks, and I began to think more and more about the possibility of taking leave of the world of chrome and chaos and carbon monoxide, and seeking refuge in a temple or nunnery. I was utterly enamored with what I had seen and heard of the Zen way of life: the reassuring rituals, the stirring chanting, the exquisite, earthy aesthetics, the preordained serenity, and the feeling of timeless harmony with the universe, both immediate and infinite. After my memorable evening in the park with Fuji Mugen, I wasn't eager to give up consorting with men, but on the other hand I figured that a nunnery might be the one place where a full-grown American virgin wouldn't be considered an aberration, or a challenge. The only other aspect of the monastic experience that gave me pause was the necessity of shaving one's head.

Upon returning from the public bath each evening, I would wrap my mass of damp hair in a towel and peer into the small antique mirror that hung in the candlelit hall, trying to imagine how I would look with a naked scalp. Not very appealing, I feared, and surely that was part of the point. I had used my hair as a cloak of invisibility and a Bohemian banner for as long as I could remember, and I knew that to be suddenly stripped of that protective thicket would require a major adjustment— not just emotionally but metabolically as well, for I suspected that a skinhead would be very chilly in the approaching winter.

Still, aside from the mandatory hair-removal and the proscription on stepping out with intriguing males, every other aspect of the monastic life, as I perceived it, appealed to me more and more. As a semi-militant virgin, I had no quarrel with sexual abstinence; it was the segregation of genders that seemed such a waste of potentially fine rapport and rare adventures. The ideal compromise, I thought more than once that fall, would be to find a sect of long-haired nuns who were permitted to have a social life—or at least to take an occasional moonlight stroll in the park with the mad monk of their choice.

S I X

LILIES IN WINTER

And might this young witch,
Upon taking the veil
Count on an aged abbess's connivance
At keeping toad-familiars
In her cell?

Robert Graves
Gooseflesh Abbey

—KYOTO

The young nun unwound the gray wool shawl from around her head and shoulders very slowly, as if she were unwrapping a precious globe of white jade, or the still-fertile egg of some prehistoric bird. There was a gentle reverence in the way she touched her bare head (long strong fingers, trembling hands), and I sensed that she was filled with wonder at the holiness of her own existence. "Deborah-san?" she said.

"Yes," I said, holding out a bulky paper-wrapped bouquet of white trumpet lilies.

"Hotokesama ni," said the young woman, taking the flowers. "I accept these on behalf of the Buddha." Standing there framed in the antique gate with her arms full of luminous lilies, the nun looked pure and pale and otherworldly, and I shivered, partly from the late-night December cold, but also from the excitement of being about to embark on a visit to an unknown realm.

As I followed the nun through the gate and along a stone path lined with mauve-leafed maples, I had a sudden attack of anxiety. What am I doing here? I wondered. Like so many of my adventures, this one had grown out of a chance remark. I had mentioned casually, that day at

"Versailles" with Fuji Mugen and Genji Masamune, that I was interested in knowing more about the daily life of Buddhist nuns. A month later I received a letter from Genji, saying it was all arranged: a friend of his mother's knew an abbess, and I was to spend a week in December at Mumyo-in nunnery. At first I was thrilled at the prospect of such a novel experience, but now, as I realized that I would have only one day at the end to see my friends and to loiter hopefully outside the Zenzenji Sodo, a week began to seem like a very long time.

After introducing herself as Yuriko (the name means "Lily Child," and I congratulated myself on my unwittingly perfect choice of flowers), the young nun led me into a sort of sitting room. The room was furnished Western-style, with overstuffed chairs covered in worn sherry-colored velvet, spindly-legged tables, and green-fringed lampshades. There was a rug of woven jute on the wood-plank floor, and the only decorations were a warty-looking white bud vase containing a single wilted daisy, and a calendar which featured a poem by Paul Reps, of all people, superimposed on a serigraph of a lemon-curd sun. I was very disappointed by the decor, for I was always hoping to find Lafcadio Hearn's idealized "faërie Japan" around every corner, and the expectations were naturally higher at temples and shrines. I was bewildered, too; I thought that all temples were oases of timeless aesthetics and undiluted Japaneseness, and this room was more like a set for one of those dreary off-Broadway plays about loud, crude, cantankerous families.

The Lily Child excused herself, and when she returned a few minutes later she was carrying a large green glass vase. As she arranged the lilies I had brought, expertly snipping the stems to the proper three lengths to signify heaven, earth, and man, I noticed that Yuriko's skull was different from those of the monks; smaller, smoother, more delicately modeled. The second thing I noticed, under the light, was that she looked very attractive, and completely feminine, without hair. If anything, the absence of fringe seemed to emphasize the flares and curves of her lovely features, and the becoming solemnity (or was it sadness?) of her expression.

The door slid open again, and a frail, diminutive, rosy-cheeked nun dressed in a simple gray cotton kimono entered the room. Like the biwa master, she was ageless, but definitely old; she appeared to be in her late seventies but she could have been as old as ninety. There was something unsettling about the round infant smoothness of the nun's bare skull, in contrast with the flushed, wrinkled face beneath it, as if the two extremes of Shakespeare's ages of man had been conflated. "Deborah-san, welcome!" she said in a surprisingly light, girlish voice. "We are so honored to have you here."

"The honor is entirely mine," I replied. It was small moments like this that made all the late nights spent studying the convoluted rules of *keigo* (polite speech) seem worthwhile. I wondered what Toozie would have said in the same situation; probably the Japanese equivalent of "Hey, like, it's really far out to be here!" While the elderly nun and I exchanged deep, zero-visibility bows, I reflected once again on the liberating ease of ignorance, at least in relation to the complexities of the Japanese language and the even more complex society it reflects.

"You must be tired," said the nun, after introducing herself as Kashibara.

"Just a bit," I replied. It was nearly eleven o'clock, and I had spent the day at school in Tokyo, taking final exams, and the evening on the bullet train. "I'm sorry if I kept you up past your bedtime," I said. "I came directly from the train station." I didn't mention my detour to find a flower shop, and the ensuing marathon-chat with the poetic proprietor about the beauty of barren branches, and the incubatory promise of winter.

"That's all right," said the elderly nun. "I find that I need less and less sleep these days—it's one of the blessings of growing old." She showed me where the bathroom was, and then, apologizing in hyper-polite language for the spartan accommodations, she led me to my room. "See you in the morning," she said, bowing her gleaming head above praying hands.

The nunnery didn't have a guest room, so I was lodged in a small cubicle that had been used for storage. The usual occupants of the room—several cardboard boxes, a tall bamboo birdcage, a red velvet chair with one broken leg, a generic ink painting of a wispy-whiskered sage on muleback gazing at a misty Chinese waterfall—had been deposited in the hall outside. After a quick dip in a stunningly hot bath I lay down in my tiny sleep-capsule with the balls of my feet touching one wall, and my untonsured head pressed against the other. It wasn't the zenith of comfort, but I was so tired that I could probably have slept like a stone in the velvet armchair, or the birdcage.

* * *

Mumyo-in was, after all, a nunnery, a place of sacrifice and self-denial, so I shouldn't have been surprised that "See you in the morning" turned out to mean prayers and prostration at five a.m. I was still half-asleep as I followed a dour middle-aged nun ("I'm Mochizuki," she said by way of greeting, "and we all know who *you* are") up a narrow staircase to a large tatami-matted room, hazy with incense, where twenty women of various ages, all bald, all dressed in gray kimono, were kneeling three to a mat. I spotted the sweet rosy-cheeked old nun kneeling on a brocade pillow beside a tall black-lacquer altar, and I realized for the first time that she must be the abbess. Mochizuki, meanwhile, had led me to a spot at the back of the room. "Just imitate the person in front of you," she whispered, before hurrying off to join the other senior nuns in the front row.

There was a brief overture for drums and bells, and then the chant began: "Namu-amida-butsu" (Praise to merciful Buddha), slurred and shortened, as the cadences rippled on, to "Namu-ami-dabu." The room was lit by candles, and the visible breath of the chanting nuns turned the chilly space into a dance hall full of ghosts. At first the soprano and contralto voices simply chanted, with eerie, ethereal harmony, but after a few moments the nuns began a sort of non-secular calisthenics: chanting "Namu-amida-bu" all the while, they would kneel down, touch their foreheads to the tatami (sweet scent of hay), place their hands on the floor palms up, then stand up, then genuflect again.

This sequence was repeated hundreds of times, and when we finally stopped I was sweating and panting for breath. If I had been familiar with the concept of aerobic exercise I would no doubt have felt very virtuous. As it was, all I felt was a strong desire to escape from the nunnery as quickly as possible, for I had realized, by the fifth syllable of the first chant, that this was not a Zen nunnery, as I had blithely assumed; rather, it belonged to the Pure Land sect of Buddhism.

The difference between Zen and the Pure Land sect may be defined, in the simplest philosophical terms, as the difference between *jiriki* and *tariki*. "Jiriki" means, literally, "self-power"; in a religious context it refers to attaining salvation or enlightenment through one's own efforts. "Tariki" means "other-power," and refers to the belief that one can be saved (the passive tense is significant) if one simply practices the proper rituals and utters the prescribed incantations.

In non-religious terms, I have occasionally explained the distinction with this admittedly simplistic example: A person who asks a friend for a favor (say, a ride to the airport) only as a last, desperate resort, is living by the principle of jiriki. A person who asks a friend for a ride before even investigating the self-powered alternatives (cabs, shuttles, public transportation) is practicing tariki. I have found that most people's behavior falls clearly into one category or the other, and I have learned the hard way that any friendship between a jiriki-purist and a tariki-opportunist is probably doomed from the start.

The differences between Mumyo-in and Zenzenji were atmospheric, too; the aesthetics, the emanations, the quality of light, even the smell of the incense at the Jodo temple seemed harsher and less sublime. I tried, in my free moments, to analyze the ambience of humorless, joyless gloom. Was it the difference in doctrine, the difference in decor, the difference in gender, or simply the difference in personnel? Or was the dark, damp miasma that seemed to hang over the nunnery like Spanish moss in a haunted graveyard the result of a communal depression over the belief that no matter how hairless and asexual they might be, no matter how early they rose in the morning, how loudly they chanted, and how assiduously they fell to their knees, women could never become Buddhas?

Much as I longed to flee, I knew that early departure was not an option. If I had left before the end of my scheduled one-week sojourn, it would have caused Mrs. Mikita (the friend of Genji's mother) to lose face, and, by extension and association, Genji and his mother would have been shamed also. There was nothing to do but stick it out.

Like the monks I had met in Tokyo, the young nuns were very curious about American pop culture and personal economics, but there weren't many opportunities for frivolous conversation. Although they were all friendly enough, I was struck by the permanent glumness of their expressions. I wondered why they had chosen to "throw away the world," as the Japanese put it, and in lieu of biographical facts I made up highly speculative stories about several of the women. I was certain, for example, that the beautiful sad-faced Yuriko had been wounded by love, while I suspected that the stern and androgynous Mochizuki, who told me she had once worked as a bank teller, was on the lam from an embezzling charge.

I was paying only about a dollar a day to stay at Mumyo-in, but even at late-sixties slave labor rates, I was more than earning my keep. I worked for several hours every morning and afternoon, pulling weeds, patching shoji screens, peeling vegetables, and cleaning the waxy wooden floors on my hands and knees. Every day after lunch I went into a schoolroom where I practiced writing kanji while the younger nuns studied sutras and scripture. Then it was time for the afternoon version of the morning genuflection ritual; the sequence was identical, but it seemed less exotic because our chanting breath was no longer visible in the warmer air and brighter light of afternoon. The ritual was repeated again at eight in the evening, just before the spiritual high point of my day: bedtime.

The food, at least, was delicious: rustic soy-sauced variations on a basic theme of vegetables, tofu, rice, and seaweed. I also liked raking leaves in the garden, wearing a borrowed kimono jacket of scratchy brown wool over my own "habit" (a thick raspberry-colored sweater and a long dusty-rose wool skirt, worn over L. L. Bean long underwear), and smelling the spicy smoke of bonfires from other temples in the compound. Eventually I began to enjoy the physical aspect of the early-morning sacred aerobics, the Buddhist jumping jacks, the Pure Land push-ups. All in all, though, it was the slowest-passing week of my life, and when I wasn't cursing myself for not having asked Genji Masamune the obvious preliminary question ("What sect does your mother's friend's nunnery belong to?") I was meditating, ruefully, on the theory of temporal relativity: The less fun you're having, the longer it takes to have it.

My last day at Mumyo-in was a Friday, and it began like all the other days: up at five, visible breath and candlelight, calisthenic chanting till the first light of dawn. Around midmorning, just as I was emptying the last bamboo scoop full of brittle worm-veined leaves into a wooden barrel, Mochizuki appeared around the corner, wearing her usual saturnine expression and making the Japanese gesture (confusingly similar to our goodbye wave) which signifies "Come here." She led me into her little office and locked the door behind us. On the desk was a towel, a pan of steaming water, a gleaming straight razor, and an old-fashioned brush and soap bowl. Oh my God, I thought, after the leap-to-conclusions portion of my brain had processed this startling still life, she's going to shave my head!

I glanced around frantically for possible avenues of escape, but the door was thick, solid wood, and the only window was a tiny frosted pane well over my head. "Well, let's get started," said Mochizuki briskly, and she picked up the towel and draped it around her own shoulders. Realizing my folly, I began to laugh, but relief turned to panic when I realized that she wanted me to shave *her* head. The nun gave me a curious look. "Have you ever shaved anyone's head before?" she asked.

"No, never!" I said eagerly, hoping that my lack of experience would disqualify me. "I always cut myself to shreds when I shave my legs," I added sinisterly.

"Don't worry," said Mochizuki. "It's simple. Just try not to perforate my brain." She chuckled at this macabre quip, but I had a sudden vision of a bright geyser of blood gushing forth from a punctured soft spot. "Are you sure you wouldn't rather have someone else do this?" I pleaded.

"You're my only hope," Mochizuki said matter-of-factly. She explained that she should have had her head shaved the evening before, but she had become engrossed in a novel and had missed the mass weekly head-shaving. Fortunately the old abbess had stayed in bed that morning with a cold, but she would be up for lunch, and it was imperative that Mochizuki, as a senior nun, greet her with a shiny, depilated head. I gathered that there was a strict rule about having the head shaved every Thursday night, and that any nuns who failed to comply would be punished by having to stay up all night chanting and touching their stubbly crowns to the cold floor.

I seemed to have no choice but to do the job ("no choice" being the leitmotif of that week), so I picked up the wooden-handled brush, dipped it in the hot water, rubbed it around the soap bowl until a rabid foam appeared, and then applied the bubbly lather to Mochizuki's lumpy, moon-cratered skull. I was surprised by how thickly the hair had grown back in only a week; it was about a quarter of an inch long and very wiry, like a suede brush.

In order to neutralize my inadvertent-lobotomy anxiety, I tried to approach the task through a gardening metaphor: the hair as lawn, myself as mower. This worked quite well until I got to the ears and remembered the graphic scene in the film *Kaidan* in which Hoichi, the medieval biwa player, has his ears non-surgically removed by the irate ghosts of drowned aristocrats. I stopped and took a deep breath, and then, several very careful strokes later, I was finished. "Thank you very much," said Mochizuki, wiping the seafoam of excess soap from her head with a towel. "You've saved me. I owe you a favor." She smiled for the first time in our acquaintance, and I counted seven gold teeth before her mouth closed again.

"It was nothing," I said, but I was still trembling and sweating, and I couldn't seem to catch my breath.

Just then the lunch bell rang; the head-shaving ritual had taken a full forty-five minutes. The abbess was seated in her place at the head of the table, but she was obviously unwell; her cheeks were pale, and she was coughing intermittently. I took my usual seat and watched as the nuns, one by one, filed by for inspection. A couple of the younger nuns received scoldings for having missed a few microscopic clumps of hair, and I couldn't help feeling a small surge of pride when the abbess passed her hand over Mochizuki's glossy, unlacerated scalp and beamed with approval.

Finally, at long last, it was time to say goodbye. The abbess invited me to come and stay at Mumyo-in anytime I was in Kyoto, but even as I made the appropriate social sounds I knew that I had no intention of doing any more Pure-Land aerobics by candlelight, or of chanting "Namu-amida-bu" with a chorus line of doleful-looking nuns, or of asking the Buddha—or any other deity—to give me a lift to the ultimate airport.

* * *

My heart felt huge with joy and expectation as I walked through the antique district, past a garish vermilion shrine-gate, along the familiar lanes of small shops and surrealistic love hotels, and entered the main gate of Zenzenji. Standing under the great canopy of catfish-colored tiles, I felt as if I were at the border of another world. I had left behind the universe of cheap sex and shallow passions, of ugly furniture and religious compromise, and before me lay a landscape filled with pure souls, free minds, artistic atmosphere, and immeasurable mystery.

The stout gatekeeper was snoozing in his little box, but he woke up, wheezing gently like an old dog, when I passed by. "Ah," he said, "okaeri nasai!" ("Welcome home!") I was thrilled by the greeting, which struck me as clairvoyant, and profound. I had chatted with the gatekeeper a few times during my summer sojourn in Toozie's little temple, but I had hardly expected him to remember me, much less to perceive me as a returning resident. As I walked along the cobblestone path through the center of the compound, I did feel as if I had come home, and it occurred to me that my enthrallment was not with Buddhism per se, or even with the sect of Zen, but rather with this particular temple: this small but infinite slice of space.

As I rounded the lily-pond corner and headed up the Sodo slope, I almost collided with a monk wearing a short black wide-sleeved koromo, his face hidden under a huge round bamboo hat. "Hooo!" said the monk (for that word, which means 'the rain of Dharma,' is the cry of takuhatsu), and then I recognized the deep, amused voice: it was Tokusan. As the line of monks, six in all, passed me, they all echoed the greeting. I felt a great surge of warmth and delight and homecoming; to quote from my starstruck journal, *I was petrified with wonder to think that I was actually acquainted with such mythical-looking beings.* And I realized then (for those were the days of 45 rpm: revelations per minute) that I didn't really want to be a nun at all. What I wanted to be was a woman—preferably the *only* woman—in a monastery full of fascinating men.

Toozie was waiting in her little room, the room I coveted more than any villa or castle or chateau, with cinnamon-dusted mochi and hot jasmine tea. "So," she said, "are you gonna become a nun, or what?"

"Not this week," I said. "And definitely not at *that* temple."

"Far out," said Toozie, through a mouthful of mochi, and then she began telling me about a strange monk named Muni Nigamomo whom she had met at a nearby coffee shop.

"He's very good-looking," she said, "and seriously weird; I can't decide if he's utterly cool or totally full of shit. He says he used to be a Zen monk, but he decided that celibacy destroys brain cells, so he left the monastery and now he just crashes in parks, or at all-night coffee shops, or with whoever takes him in. He meditates a lot, and he walks everywhere—he's got great legs!—and he practices his own version of Tachi-something, some kind of sexy Buddhism. Have you heard of it?" I had, just barely. I shared what little I knew of the Tachikawa-ryu, a sybaritic splinter-religion, surviving from the Middle Ages, which is based on the Tantra of Desire: the explicitly-stated belief that sexual intercourse is the "supreme Buddhist activity."

"Oh, wow," Toozie said, laughing, "that would explain why he kept staring at my chest and then looking up and giving me these piercing pink-eyed looks. I thought he had, like, conjunctivitis or something, but I guess it was just lust. But he's so strict in other ways—like he refused to sit on a zabuton, saying it was too soft, and he wouldn't eat the wheat cracker I offered him because it was 'impure food' or some bullshit like that, which really pissed me off."

Just after sunset, when the garden beyond Toozie's interior door was shadowed with the inky blues and violets of December dusk, Karen McKie stopped by. She was wearing a quilted kimono-jacket (lustrous padded patchwork squares of pistachio, teal, and rose) over a long denim skirt; her usually frizzy hair was in a sleek chignon, her Botticelli face was beatific, and I thought wistfully that she looked like the radiant paradigm of a fulfilled artist, well-loved woman, and happy human being.

"Tatsuya has a meeting tonight, and I can't face those ghastly dormitory pickles alone," Karen said. "Where shall we go to eat?" After twenty minutes of lively partisan discussion we still hadn't managed to agree on a restaurant, so we compromised by going to three. We began with hand-made noodles at my favorite *sobaya*, followed by *chawan-mushi* (a gossamer egg custard, loaded with savory morsels of vegetables, gingko nuts, and mushrooms) at a closet-sized bistro of Toozie's choice, and a few crisp rolls of cucumber sushi at a fifth-floor aerie, overlooking the dark river, where Karen and Tatsuya had gone on their first date.

Finally, by enthusiastic consensus, we stopped at a sidewalk stand, its calligraphic curtains flapping in the wintry breeze, and bought three greasy parchment bags of "yam candy" for dessert. The confection was actually made from sliced sweet potatoes, not yams, cooked in a vat of boiling sugar syrup; when the sweet potatoes cooled the crust became crisply caramelized while the Halloween-orange interior remained soft, sweet, and mealy. (Overcome by nostalgia one summer in the 1990s, I spent an entire afternoon searching for the yam-candy stand. A woman at a nearby florist's finally took pity, after I had wandered by her shop for the tenth time, and told me that the place I remembered had gone out of business in the early seventies. "People don't want to eat such simple food anymore," she said. "It reminds them of the war.")

After seeing Karen onto her bus, Toozie and I walked through the silent grounds of Zenzenji and tiptoed into the sleeping sub-temple of Kaiko-in. "What's this, a mash note?" I said, picking up an envelope which had been left in front of Toozie's door.

"Good guess, Sherlock," said Toozie as she scanned the page, then passed it to me with eyebrows raised so high that her forehead resembled Tijuana tuck-and-roll upholstery.

The letter was from the pink-eyed monk, and it was written in fluid Roman letters on a slightly crumpled piece of Miyako Hotel stationery. *Dear Mrs. Tuzi*, it read. *To meet you has been my favorite miracle. Your flowering flesh is zabuton of my restless soul. Please to meditate with me most soon. Om mani padme hung. With purity of passion, your humiliating servant, Mr. Muni Nigamomo. P.S. I will waiting tonight until midnight at same coffee shop you remember we met one other day.*

We laughed about the misprint of "hung" for "hum" ("Or maybe it's an incredibly clever pun," Toozie mused. "Either way, it's a mantra to live by!"), and then I said, "Well, Mrs. Tuzi, are you going to meditate with your passionate servant tonight, or not?"

Toozie shook her head. "Mmmm ... I don't think so," she said slowly. "Even though he is attractive as hell, and I *am* kind of curious about the Buddhism-in-the-dark trip."

"Then why not?" I asked: the virgin as procuress. "Because he didn't take a Wheat Thin when I offered it," Toozie said gravely.

"You know," I said, "sometimes I really feel sorry for men. I mean, if they only knew what trivial details determine their sexual fates! He would have had a better chance with you if he had been a parrot."

"A parrot? I don't get it," said Toozie, pulling her futon out of the closet. She climbed under the covers, fully dressed, and by the time I had finished belaboring the Polly-want-a-cracker connection, she was fast asleep.

* * *

The next day was crisp and clear and mild, a glorious throwback to fall. I was planning to return to Tokyo on the evening train, and to catch a plane the following morning for Los Angeles. From there I would follow the *fêngshûi* dragon-lines home to Sedona, Arizona for a family reunion. Around noon I walked over to the Sodo, hoping to see Toku-san, and wishing secretly that Mugen would be around as well. I hadn't heard from Mugen since that evening in Shinjuku Park, and my feelings for him had fallen into a state of volatile dormancy, like a dug-up daffodil bulb languishing in a winter basement, ready to burst into bloom at the slightest sign of warmth.

I hung around outside the gate for a while, but there was no one in sight. No black-robed spy-hatted monks setting out on takuhatsu; no white-kerchiefed unsui trimming the trees; no sound of chants, no smell of incense. The only sign of life was a ribbon of smoke from the chimney, so I finally summoned up all my courage, ducked through the gate, and tiptoed into the dim kitchen. An unfamiliar monk (short body, long face, tree-mushroom ears) was stirring a pot of *miso*-and-seaweed soup, and he was so startled to see me that he dropped his cast-iron ladle into the vat and had to roll up his sleeve to fish it out.

"Is Toku-san here?" I asked. "He's eating lunch," the monk said, as he washed his soupy forearm in the big metal sink.

"Oh, I'm sorry," I whispered. "I'll come back later." I felt a rush of embarrassment as I thought of the monks eating in the room next door, the ritual silence of their meal shattered by my ill-timed intrusion.

"No, don't go," said the monk. He pointed in the direction of the far door. "Just wait out there for a minute, please." He disappeared, and I walked out to the unpaved courtyard.

After a few minutes I began to doodle in the snuff-colored dust with a stick I found nearby; I drew a sorcerer's logo (crescent moon with a star in the curve), and then I began to draw one of my favorite design motifs: a worm (or snake) devouring its own tail, with a camellia-leafed tree inside the circle. It was the same thing I would have drawn in the privacy of my room, but I was also hoping that a monk—any monk— would come out and see my glyphs and be impressed by the symmetry, or the symbolism.

Just as I had finished adding the leaves to the tree of life, a large, thick-torsoed monk emerged from the back door of the kitchen. "Wait a bit longer," he said, with a belligerent scowl. "Toku-san will be right out." While he was speaking, the fierce-looking monk rubbed his zori-shod foot in the dirt, obliterating every trace of snake, and tree, and Turkish flag. I felt as if I had been slapped, but it was an oddly salutary blow; I became conscious of my own hubristic motives in drawing the picture in the first place, and I felt grateful to the intimidating unsui for pointing out my vainglorious behavior.

A few minutes later Toku-san came out, followed by several other monks, including Zo-san, the human *luminario*. Then a young monk with boomerang-shaped eyebrows came running through the gate, carrying a box filled with *manju*, white-flour buns filled with bean paste.

When he passed the box to me, I recognized him as Ryu-san, the Motown-music fan I had met in Kyoto. "Thanks for dropping by; you're the only reason we got dessert!" Ryu-san murmured. Then he added, in an even more muted voice, "I hope to talk to you soon, in private—I want to ask a favor!"

When I told the monks that I was going home to Arizona and wouldn't be back for several months, they became sweetly solicitous. "You will come back, won't you?" Zo-san said.

"Of course," I said. "Japan is my *dai-ni no furusato* (second home)." Suddenly, all the monks began talking at once.

"We should give you a present, some souvenir of Kyoto. What would you like?" asked Zo-san. "How about a Japanese doll?" said Ryu-san. "Or some kimono cloth?" suggested Nu-san, the Valentine-eared monk, who was doing laundry by hand in a large outdoor sink. "Let's give her one of the Sodo umbrellas," said Toku-san. I would have loved to own one of those gorgeous bamboo umbrellas, waxy gold parchment decorated with scarlet lacquer trim and functional Zen calligraphy. But in those days I was sincerely striving to be non-materialistic, and, since vanity springs eternal, I also hoped that the monks would be impressed by my un-American austerity.

"Thank you very much for the generous offers," I said, "but I really don't need any material objects. Just to be standing here with all of you, at this moment, is the best possible souvenir." There was a general murmur of disappointment at this ostensibly noble and, I thought, impeccably Zen-like sentiment, and it occurred to me then that perhaps receiving was not a vice to be transcended, but rather an art to be mastered. Unfortunately it was too late to say, "On second thought, I *will* take that umbrella, and the doll, and the cloth, and anything else you might happen to have lying around," so instead I changed the subject. "What can I bring from America for the Sodo?" I asked.

"A washing machine," said Nu-san, who was hanging hand-washed gray cotton jackets on a clothesline made from braided green twine.

"No, seriously, what would you really like?"

"Two washing machines," said Nu-san.

THE LIZARD KING
AT L.A.X.

*I never travel without my diary; one should always
have something sensational to read in the train.*

Oscar Wilde

—PACIFIC OCEAN

I n the spring of 1970 I had never heard of biophilia; I only knew that
the moment I stepped into the chrome-and-glass chaos of Los Angeles International Air Terminal I wished I were back in the rosy,
mythic hills of Sedona. After an idyllic three-month visit with my endear-
ingly neurotic family in northern Arizona, my elusive visa renewal had
finally come through, and I booked passage on a train to Los Angeles, an
airplane to Honolulu, and a ship to Yokohama. I was standing in the
middle of the lobby at LAX, clutching my scratchy Japanese wicker and
Mexican striped-straw bags, trying to figure out where to board my
flight to Hawaii, when a voice behind me said, "Hey, baby, what's hap-
pening?"

I turned around, ready to glare at whoever had the temerity to
approach me with such a tired honky-tonk line, and found myself face
to seraphic face with Jim Morrison—lead singer of the Doors, dope
fiend, drunkard, Franco-Floridian imagist poet, and erotic loose cannon.
The quintessential rock and roll embodiment, I wrote that night, making
the obvious connection, *of Rimbaud's "complete disordering of the
senses." Perhaps* A Season in Hell *is another of those books—like the* Tao
Te Ching—*that should be available by prescription only.*

I knew at least one woman who would have given her spleen, on the
spot, for a chance to converse with Jim Morrison, but the encounter was

wasted on me. I found "Light My Fire" an energizing car-radio anthem, but I was neither a fan of the Doors nor a disciple of the cult of self-destructive debauchery. In fact, a self-styled "peyote poet" whom I met at the first Human Be-In in Golden Gate Park had called me unhip and reactionary because I refused to acknowledge Narcosia—his reverent name for the goddess of druggy glossolalia—as a valid muse. He later called me frigid, too, when I declined to spend the night in his fetid mushroom-grotto digs on Cole Street. "I'm not frigid, I'm a virgin," I said. "Yeah," he sneered. "I rest my case."

I wish I could say that I responded to Jim Morrison's greeting with some pithy, epigrammatic profundity that later showed up in the lyrics of one of the Doors' greatest hits. Unfortunately real life, while often more bizarre than fiction, is seldom so satisfyingly symmetrical. What I did was to point at a sign above a nearby counter which read "Information about Future Flights" and stammer lamely, "Um, I was just wondering whether this afternoon is considered the future."

"I wouldn't know—I always try to live in the present," said the rock star. Just then his entourage came along in a whirl of beads, beards, long hair and leather, and swept their leader away. "Have a good trip!" the Lizard King called over his shoulder with typical sixties ambiguity, and then he winked. Sixteen months later, as they say in those portentous rock biographies, he was dead.

I was no stranger to the ocean voyage; when I was sixteen years old, I had gone around the world on a Slovenian freighter with my sister, as her guest. (She ended up marrying the captain, and I ended up learning to speak Serbo-Croatian well enough—or badly enough—that when I visited Montenegro several years later, I was repeatedly mistaken for a *Slovenka*.) But the *Amazon-Maru* was very different from a twelve-passenger freighter; it was primarily a passenger ship, carrying hundreds of South American–born Japanese back to their ancestral homeland. I envied them that journey of discovery, but I also pitied them, for I had heard from other *nisei* that it can be very difficult and disheartening to be in Japan as a Japanese-looking person who grew up elsewhere, and doesn't know the cultural passwords.

I stowed my luggage in the narrow six-bunk cabin to which I had been assigned and went up on deck to watch the Oahu shoreline recede into the shimmering tropical distance. During my brief stopover in Honolulu I had found the warm, humid, plumeria-scented air almost anaesthetic, more conducive to heliolatrous languor than to liveliness of art or of intellect, and I speculated that it might be harder to struggle and suffer and grow in Hawaii than in a place with a more challenging climate. *An almost hypnotic ease in the air,* I wrote. *How can anyone concentrate amid such seductive tropical fecundity?* Years later, when I lived there, I learned the answer: by sequestering themselves in offices with hermetically sealed windows and gale-strength air conditioning.

I quickly made a few friends; oddly, more distinctly than their faces, I remember the words with which they approached me. "'Picture yourself on a boat on an ocean ...'" That was Elijah Ruskin, an architectural historian who was going to Japan to research a book on the curious architecture and risqué-rococo decor of love hotels. He was a gray-bearded gray-tweeded man in his late forties, with a wide gold wedding band on one hand and one of those hideous red-stoned Harvard class rings on the other. "So," he said, when he had finished presenting his verbal résumé, "are you going to Japan to study Zen?"

"*Mu,*" I said, but he didn't get the joke.

"Howdy! I see by your outfit that you are a gaijin! Have y'all been seasick yet?" That was C. J. Holcomb, a bouncy blonde Texan of about my age, with a turned-up nose, turned-up mouth, and dense eyelashes, so curly they were almost tubular, above Adriatic-azure eyes. She had been in Japan before, teaching English, but now she was going back on a student visa, to take courses in Japanese cooking at an academy in Kyoto. "Have you seen any cute guys around?" C. J. asked. "I'm dying; it's been at least three days since I last fell in love, or into bed."

"Hey, wow, I dig your gnome-boots." That was Lewison Lear, a self-described shoe fetishist who had been hired to take the photographs for Elijah Ruskin's love-hotel book, commenting on my rose suede shoes. Lewison was a large, soft-bodied man with tanned skin, a bushy full-face brown beard, and long brown hair combed straight back from an attractively-receding hairline in the approximate shape of the French side of the English Channel. He was wearing a cinnamon-colored corduroy suit, a purple cotton shirt, a wide brown velvet tie, and a pair of incandescent hand-stitched boots of Spanish leather (polished daily, he told me, with an aromatic mixture of beeswax and Darjeeling tea). After a brief biographical volley and a rhapsodic discussion of the Filene's Basement shoe department, he excused himself, saying, "I gotta go commune with the rest of my shoes."

"It's been nice talking to you, Lewison," I said.

"Oh, please, call me Lui—that's L-U-I," he said, spelling it out.

"As in Lui Lui?" I asked.

"Right on," he said. "Well, baby, I gotta go." I had barely had time to digest this rock-and-roll witticism when I felt another presence at my elbow, and heard another friendly voice.

"Did you by any chance have occasion to sew that very nice velvet skirt yourself? And also I love your striped-silk belt, where in the earth did you obtain that thing?" This was Ramon Furuta-Fuentes, a half-Japanese, half-Incan man with a billowing rusty-black Afro above broad, exotic features. He was on his way to Kyoto to learn to make kimono, and to continue his study of the language of his maternal ancestors. He spoke courtly, convoluted English and charmingly bizarre Spanish-accented Japanese, with every "n" pronounced as an "ñ." Ramon was a tailor by trade, and he hoped someday to become, as he put it, "a highly dramatic fashion designer of international well-repute."

Exhausted from so much socializing and self-revelation (for I had been called upon, again and again, to answer the same questions about my personal when, why, and whatever), I wandered toward the stern of the ship. The sun was setting directly ahead, and the sky was filled with a bestiary of rose-and-violet clouds. An Afghan hound was fleeing from a spiny-backed sea monster, a charcoal bird with wings of smoke sat on the head of a sacred elephant, a kangaroo waltzed with a biped bear. Beneath this zoomorphic procession the sea was smooth and green and celadine, and sleek brown albatrosses dipped and skimmed in the foamy wake.

All the other passengers seemed to be inside, or else leaning over the bow, for that was where you could see the fluorescent flying fish, and get drenched by spumes of salt-spray, and shout John Masefield poems into the wind. There was only one other person on the stern of the ship: a young man with long black hair and wide, square shoulders, dressed in a sunset-orange cotton shirt. He was sitting in the lotus position with his back to me, but by straining the limits of peripheral vision and proper etiquette I could see that his eyes were closed and his hands folded in his lap. After a moment I realized, with a *frisson* of affinity, that he must be doing zazen meditation. Not wanting to disturb him, I crept away to join the exuberant fish-spotters at the front of the ship.

The crossing took a week and a half, and by the third day a certain sea-birthed cadence had evolved. If I woke up early enough, dawn was for seated meditation on the back of the ship, and for watching the strange, fragmented sunrise, which began as a cluster of small flares on the silvery seam between sea and sky. Mornings were for studying and reading (H. H. Munro, Italo Calvino, Ryunosuke Akutagawa, Isabella Bird); afternoons were for hanging out; dusk was for strolling around the deck, and for surreptitiously admiring the strong samurai profile of the young man who always did zazen, dressed in bright equatorial colors, on the stern of the ship under a color-coordinated sunset. I never saw him at any other time; not at meals, not in the halls, not in the lounges, not even, lamentably, in my dreams.

Evenings were for terpsichorean excess: for dancing till we dropped. There were three factions: the young and the feckless (us); the tango crowd (three vividly made-up Japanese-Brazilian women and their tight-trousered, slick-haired partners); and the watchers (everyone else). On the second night, a subtle power struggle took place; our group won, by virtue of audience applause, and the tangoistas slunk off to a smaller lounge with a scratchier record player.

The ship's record collection, for some unknown reason, consisted of a single disc: the Rolling Stones' "Let It Bleed." Fortunately, we all loved that album, and we played it over and over, dancing to every song. At first we just did an amorphous no-partner bop, but by the fourth night, buoyed by the response of the watchers, we had begun to improvise some comical choreography: square-dance satires, a Fantasia-inspired ballet routine, an Isadora Duncan free-for-all (grand jetés and hamadryad poses), and revivals of such vintage steps as the Stroll, the Rocka Conga, and the Chalypso.

Occasionally, as I was leaping around on the not-quite-level dance floor, feeling the ocean's mysterious motion five floors below, I would suddenly think about Zenzenji, and the monks, and the quiet precision of monastery life, and I would wonder if I should be off merging my soul with the sky or doing zazen or practicing calligraphy. But then I would remember the quote from Hakuin, the feisty Zen master: "Both music and dancing are voices of the Way," and I would grab a couple of star-tled spectators from the shadows. "But I'm a really bad dancer," the reluctant recruits would always protest. "The only bad dancer is some-one who refuses to dance," I would declare, and then I would try to teach them the intricacies of the Boogaloo or the Shing-a-ling, while

Mick Jagger sang "Come on, baby, don't you wanna live with me?"

Other popular shipboard activities were playing board games, especially Scrabble; walking laps around the slick, salty deck; taking naps; counting the minutes till mealtime; and staring dreamily into the misty blue distance. One day, numbed by an excess of leisure, I sat down on a deck chair under a sunless zinc-colored sky, and began browsing through my journal. The Kyoto entries made me long for Zenzenji, while the Arizona notes made me homesick for my family in Sedona, and I felt fortunate to have so many homes to miss.

Oak Creek is my roshi, I had written in early March. *Wild asparagus sprouting on the riverbanks, fussed over by flocks of whirring winged insects reminiscent of the dweller-under-sundials in* Alice. *Mistletoe, dried to the color of a Tibetan lama's robe, crumbles into saffron powder. The ground golden with sycamore leaves; the evening sky the velvety blue of a Navajo squaw dress; wispy clouds like smoke from the pipe of the Old Man of the Mountain; and everywhere the shooting green and wildflowering of spring.*

I closed my journal with a sigh and peered into the manila envelope containing the correspondence I had received in Sedona. There were several earnest, relentlessly lyrical letters, postmarked Vermont and Boston and Mendocino, from young American men; the obsolete crossed-out addresses bore untidy testimony to my constant movement, and, I thought, to the fragility of post-romantic friendship. There was a postcard from Izumo, the kanpoyaku-monk I had met in Tokyo: a photograph of irises in bloom, with a message in stylized squarish calligraphy on the back. *Hope you return in time to see the cherry blossoms. In the meantime, beware of caffeine!*

There was also a letter from Toozie Zane (green ink on mauve paper) written in surprisingly dainty script. *Well, here I am on a literally far-out island in the East China Sea, practicing gentle perversions in a grass shack, with rain falling on a tin roof—and on our naked pagan bodies! The roof leaks, but that's cool, 'cause we do, too ...* That was how the letter began; it ended, several uninhibited pages later, with the salutation, *Love and Snickers, 2-Z.* I was trying to imagine what Toozie meant by "gentle perversions," when I felt a tap on my shoulder.

"Hi," said C. J. Holcomb. "Can we talk?" She was wearing red shorts and what Toozie might have called a shit-eating grin, and she bounced around on her slatted wooden deck chair as if it were a trampoline.

"You're awfully cheerful today," I said. "Did something good happen?"

"Something fantastic happened," said C. J. "I got laid."

"Oh, um, congratulations?" I wasn't entirely at ease with the topic, but I was mildly curious about the identity of the man. "Anyone I know?"

C. J. shook her head. "No, I don't think so," she said. "He's never around. His name is Yukio, and he's absolutely gorgeous and very intelligent and astonishingly passionate. I had only seen him once before, doing yoga or something on the back of the ship—" (Oh no, I thought, not *him*) "—and then last night when I went into the communal shower area he was there, looking incredibly sexy in a summer kimono. Our eyes met and then we both took off our robes and got into separate stalls, right next to each other, and after a few minutes under the hot water, thinking about his spectacular body, I said, 'The heck with this, what have I got to lose,' and I decided to visit him in his shower, and I met him on the way—it turned out he had the same idea and was on his way to visit me! And we did it right there under the hot water, standing up, first in his shower stall, then in mine, then in a lifeboat, then on the rug in the lounge—we couldn't go back to either of our rooms 'cause of the dreary roommates, you know—and then in the hold on a scratchy burlap bag, surrounded by animal sounds. (Or maybe that was us!) I had a few other ideas—the engine room, the captain's table in the dining room, the walk-in freezer—but he said he was tired and he had to get up early to feed a cow or something. I guess I'm what you'd call experienced, definitely a double-digit non-virgin, but I don't think I've ever spent such a fabulous night with anyone. We didn't talk much, and it wasn't exactly the height of comfort, but it was still unbelievably pleasurable. I mean, I've been with two men at once, and that was fun—I never knew whose hands were whose—but it wasn't any more exciting than last night. Yukio is such an unbelievably powerful lover, he turned me inside out like a, uh—like a reversible raincoat."

Ordinarily I would have been amused by the absurdly anticlimactic simile, but my sense of humor had been temporarily short-circuited by feelings of envious infatuation, manifested as nausea, shortness of breath, and the complete atrophying of all social skills. "I have to go," I said abruptly, and I ran off to seethe and mourn in my cool, dark cabin.

When I came back an hour later, armed with a semi-true excuse about a sudden headache, I found C. J., still wearing the residual bloom from her wild night, engaged in a game of Scrabble with Lewison Lear. When I peered over Lui's bulky brown shoulder, expecting the customary ladder of vowel-rich words like "liqueur," "gouache," and "innocuous," I was startled to see that they were playing a scatological version of the game: "shit," "crap," "fart," "whiz," and "feces" were just a few of the words on the board.

"Too bad, if you had five more letters you could make 'coprophagy,'" I whispered in C. J.'s ear, and then I went off to watch the flying fish, and the supernatural sunset.

That night we were all dancing, as usual, to "Let it Bleed." When "You Can't Always Get What You Want" began to play, we formed a conga line. Elijah Ruskin was behind me, with his overheated hands cinched tight around my waist, like a thermal corset. When the title line came up, he leaned over my shoulder and whispered, "I want *you*." I was horrified, and I rushed from the room, climbed a flight of outside stairs, and plopped down in a deck chair. I had thought of Elijah Ruskin as Just a Friend (he was a married man, and not my type in any case), and I felt that my friendship had been betrayed and my trust violated. I was trying to sort out my reactions to this shocking development, and I had identified anger, sadness, and revulsion when I heard a voice in the shadows.

"I don't know why you're sulking, but I have just the thing to cheer you up," said Lewison Lear. "Come on, follow me."

He led the way to the first-class stateroom he shared with Elijah Ruskin, and I gazed enviously at the mahogany paneling, the burnished-brass trim, the gumdrop-colored dahlias in malachite vases. "I don't usually do this," Lui said, "but I know you can dig the finer side of life, so I'm gonna show you my collection." He pulled a suitcase of amber leather from the closet, unlocked it with a small gold key which he wore on a thong around his neck, and flung open the lid with a flourish.

Inside, reclining against the regimental-striped rayon lining, were twenty pairs (I counted) of exquisitely-detailed shoes, in bright canvas, soft suede, and luminous leather: forty works of the cobbler's most inspired art. "Every pair has a story," Lui said, and he proceeded to tell me ten or twelve of the best ones. The tales were somewhat formulaic; most began, "I was walking along a street in Barcelona (or Milan, or Paris, or Westwood) when I passed the most amazing shoe store," and ended, "And so of course I bought them. Hey, I can't help it; I just really, really dig shoes."

When Lewison had finished, I felt that I should reciprocate in some way, so I pointed at my dancing shoes—square-heeled black pumps with multiple intersecting straps and silver buckles—and said, "I have a shoe story, too."

"Do tell," said Lui, and tell I did.

"A couple of years ago," I began, "when I was living in Cambridge and working at the Wursthaus (a time I now think of as my pastrami, psychotherapy, and Rilke period) I was invited to a Halloween party. My roommate Ursula decided to go as Vanessa Bell, so it seemed natural that I should attend the party dressed as Virginia Woolf. It was an easily assembled costume: a high-necked blouse with an antique brooch at the neck, hair in a bun, a long velvet skirt, my strappy black pumps, and a baggy cardigan with rocks in the pockets. I worried that the costume might appear to be disrespectful to the writer's troubled spirit, because I intended it to be a sympathetic tribute as well as a ghoulish joke. As it turned out, the party was light on literati and everyone thought I was impersonating the daguerreotype dowager on the Grandma's Molasses label. I didn't bother to correct that monumental misreading of my costume, and when no one was looking I dropped my suicide stones, which were surprisingly heavy and more than a little depressing, into a potted plant."

"That's a groovy story," said Lui absently, and then, in one fast, fluid movement, he turned off the lamp, sprang from his chair, and pressed his furry werewolf-face to mine.

"What are you doing?" I cried, and I ran from the room. This time I went and sat under a lifeboat, where I tried to figure out what it was about this full-moon night that had turned all my supposedly platonic male friends and dance partners into spring-loaded satyrs.

"Hello, you missing person under there," said a soft voice, and I looked up to see the epic-featured face of Ramon Furuta-Fuentes, shining in the moonlight. "May I join you in your shelter?"

"Oh, hi, Ramon," I said. I was happy to see him, for he was unfailingly gentle, courteous, and fun to talk to, and besides, I had been led to believe by shipboard gossip that he was not romantically interested in me, or in anyone of my gender. Ramon crawled under the lifeboat and pulled a tarp down so that we were completely invisible to passers-by.

We chatted for a while about odd, disconnected things, and then Ramon said, "Uh-oh, I think some object is inside my eye." I peered into his large, liquid-pupiled brown eye but all I could see was a contact lens, floating around like a visible ozone layer.

"I don't see anything," I said, but before I could pull away, Ramon put his arms around me and kissed me, rather wetly and not quite on center. "Jesus!" I said tactlessly, as I pulled away, wiping my mouth on my sleeve. "You too? I thought you were, um, er, ah—"

"Attracted to men?" said Ramon, providing the euphemism I had failed to think of. "I am. Please forgive me my trespass."

"Wait a minute—I'm confused."

"Haven't you ever heard of AZ/DZ?"

"You mean AC/DC? Oh, you're bisexual?" Ramon nodded. "But why me?" I asked.

"Because I love your velvet skirt, and because the moon is full. And because the handsome gaucho turned me down." We laughed at that, and then, our friendship intact, Ramon and I went off to one of the lounges, where he set up his portable sewing machine and rummaged through his spectrum-catalogued spools of colored thread and then sewed for me ("as apology for my unpolite assault," he said sheepishly) a marvelous medieval blouse. It had a low square neck, full sleeves, and a gathered bodice, and it was made from a piece of antique indigo-dyed cotton, screen-printed with chrysanthemums, which I had been using as a *furoshiki* to wrap my notebooks and diaries in.

When I got back to my room, it was nearly two a.m., and the entire ship seemed to be asleep. There was a note under my door, written in blue ink on both sides of a sheet of yellow legal paper. *Dear Debora*, it began, *I am Elijah Ruskin & there is only one me. I am not a kindly all-knowing father type & I am not an ogre. I'm not a sex maniac & I'm not a celibate when away from home. I'm Elijah Ruskin.* It went on and on, in that not-quite-apologetic vein; I still have that letter, and I still think it is one of the sweetest, saddest, most sensible messages I have ever received. I even liked the misspelling of my name.

The next day, feeling the need of a respite from adult male company, I spent the entire day "venturing," as we called it, with my young friend Dylan. He was a beautiful brown-eyed butterscotch-haired nine-year-old from San Francisco, the son of a languorous lace-draped mother named Moireen, with whom he was traveling, and a Japanese carpenter-father who had gone on ahead to look for work in Tokyo. The mother and son were my only roommates in a six-bunk stateroom, and since

Moireen spent most of her time reading, sleeping, and doing complex monochromatic macramé, I ended up keeping young Dylan (whose full name was Dylan Denzaburo Suginami-Jones) company quite often. Like many children of unconventional parents, Dylan was conservative, reflective, and almost compulsively well-organized, but he also had a wily sense of humor and an infinite reservoir of curiosity and wonder.

On this day, we began with Twenty Questions, moved on to Scrabble (Lewison Lear dropped in on the game for long enough to make the words "unreal" and "futile," and then wandered off in his green-and-oxblood alligator-skin saddle shoes), played an antic hour of hide-and-go-seek, stopped for lunch, and then spent the afternoon exploring the lower intestines of the ship. ("It's rude to say bowels," Dylan had admonished me earlier.) We marveled at the din and the gigantic pounding pistons of the engine room, indulged in macabre speculation about the contents of some suspiciously lumpy burlap bags in the hold, and sniffed the aroma of banana-pecan cupcakes baking in the vast and pristine kitchen. After a tea-break, we climbed down a narrow stairway and found ourselves in front of a door marked LIVE ANIMALS. DO NOT ENTER! Naturally, we went in.

"Wow! A cow!" said Dylan. "And a dog! And a cat! And a parrot!" We heard a clanking noise, and a low "moo," and then from around the corner there appeared a strange mythological hybrid: a creature with the head of a calf and the body of a man. The illusion was soon dispelled, as we realized that the adolescent Minotaur was just a man carrying a calf at eye level so that he could inspect, as Dylan whispered to me, "its silly parts."

The man, who had evidently not yet noticed our presence, turned his back and lowered the calf gently onto a bed of folded burlap bags. In one of his back pockets was a baby bottle filled with a milky fluid, in the other was a large thermometer. "Hi," said Dylan in a loud voice. The man looked up in surprise, and when he took off his wide-brimmed suede hat I saw that it was Yukio Yanagida—practitioner of sunset zazen and C. J.'s passionate subaqueous lover. "Hello," he said, and then, to Dylan, "Would you like to feed the calf?"

"*Would* I!" said Dylan, in classic boy's-true-adventure style.

The young veterinarian-to-be and I chatted, first in English, and then, after a subtle linguistic power struggle, in Japanese, while Dylan bottle-fed the calves. There were three of them, samples of a special

Argentine strain that Yukio was taking back to be raised at the country adjunct of his vet school in Tokyo. He was returning—reluctantly, I gathered—to Japan after two years of working as a gaucho on a cattle ranch in Argentina. (So *this* was Ramon's unreceptive gaucho!) Yukio pronounced the word "Arhentina," and I was impressed. Seeing him up close for the first time, I was startled by how much his fine bones and symmetrical features reminded me of the handsome cad Kuri, but I felt certain (his wanton conduct with C. J. notwithstanding) that this man was not a playboy, heartless or otherwise.

When Yukio interrupted our conversation to help Dylan refill the bottle, I found myself visualizing the early stages of his shower-encounter with C. J.—the galvanizing eye contact, the first pyrotechnic kiss, the slippery embrace—and I had to take a deep breath and shake my head, like a dog with ticks in its ears, to banish those unseemly voyeuristic thoughts. At the end of thirty minutes I knew 100% more about Yukio Yanagida than I had known before, and I suspected that I knew at least 98% more about him, in a biographical sense, than his watery moll, C. J. Holcomb.

That night at dinner, Yukio was absent as usual, but now I knew why: he always took a boxed meal down to the kennels and ate it by lamplight, in the company of his calves. It felt good to know his secret, and to think of him, so noble and philosophic (and so very good-looking), pursuing his singular dream. I sat between C. J. and a red-haired Canadian woman named Maggie; their plates held some pallid cold cuts and a tumulus of potato salad, while mine was piled high with hearts of palm and artichoke; marinated cucumbers and carrots; tofu in miso sauce; brown rice with sesame seeds and raisins; and crisp, lacy vegetable tempura. I had had the foresight to request a vegetarian diet when I booked passage on the *Amazon-Maru*, but I hadn't expected to be served wildly artistic feasts while my friends sipped their suety commoner's gruel and gnawed on vaguely anthropomorphic-looking bones. The contrast wasn't quite that dramatic, of course, but it was noticeable enough to stir a nightly outbreak of what Lui called "veggie envy" among my tablemates.

After a week, it had become a ritual. My friends would gaze covetously at my plate; then, one by one, they would call a white-shirted Japanese waiter over and say, "Could I please have what she's having, instead of this?"

"I'm sorry," the waiters invariably replied, "there was only enough for one portion." As I consumed my vegetarian delicacies amid vibrations of envy, resentment, and resignation, I was always reminded of the midnight dormitory-scene in *Madeline*: "And all the little girls cried, 'Boohoo! We want to have our appendix out, too!'"

The Honolulu–Yokohama crossing took exactly ten days. When we finally sighted land there was a communal sense of relief, but there was sadness, too. For a ship is like a small, strange, self-contained nation, complete with politics, love, fads, feuds, slang, in-jokes, pariahs, royalty, subterfuge, and sex, and once the ropes are looped around the pier, that curious, ephemeral country ceases to exist, forever.

E I G H T

THE COLOR OF
CHERRY BLOSSOMS

A samurai should know his own stature,
pursue his discipline with diligence,
and say as little as possible.

Yamamoto Tsunetomo
Hagakure

"I have some excellent news for you," said Father Bonini. He removed a fat unlit cigar from between his haggis-colored lips, and blessed me with a weary, benevolent Jesuit smile. Father Bonini was a large man in his mid-forties with a complexion like a well-used wooden dart board, a scimitar-shaped nose, and gnostic brown eyes, the color of half-cured tobacco. (*Dante's*–Inferno *eyes,* I wrote, *set in a holy-desperado face.*) I had always found Father Bonini very attractive, particularly since I knew he had taken a vow of lifelong celibacy.

The "excellent news" was that some not-quite-bilingual front office clerk at Sophia University had made an error in totaling my credits (no wonder, for I had attended four colleges and three language institutes before enrolling at Sophia), and I only needed six credits to graduate, not twelve as they had originally thought. These could be picked up in the second session of summer school, leaving me with the entire spring and most of the summer unexpectedly free.

"What will you do with this gift of time?" Father Bonini asked as he saw me off at the university's big wrought-iron gate.

"I'm going to go to Kyoto," I said.

"Ah, Kyoto," sighed Father Bonini. He removed the cigar from his mouth and kissed his thick, callused fingertips.

"That's the way I feel, too," I said. It seemed like a deliciously ambiguous adult conversation, and I was pleased, when I looked back after taking my leave, to see Father Bonini still standing under the gate, chewing on his cigar and watching me with those meditative Mediterranean eyes.

Ten minutes later I was standing on a busy corner in Yotsuya, trying to decide whether to go to a classical-music coffee shop for a cucumber sandwich on etiolated Wonder-clone bread, or to my favorite Japanese restaurant, where I could sit at the counter and munch on vegetable tempura while gazing into a tank full of silver-and-goldfish with gauzy, diaphanous tails, like fairy-princess ball gowns. I heard a voice calling my name, and when I turned around I saw Yukio Yanagida, the extraordinarily appealing (and, I immediately remembered, "astonishingly passionate") Japanese gaucho from the *Amazon-Maru*. He was taller than anyone else on the street, and his long hair and exotic clothes (loose white trousers, a colorful toucan-print shirt, and the battered suede pampas hat he had worn on the ship) made him stand out even more.

I held out my hand, but to my surprise Yukio gave me a quick, spontaneous, scandalously un-Japanese hug. I couldn't help noticing, as we brushed cheeks, that he smelled completely natural and unperfumed. This discovery enhanced my already favorable opinion of him, for I have always believed that the most desirable scent a man can exude, besides the subtle musk of monasticism, is his own unembellished maleness.

Yukio's first words to me were as surprising as the hug had been. "Do you believe in Fate?" he asked.

"Now more than ever," I replied, and with that brief exchange we moved from the neutral arena of friendly acquaintanceship into the faradized, perilous, promising realm of romance.

* * *

When I arrived in Kyoto early the next morning the sidewalks were still dark and shiny and strewn with amputated branches from an all-night storm, but by the time I stepped off the bus at the stop nearest Zenzenji, the sky was a pale slip-glazed blue, with just a few pewter-colored clouds. I had no idea where I would live in Kyoto; I only knew that I craved the sight of the Sodo's crumbling saffron wall the way a malnourished pirate might crave a blood orange. First I'll walk around Zenzenji,

I thought, and then I'll call some of my friends and see if anyone needs an eccentric, insomniac roommate.

"Deborah-san?" My reverie was interrupted by a sweet, familiar voice.

"Okusan!" I said, for it was the wife of the priest of Kaiko-in, the sub-temple where Toozie lived, carrying a basket filled with a scurvy sea-man's dream come true: tangerines, lemons, grapefruit, limes. I followed her back to Kaiko-in, and over tea and sugar-frosted rice crackers I explained what had brought me, unexpectedly, to Kyoto. "I suppose Toozie's at work now," I said.

"No," said the Okusan (the term means, loosely, "mistress of the house"), "Toozie is in the United States. Her father had a mild stroke, and she had to rush home. She said she plans to come back, but she wasn't sure when."

"Oh dear," I said, "how terrible." Even as I spoke, a shamefully self-serving thought leaped into my mind, but the Okusan's prescience saved me from having to put it into words.

"Would you like to stay in Toozie's room until she returns?" she asked. "As you know, it's very small, and it's a dreadful mess, but ..."

"*Would* I?" I exclaimed in classic girl's-true-adventure style. "There's nowhere in the world I'd rather live!" I often spoke in such hyperbolic terms, but this time it was the absolute truth. I wished that my dream hadn't come true at the expense of Toozie's happiness and her father's health, but once again I thought I saw the hand of Fate at work.

Toozie had obviously left in a hurry. The room reminded me of one of those fossilized-lava tableaus at Pompeii with the food on the plate, the pot on the hearth, the dog asleep (forever) by the fire. There were dirty dishes on the table, and candy wrappers and newspapers and cor-respondence (including a postcard I had sent from Sedona of the apoc-ryphal jackalope) were strewn around the room. It took most of the day to clean up the mess and pack Toozie's things away in boxes, but that task was leavened by a series of welcome visitors.

First, there was Mondo, the Maedas' solemn-faced oldest son. He was tall and muscular, with thick, perfectly horizontal eyebrows above intelligent eyes, and his perpetual unsmiling grumpiness, I soon learned, was due to the sleep deprivation that went with studying to be an engi-neer. Toozie had once confided that she found Mondo very sexy, and I could see what she meant, although I agreed with her that there was something vaguely wicked about having such thoughts about the son of a priestly household which had made us both so welcome. On this day Mondo just stuck his head in my door and mumbled, "Glad you're here—hey, I can actually see the floor!" before disappearing into his lair across the hall.

Next came shy, studious Musashi, the middle son. He was in the midst of the ordeal of studying for college entrance exams, so he was under even more academic pressure than Mondo. He poked his head in as I was dislodging a clot of melted chocolate, caramel, and peanuts from the tatami and said, "Do you understand calculus?"

"Zenzen (not at all)," I replied. "I never even took that course, because I got a C in high school geometry, and when my parents sent me to summer school to improve my grade, I got a D in the same class."

"Oh," said Musashi glumly. "But you do speak English, don't you?"

"Like a native," I said, and his face brightened.

"Please think of me as your resident English tutor," I added, taking the hint.

The youngest son, Migaku, a noisy, loose-limbed thirteen-year-old, didn't pay me an official visit, but he set up a Ping-Pong table in the tatami hall outside my door and, like some preadolescent male Medusa, waylaid everyone who passed by and taunted them into playing. He was very good at Ping-Pong, with a wildly antic style of play: physically lively to the point of hyperkinesis, and punctuated every few seconds, whether he was winning or losing, by the most amazingly varied outbursts of profanity.

My present knowledge of Japanese curses derives from three sources: chanbara (samurai) movies; drunken-salaryman mutterings overheard in the back alleys of Kabukicho; and young Migaku Maeda's colorful conversation—or monologues, for his impromptu outpourings of scurrility didn't seem to require an audience. It was Migaku whom I first heard using *kuso* ("shit") as an expletive—a minor revelation, since several of my Japanese-language teachers had assured me that the word was used only in a clinical sense. All I have to say to those ethnolinguists who claim that the Japanese language is devoid of swear words is: Obviously you have never played Ping-Pong with Migaku Maeda.

There was one other paying boarder, besides me. His name was Inaka Hakamune, and he was the only son of a doting calligrapher-mother and a priest of the mystical Shingon sect. Inaka was studying for the priesthood at the Shingon university in Kyoto, and almost every day the postman (who rode an old black bicycle with leather saddlebags) would deliver a box of fruit or seaweed or *shiitake* mushrooms or seasonal sweets, addressed to Inaka in his mother's delicate cursive hand. On that first day he had just received a box of cherry-blossom dumplings, and he gave me three to eat later, with my tea.

Inaka had a plum-colored birthmark that covered half of his face, in almost the exact configuration of a yin/yang symbol, but he seemed to be totally unself-conscious about it. (I found it startling, and artistic.) After he had told me about his rural background, I said, "How wonderfully appropriate that your parents named you Inaka!" "Inaka" means "country," in the pastoral sense, in Japanese.

"Oh, but my name doesn't mean 'country,'" Inaka said with a smile. "It's written with entirely different characters."

"Oh," I said, "I should have known." For a foreigner who hasn't mastered the complexities of kanji (Chinese ideographs), the Japanese language can be homonym hell. I still remember my feeling of linguistic bereavement when I learned that the useful contranym "zenzen" (which can mean either "absolutely" or "absolutely not") is not written with the same characters as Zen, as in Buddhism.

The Okusan popped in several times, bringing me glasses of iced barley tea, as well as an assortment of cleaning supplies. Late in the afternoon, she appeared in my outside door (which opened onto a verandah, with a garden beyond), silhouetted against the muted golden light. Behind her stood a tall, elegant, straight-backed, kimono-clad woman whom I was thrilled to recognize, when the two stepped over my newly-scrubbed threshold and into the light from the overhead bulb, as the woman whose carriage and aura had so impressed me when I saw her walking through the temple grounds, under a peony parasol, nearly a year before. "This is my mother," said Mrs. Maeda. "You can call her Obaasan [Grandmother]."

"Oh! Now I see," I said. The beautiful mother and daughter sat down at the low table, and we drank green tea and ate Inaka Hakamune's country-style cherry-blossom dumplings. Then the Okusan excused herself (for she was very busy as the wife of a priest, mother of three, keeper of a temple, and pursuer of her own interests in cursive calligraphy and flower-arranging), and I was flattered when the Obaasan chose to stay behind and chat with me while I continued my reclamation project.

"Would you like to hear some stories about this temple, and its inhabitants?" she asked, in her soft, strong voice.

When I said, "By all means!" the Obaasan proceeded to tell me, with a graceful, slightly old-fashioned vocabulary and many poetic turns of phrase, how she and her daughter had come to live at Kaiko-in. Her husband, who was a successful textile merchant, had been "spiritually sick," and so, many years before, he began to attend zazen sessions at Zen-zenji. His wife (the Obaasan) didn't like staying home alone, so she began going to zazen as well. After her husband died, she continued to attend, every week for sixteen years. She was given koan, and she went to dokusan audiences with the previous roshi. I longed to ask what koan she had solved, and how, and what form the climactic moment of satori had taken (for I was certain that she was enlightened), but I felt that such questions would be inappropriate.

She told me that the Osho-san, the priest of Kaiko-in, who was the husband of the Okusan and the father of Mondo, Musashi, and Migaku, was an orphan who had been brought up since early childhood at the Sodo. (I had met the Osho-san only once, briefly, but he had impressed me as a gruff, gentle, imposing-looking man.) He had met the Obaasan's daughter, now the Okusan, when she accompanied her mother—reluctantly, of course, for all great romances must have the element of initial resistance—to one of the roshi's lectures. They had married when the Osho-san "graduated" from the Sodo and became the priest of Kaiko-in.

"Do you still go to zazen?" I asked.

"No," said the Obaasan wistfully. "My mind is willing, but my body won't cooperate any more. I find that it's all I can do to take my daily walk."

As she stood up to leave ("It's time for my nap," she said), I wanted to say: *When I am your age, I hope I will be half as gracious and serene and at ease with myself as you are,* but I had become self-conscious about my tendency to spout hyperbolic superlatives, so I just said, "It has been a real pleasure to talk to you." In retrospect, I wish I hadn't kept those compliments to myself, but I would like to think that the Obaasan sensed my admiration and respect, and later, my fondness.

That evening, my charwoman-chores at an end, I traipsed off to the public bath for a restorative soak. When I returned to Kaiko-in, Musashi was waiting at the gate. "Hurry," he said, "you have a phone call."

* * *

An hour later, I was sitting in a cacophonous red-lit nightclub called Popeye, shouting above the recorded din of "Born To Be Wild" played at maximum volume. On my left sat C. J. Holcomb; Ramon Furuta-Fuentes was on my right, and across the table was Arasuke Karasumaru, C. J.'s rakish-looking and exceedingly intelligent Japanese boyfriend. The other tables were packed with young Kyotoites with psychedelic clothes, hennaed hair, and heavy eyelids. *Woodcut children in a red electric forest, too full of music to ever grow old,* is how I described them in my journal, later that night. Those slack-faced, nodding children were probably full of beer and whiskey and airplane glue, too, but I chose not to record the unlovelier aspects of life.

It had been C. J. on the telephone; she had lost my Tokyo contact number, and had called Toozie (whom she knew slightly) to try to track me down. "This is amazing," I said, shaking my head. "I was trying to figure out how to find you, too." C. J. nodded.

"Amazing," she mouthed, for the music was very loud. Arasuke, who had lived in Los Angeles for six years and spoke almost eerily fluent English, leaned over and shouted, or rather sang, something in my ear.

"What?" I shrieked.

"Born to be de-e-e-e-eaf," he repeated. I smiled and nodded my agreement, and then I caught C. J.'s eye and pointed to the door.

We went outside—she in a short, low-cut red dress that she called her "trollop frock," I in a four-gore black velvet skirt, my gray suede boots, and a purple turtleneck sweater. Popeye was located in the midst of the lively Pontocho night-life district, but it was next to a pretty little pocket-park, with trees and swings and slides and a sandbox surrounded by the dark parabolas of bisected truck tires. We sat on the swings for a few moments, savoring the relative silence.

I had something very important and very delicate to say, and I wasn't sure how to begin. To my relief, C. J. spoke first. "It's about Yukio, isn't it?" she asked. I was dumfounded.

"How on earth did you know that?"

"Don't worry," laughed C. J., "I'm not clairvoyant—the opposite, if anything. I just called him earlier to ask if he might have your Tokyo number, and he told me that he ran into you and that he thought he was going to, uh—" she paused for a moment, choosing her euphemism

"—going to be *seeing* you when he came to Kyoto next week."

"And you don't mind?" I was afraid that C. J. might have some pos-sessive "I saw him first" feelings about Yukio, and I wouldn't have blamed her a bit.

"Of course I don't mind," she said. "That was just a shipboard fling. He's much more your type, anyway. Besides, I have my hands full with Arasuke and, uh, Arasuke." I was so relieved by C. J.'s disclaimer that I didn't even stop to wonder what she meant by "Arasuke and uh, Ara-suke." It seemed an insignificant detail; I was in Kyoto, it was a soft spring evening, and I had just been given *carte blanche* to fall in love with Yukio Yanagida.

* * *

The next day I went to the Sodo to deliver the souvenirs I had brought back from Arizona. In response to the shopping-koan "What do you buy for the monk who has nothing, and everything?" I had hit upon what seemed a logical answer: incense. It doesn't occupy much space, it has a place in Buddhist ritual, and (to borrow a line from Eric Dolphy) after you burn it "it's gone, in the air; you can never capture it again." He was talking about music, of course, but I think of incense as olfactory music.

The incense I had brought from the United States wasn't the usual mix of myrrh and frankincense, spices and sap; it was piñon, made in Santa Fe, where I was born, and it took the form of ligneous honey-col-ored rectangles the size of throat lozenges. "This is the smell of my *furusato* (homeland)," I told Zo-san. He sniffed the box dubiously.

"It smells like—wooden soap?" he said. I realized with a sinking feel-ing—what I used to call a "negapiphany"—that I had made a mistake; I should have brought something immediately useful, or some exotic foodstuff. No one in the Sodo would ever put match to my silly Southwestern incense; they would just laugh and throw it away.

I peered into my paper shopping bag (emblazoned with the words "JAMES DEAN REAL COOL MAN") at the other boxes of incense, which I had intended to share with a number of friends. They probably wouldn't use it, either, I thought. Impulsively, I thrust the bag into Zo-san's hands. "Please use this as you see fit, or else just throw it away," I said, and I fled, feeling, as I so often did, that my social skills and instincts were hopelessly inadequate.

"Come back any time!" Zo-san called after me. I glanced back and saw him standing in the door, dressed in gray homespun, holding a box of piñon incense up to his nose and looking bemused, if not bewildered.

* * *

The cherry blossoms came early that year, and it seemed perfect—better than fiction—when C. J., who had been staying at a run-down inn in the Shinmonzen antique-shop district with Arasuke and Ramon, called and said, "We've found a wonderful place on Cherry Blossom Lane, you must come visit as soon as you can."

"I'll come tomorrow," I said. "Tonight I've been invited to a zazen session at the monastery next door."

"Who invited you?"

"The head monk."

"Hmm," said C. J., and I could tell that, to her, the word "monastery" meant a building full of single, sex-starved men. "Are there any cute monks?"

"Not really," I said. I realized with a slight twinge of guilt that I didn't want to share the Sodo with anyone, least of all with an attractive, vivacious, Japanese-speaking *gaijin fatale* like C. J. "I wouldn't call them cute, at all." What I would have called them, every one, was beautiful, mysterious, and infinitely intriguing, but I kept that provocative thought to myself.

"We sit at seven o'clock," Toku-san had said the day before when I met him on the Sodo slope, surrounded by rosy light and iridescent doves. "Why don't you come?"

"I'd love to," I said, "but what should I bring?" I automatically ask that question when I'm invited somewhere, which is probably why a cynical friend once accused me of having a "compulsive-potluck mentality."

"Bring?" Toku-san looked blank for a moment. "Just bring your legs." And off he went into the rubescent sunset, with Shiro frisking whitely at his heels. I flushed with embarrassment, for I had done it again: said something moronic to someone I wanted desperately to impress. Foolish woman, I thought. What would you take to a zazen session, anyway—a tuna casserole?

* * *

I still remember the feeling I got as a child of eight when I walked through Carlsbad Caverns, feeling the chilly benediction from a slow-dripping stalactite on the top of my head, and gaping at the phantasmagoric landscape of eternal accretion. This was here when I was born, I thought, and it will be here when I die: this cool, secret world, this enchanted forest of unicorn-horns. I felt the same way, awestruck and humbled and utterly mortal, as I followed Zo-san through the smooth, silent halls of the monastery. The immaculate garden was quiet except for the subliminal shrill of cicadas, and the Sodo was as still and dark as Carlsbad Caverns after closing time. (I used to fantasize about hiding behind a stalagmite and exploring all night, by bat-light.)

"Seven o'clock," Toku-san had said. Determined to be early, I had left Kaiko-in when my not-entirely-reliable alarm clock read 6:50, but as soon as I heard the stillness in the genkan I knew that something was wrong. No one was around, and from the direction of the Zendo I heard the tinkle of a bell. I was obviously late, and I was faced with a dilemma. Should I stay and make a conspicuous entrance, or leave and risk offending Toku-san? The second option vanished abruptly when Zo-san appeared from the kitchen, drying his hands on a rough cloth. "Oh, you came!" he said. I began to stammer excuses and explanations, but he just put his finger to his lips and beckoned to me to follow him down the long breezeway to the Zendo.

There were no guests that night, so Zo-san placed a burgundy zabuton in the center of the tatami-matted guest meditation area, which was perpendicular to the Zendo and thus faced directly into the zazen hall. He motioned for me to shed my slippers and climb up on the ledge, and watched approvingly (I hoped) as I easily twisted my legs into the full lotus position, thanking providence for ballet lessons and double-jointed ancestors. I arranged my hands one over the other, thumbs barely touching, and Zo-san gently reversed the layering: "Left over right, like the lapels of a kimono," he said. "That's how we remember it." (A very handy mnemonic device, except that I always got the lapels of my kimono wrong, too.) After aligning my shoulders, Zo-san nodded and went back the way we had come, down the long dark empty hall.

While I was getting settled, I had been staring straight ahead, into the Zendo. The sight I saw was so beguiling that if cast-down eyes hadn't been part of the zazen prescription I might have spent the entire forty minutes gaping in wonderment. The monks, all dressed in black robes with a strip of white showing at their necks, were sitting in two long rows on the tatami, facing each other across the wide hall. A small amount of gray-blue illumination, the crepuscular sheen of zodiacal light, came through the bell-shaped windows along with a swelling chorus of cicadas. The open door into the garden yielded a gentle green glimmer, but there seemed to be another source of light. After a moment I realized that the shaved heads of the monks appeared to be glowing from within, with the alchemical phosphorescence of enlightenment. They all had their eyes cast down, but I was certain that my late arrival had not gone unnoticed, or undisapproved of.

In my earliest attempts at meditation I had tried to focus on an imaginary light at the end of a metaphysical tunnel, but I had read quite a bit about Zen in the interim (too much, Toku-san always said), so I decided to put my newfound knowledge to work. Eyes three-quarters closed, hands overlapped, legs intertwined: the purpose of this position was to "reduce the claims of the unruly body to the minimum." But what of the unruly mind? I knew that the monks were all meditating on koan assigned by the roshi, and I felt an outsider's envy of the elite initiates. I remembered that one of the basic koan was "What was your face before your parents were born?" so I decided to think about that.

First, though (I had read), you were supposed to give your mind free rein to sort through the conscious detritus and subconscious effluvia which might interfere with concentrating on your koan. So I began to free-associate; or rather, I began to daydream about my romantic future with Yukio while, on another level, the sound of the cicadas dying loudly of song reminded me of an Edgar Lee Masters poem I had once memorized: "The earth keeps some vibration going/There in your heart, and that is you ..."

I must have dozed off, because the next thing I remember is feeling a tap on my shoulder. I opened my eyes and saw a monk with black-rimmed glasses standing in front of me, bowing. I was a bit disoriented but I bowed back, automatically, and then I felt a sharp pain on my right shoulder blade, as a long stick came slicing through the air like an executioner's sword and landed on my flesh. "Ow!" I said in English, and I thought I saw a brief, slight upward motion at the corners of the mouth of the stern bespectacled monk who had struck me. But he didn't smile;

he just bowed to me and walked away, holding his stick in front of him with two hands, like the flag-bearer in a Fourth of July parade.

I felt confused and humiliated, but a few minutes later I heard the sound of the stick hitting a monk inside the Zendo, and then another, and I realized that I hadn't been singled out for abuse simply because I was an inept, scatter-minded interloper who couldn't even meditate without falling asleep. I closed my eyes again and tried to focus on the koan, but all I could think about was the shame of arriving late and then promptly dozing off, the shock of waking up in a strange place to be struck by a strange monk with a big stick, the pain in my *latissimus dorsi*, and the ultimate loneliness of being a foreigner in Japan.

At the end of the session I unwound my legs and shuffled off down the hall without speaking to anyone. *I really blew it*, I was thinking morosely. *I'll never see the inside of this place again, and I'm not even sure I want to. Maybe I should go back to America right now and get on with my real life. There's nothing for me here.* As I was putting on my shoes in the genkan, a voice behind me said, "How was it?" It was Toku-san. I shook my head and made a hopeless face, and he smiled and said, "The first time is always difficult. Please come again tomorrow."

"I'd love to!" I said, and I ran home in unambivalent jubilation.

* * *

Cherry Blossom Lane was two or three miles from Kaiko-in, so I borrowed Mondo's old red bicycle for the journey. ("Use it any time," he had said. "I don't need it anymore, since I got the scooter.") I rode along the banks of the Kamo River, where the wide ribbons of aniline-dyed cloth—bright spring banners of red and purple and turquoise and yellow-orange—were laid out to dry; past the tall riverside teahouses hung with pink lanterns; past bridges thick with roosting doves. Then I rode across one of those feathery murmuring bridges, down a narrow lane, and into a scene of staggering loveliness.

There was a clear cobblestone-bottomed stream, forded at intervals by arcing bridges of rough gray stone that led to old-style walled houses, and overhung by hundreds of cherry trees in frothy, precocious, pale-pink bloom. On the other side of the canal I saw a procession of kindergarten students, dressed alike in blue smocks, yellow hats and boots, and red backpacks. All the children were carrying necklaces of bright-colored paper rings, draped carefully over their outstretched hands like the first stage of a cat's cradle.

As I rode along, I thought about the trees in the cherry orchards of my childhood. I remembered appreciating the cumulus cloud of flowers, and then thinking, when the blossoms dropped off: That was nice while it lasted, but if flowers fall, can fruit be far behind? The Japanese have given much more thought, and considerably more feeling, to the matter of cherry blossoms. The perception of the delicate blooms as a symbol of the fragility, evanescence, and heartbreaking beauty of human life is instilled in Japanese children at an early age, along with the Sunset Song and the elemental triumvirate of paper/scissors/stone. Many Japanese also see the annual appearance of the cherry blossoms as an excuse to drink large quantities of saké and sing mournful regional ballads, and several balloon-trousered workmen were doing just that, under a huge, bouffant, umbrella-shaped cherry tree, as I passed.

"Excuse me," I said, "could you tell me how to get to Cherry Blossom Lane?"

They looked at me incredulously; one muttered "Hen na gaijin," one snickered, one merely belched, while the fourth, gesturing at the street in front of us and shaking his head, said scornfully, "What do you think *this* is, gaijie, the Ginza?"

Q. What was the color of your face before your parents were born?
A. A very bright cherry-red.

The house that C. J. had found was right on the canal, with a glorious view of cherry blossoms, drunken laborers, and gentian-blue sky. It was actually the second floor of an immense old house with polished-oak floors and tattered shoji screens patched with colorful advertisements cut from magazines. All the rooms had a curious nineteenth-century–museum smell: an amalgam of old lacquer, mildewed paper, concentrated essence of incense, and the earthy forest-fragrance of cryptomeria. The landlord, Mr. Kawazoe, was a former concert pianist, specializing in Schumann and Rachmaninoff, who had married into a wealthy family; a black-sheep older brother on his wife's side had squandered the family fortune on dog races and bar hostesses, and now Mr. Kawazoe found himself, in widowhood and retirement, forced to rent out half of his house to strange foreigners.

"Look at all this space!" C. J. said. When I arrived she was standing on a ladder, dressed in a short pink sundress ("Neiman Marcus, half-price!"), polishing an elaborate carved-wood room divider with pungent-smelling sesame oil. "I have a room, Arasuke has a room, Ramon has a room, and there's space left over—you're welcome to move in too, of course."

"The boys," as C. J. called her housemates, had gone off to an antique fair at a nearby temple, so we had the place to ourselves. We sat and drank tea and ate Oreo cookies ("From the Fort Worth Safeway to Cherry Blossom Lane," said C. J.) and talked about our respective good fortune in finding such atmospheric, "Japanese-y" places to live in Kyoto. I envied C. J. the space, and the cherry-blossom view, but I wouldn't have traded my tiny windowless room at Kaiko-in for the Imperial Suite at the Miyako Hotel, or for ex-King Farouk's three-acre blue-mirrored bedroom in Alexandria.

In the midst of our Oreo-orgy we heard wild hoots of drunken laughter, and we jumped up and ran to the window. There, promenading along the canal dressed in high geta and splendiferous gold-embroidered antique kimono, were Ramon and Arasuke. This was my first daylight glimpse of C. J.'s main squeeze, and I was impressed anew; with his *Yojimbo* scowl and his long black hair caught up in a loose topknot, he reminded me of a medieval outlaw-swordsman. The saké-drinking workmen were almost apoplectic with mirth at this strange sight, but the two gaijin were unperturbed. (Arasuke was Japanese, of course, but he had spent so much time in the United States that C. J. had dubbed him an honorary strange foreigner.) The boys just tipped their hats—Ramon wore a straw boater, Arasuke a black Stetson—and sauntered by with the impermeable dignity that comes from knowing you are morally superior, and dressed to kill.

By the time Ramon and Arasuke entered the room where we were waiting, the odd procession had swelled to three, for they had been joined by the landlord, Mr. Kawazoe. He was a small, slender man with a Heian-courtier face (delicate features, feathery moustache) and shoulder-length silvery-gray hair under a raspberry wool beret. He was dressed in an ivory turtleneck, butter-pecan flannel trousers, and a knee-length gray cardigan with bulging, distended pockets.

After a lively polyphonic conversation ("You-all look great—like a couple of samurai in drag!" "Please do look at these smashing sewn-by-hand seams!" "How much did those outfits cost, anyway?" "Did you see the way those cherry-blossom drunks were looking at us?" "When's the next antique fair? I absolutely have to go!") the boys went off to the public bath, for it was a warm day, and antique brocade works on the same principle as thermal underwear. C. J. retired to her bedroom to change her clothes, and I was left alone with the landlord.

Mr. Kawazoe fumbled nervously in his pockets for several moments, a displacement activity which produced a crumpled plaid handkerchief, a clump of stuck-together postage stamps, a lint-frosted dog biscuit, and a fragment of sheet music. Then he turned to me and said softly, almost in a whisper, "Sometime when I've had a bit too much to drink I will sing my famous song for you. It's called 'How I Pretended to Be a Foreigner.'"

"That sounds delightful," I said. "Can I buy you a beer?"

* * *

According to one of my more quixotic Japanese-English dictionaries, *okonomiyaki* means "a frizzled flapjack." It is a large pancake of shredded vegetables (carrots, cabbage, bean sprouts) in a light batter; the addition of shrimp, beef, or pork is optional. The pancakes are cooked on a hot oiled grill in the center of the table, and when they are brown on both sides they are slathered with a sweet, enigmatic sauce, sprinkled with an assortment of colorful condiments (green seaweed, pink ginger, tawny fish-shavings), cut into pie-slices, and gobbled up between sighs of rapture and sips of beer or "saidaa," a pale, fizzy beverage which bears no resemblance to its namesake, cider. Okonomiyaki was one of the staples of every foreigner-on-a-budget, for it was cheap, filling, and relatively nutritious.

On that lambent spring evening we went to a very old okonomiyaki restaurant in the lively Gion district. It was paneled with convex half-stalks of bamboo, so mellowed that the original gold had been transmuted into a deep burnt sienna, and the tables were set on raised tatami platforms. The proprietor, a statuesque woman with a complex geisha-style hairdo, talked freely about the men in her life (gamblers, cads, and grifters, every one), but she refused to divulge the secret of the dark, delicious sauce.

The frying of the pancakes is a time-consuming ritual, and we passed the time in reminiscing about our time on the ship (Ramon did several hilariously uncharitable imitations of some of the less personable passengers) and congratulating ourselves on our cleverness in arranging to be alive in Kyoto during that miraculous cherry-blossom spring. We were having so much fun that I forgot to monitor the time. "Does anyone have a watch?" I asked, after finishing off the last bite of my gigantic pancake. "I have to be at the Zendo at seven o'clock."

"Well, unless you brought your magic cape, it looks like they're going to have to start without you," said Arasuke, pulling back his red leather jacket-sleeve to reveal a Mickey Mouse watch which read 6:59.

"Oh, no!" I cried, jumping up. But then I sat down again, realizing that there was no possible way I could make it on time.

"That's okay," said C. J. "You can come to Maruyama Park with us instead; there's a free rock concert."

"All right," I said glumly, but my mind was full of the images and sensations I was going to miss: the meditating heads aglow in the shadowy violet dark, the cicada-chorus, the smell of the incense, the musical bells, the prowling monk with his painful but exhilarating antidote to torpor.

Even though it was out of the way, Ramon insisted on stopping at Kaiko-in to get his camera (which I had accidentally carried home from Popeye) so he could have his picture taken with some second-tier rockstar, a strident-voiced Japanese girl with sacrum-length bleached platinum hair, like a kewpie doll. As we walked past the monastery I heard the ting of a bell, signaling the end of the zazen session. It seemed to me at that moment that the Sodo was the existential Super Chief, bound for wisdom and truth and enlightenment, and I felt, with typical hyperbole, that I had just missed the mystery train, forever.

LIKE A DANCER ASLEEP
IN THE SUN

Give me chastity, but not yet.
St. Augustine

—KYOTO

Temples, like aging courtesans, tend to look their best by crepuscular light; the gloamy dimness seems to emphasize their elegance while obscuring the flaws and fissures of antiquity. Dusk was one of my favorite times at Zenzenji, and I loved to wander around the temple grounds in the dreamy blue-violet haze which has inspired so many poetic sobriquets: rushlight, zodiacal light, blind man's holiday, *entre chien et loup.*

In those days Kyoto still had mobile tofu sellers who rode around the restaurant-streets and residential alleys on bicycles with a water-filled wooden bin on the back. The tofu-man who came to the alley outside the entrance to Kaiko-in always arrived at the same time of day, just as the miraculous gold of late afternoon was beginning to fade, and so I mythicized him as the bringer of twilight. Like his Tokyo counterpart, the Kyoto tofuya-san was heralded by a brass horn, but his cry was very different: more musical and more inflected, it reminded me of a muezzin's minor-key wail, riding lightly on the wind from the mosaic minaret of some gleaming gilded mosque.

I was metabolically inclined to stay up late and to sleep well past the opaline light of dawn, but I was a fitful, suspicious sleeper, and the first sounds from the Sodo—drums and bells and muffled chanting—almost always woke me up around four a.m. Sometimes I fell asleep again, but often I would get up, with a sleep-deprived sigh, and putter around my room, drawing and writing and drinking herbal tea, until I felt sleepy again, or until I gave up on sleep and went out to face the day.

About a week after I moved into Toozie's room at Kaiko-in, I became obsessed with trying to make a good impression on the inhabitants of the Sodo. I would rise with the pre-dawn drums, wash my face, brush my hair, and get dressed, and then I would go out for a long walk around the temple grounds. It was always wonderful to stroll through the medieval mist in what had become (like Sedona, and Fiesole, and Santa Fe) the landscape of my heart, but the activity was marred by self-consciousness, and by desire: I wanted to project an image of myself as a pure-souled early riser, and I hoped that image would be favorably perceived by the men next door.

Although I considered all the monks to be perfectly virtuous, god-like beings, I had made one shocking discovery. (In those impressionable days, I had almost as many shocks as revelations.) One morning when I passed the Sodo, I noticed a small bottle of milk tucked away—almost hidden—in the corner of the gate, and I soon deduced that a new bottle was left every day. I knew that the lowlier monks wouldn't have the authority to order milk-delivery, and I didn't want to believe that any of the senior unsui were choosing to violate the dietary rules of Buddhism, as I perceived them. I decided that the contraband beverage must be a treat for the milk-white dog, Shiro, but in my heart, I knew that Japanese do not give milk to dogs.

For nearly a week I followed the same masochistic early-riser routine, but I never saw a single monk outside the Sodo walls during those pre-dawn walks, and I was certain that no one ever saw me. "This is silly," I said to myself one day after splashing along in the rain, under a bamboo umbrella with a pattern of purple wisteria painted on the ambergris-colored oil paper, for a dark, lonely hour. "I give up." I went home, took off my wet clothes, put on a crisp clean yukata, and went back to bed.

The next morning the drums wakened me as usual. "Go back to sleep," I told myself, but my self responded, surprisingly, "No, thank you, I think I'd rather go for a walk. Not to see or be seen, but just to greet the light, and to have the temple grounds to myself." It was a clear morning, and as I walked out under the starry sky I felt a curious peace in knowing that I was doing this for the pleasure and not for the picture it created. I wandered around in the lavender light, listening to the coo and cluck of gray flannel doves and stepping over the puddles of the previous day's rain (likened later, in my journal, to blobs of fugitive mercury from the broken thermometer of the gods).

At one point a long-haired white cat crossed my path, carrying a dead bird in its mouth; after my initial horror at seeing the food chain in action I realized that I, too, was feeling a bit peckish, and I headed back to Kaiko-in. As I passed the Sodo gate I purposely looked away, so I was startled when a voice said "Ohayo gozaimasu!" It was Nu-san, the kindly washing-machine monk with the half-a-heart-shaped ears. "Please come in," he said, and I went, without question. Zo-san was chopping *tsukemono* (pickled vegetables) in the dim kitchen—I had heard the odd fairytale sound from outside, and wondered—and while we talked of easy morning things the monks came into the dining hall beyond and sat down to their daily gruel.

After they had chanted, eaten, and departed, I was ushered into the empty dining room and given a glossy black lacquer bowl filled with gruel (just white rice, salt, and water, but amazingly hearty and delicious) and a little dish with the round translucent viridian-yellow slices of *takuan* (pickled *daikon* radish, homemade at the Sodo and surely the best in the world). I was excited to be sitting at the long low table used by the monks, and I enjoyed my simple solitary meal immensely. I didn't do anything to embarrass myself (or perhaps I should say I was unaware of my faux pas, whatever they may have been), and for once I left the Sodo with a face the color of cherry blossoms, and not of cherries.

When I had passed by earlier, in the dark, I had noticed a large bundle in one corner of the gate—the opposite corner from the daily milkbottle—and I had assumed that it was a sack of rice or vegetables, donated by some anonymous Samaritan. In the light of morning, I saw that the bundle was in fact a person: a young man with very long legs and very broad shoulders. He wore the shaved head, black robes, and straw traveling-sandals of a religious pilgrim, and he sat in the shadow of the ancient wall, bowed head resting on a satchel, with his sea urchin shell–shaped bamboo hat beside him. A fragment of a possible poem flashed across my mind: *Except perhaps a weightless weight/From waiting at the Gateless Gate …*

"Good morning," I said. "Are you all right?" but the monk didn't respond. His posture of humility and supplication reminded me of an illustration I had seen in a book called *The Training of the Zen Buddhist Monk*, which I had bought recently at a second-hand bookstore, and I rushed home to look it up. Just as I was about to duck through the low door into the courtyard of Kaiko-in, I heard a voice say "Welcome home!" I turned and looked into the irresistible aristocratic-lizard face of Fuji Mugen.

"I thought you were spending the summer in Tsuwano," I stammered.

"I am," he said, "but sometimes I come back. This is one of those times; let's walk."

We walked in silence up a long hill to a famous temple. I didn't want to say anything silly or girlish or unenlightened, but I kept up a lively (and silly, and girlish) discourse with myself. *My God*, I thought, *I love this man, and I haven't even thought about him in days. Maybe weeks; certainly not since I saw Yukio in Tokyo. Can love be so fickle, so schizophrenic, so amnesiac? (Yes.) Or is it just infatuation? Does it matter? (No.) What would the monks think if they knew that I was having unseemly thoughts about their "freeloader" while my stomach is still full of their sanctified gruel? Maybe I should tell Mugen that I just want to be friends. But that's the problem: I don't want to be just friends, I want to be just ... something else.* We walked up winding cobblestone streets, past shuttered pottery shops and teahouses with their reed blinds drawn, for it was still very early. At the top of the hill we paused to gaze over the gray and green checkerboard of the city. Suddenly, the ethereal sound of a bamboo flute floated over the still-blooming valley, like *kagura*: music of the gods.

We took another route down the hill, past a red-gated, incense-clouded monkey shrine, then through a vast graveyard that sloped down to yet another large, splendid temple. The absence of conversation was beginning to make me nervous. Had Mugen invited me out so we could have The Talk? "My marriage has been arranged, will you congratulate me?" or "I didn't mean to lead you on that night in Shinjuku Park, but it wasn't me talking—it was the moonlight" or "I'm sorry, but the height difference is just too absurd."

About halfway down the hill there was a green wooden bench, splattered with the usual variety of bench-stains. Mugen stopped. "Sit," he said. Not "Please sit" or "Shall we sit?" but just the inarguable imperative: *Sit*. He was treating me like chattel, like a subordinate, like the family dog, and I was oddly thrilled, for that is how traditional Japanese men address the women they love. Mugen carefully placed a clean handkerchief on the bench and smoothed out the wrinkles with his large, beautiful hands. How gallant, I thought, but then he sat down on the square of white cotton himself, folding his lichen-colored silk kimono around his legs. How Japanese, I thought. I was wearing a sleeveless polished-cotton dress of green-and-gold paisley; I didn't have a handkerchief, so I sat down directly on the bench, taking my chances with bird droppings and melted chocolate. Mugen looked so serious that I was about to say, "Are you mad at me or something?" but he spoke first.

"I've been thinking," he said, "that you are probably my red-thread soulmate." I was speechless, which was just as well, for he quickly added the inevitable coda: "But unfortunately we live in a very narrow-minded and complicated world where soulmates can't always be lifemates." And then he leaned over, with his hooded eyes closed, and gave me a very light, almost disembodied kiss on the lips. The touch of his sculpturesque mouth on mine reminded me of that night in the moonlit park, and I realized once again that restraint can be infinitely more erotic than a full frontal assault.

As we pulled apart and opened our eyes, I became aware of two tiny, bent old women in sardine-colored kimono, each with a bucket of water in one hand and a branch of glossy camellia leaves, to decorate the graves, in the other. The women were sneaking glances at us, and when we stood up and they saw the difference in our height, they gaped for a long heartbeat-second, and then turned away in modesty, or in shame. Mugen gave them an elegant nod, and as we walked away I heard one of the old women say in a scandalized, titillated whisper: "Gaijin to bozu!" ("A foreigner and a priest!") It occurred to me later that with a reversal of word-order, that phrase would be a perfect title for an Oriental-Gothic novel of doomed but ineffably thrilling love. *The Priest and the Foreigner*; I still think that has a certain glamorous, gloomy ring.

Mugen walked me to the gate of Kaiko-in, said "Mata" ("Again," as in "See you later") and then he was gone, without a touch. I felt slightly dizzy from our ambiguous but undeniably romantic encounter, and it wasn't until I was back in my little room, scribbling fervent dualisms in my diary, that it occurred to me that I had just received my first Japanese marriage proposal: almost, sort of, in a weird oblique way.

I was too confused and elated to study, so I decided to borrow Mondo's bicycle and pay an impromptu visit to my friends on Cherry Blossom Lane. It was a clear, cloudless, pale-sun morning, and the cherry trees were in full fantastic bloom. The unexpected treat of breakfast at the Sodo, the even more surprising encounter with Mugen, and the loveliness of Kyoto in spring, had left me feeling that I was living an enchanted existence, and that human contact was life's most precious treasure. In this euphoric mood I let myself into C. J.'s house and walked upstairs. The house was completely silent, and I wondered if my friends might have gone somewhere.

As it turned out, they were asleep, all three of them, curled up very close together, with C. J. in the middle and the two men on either side. I knew that C. J. was sleeping (in the euphemized sexual sense) with Arasuke, but I was shocked by Ramon's presence in the bed. Maybe he had a bad dream, I thought, for Ramon impressed me as the type of person who might need to crawl into bed with the nearest mother-figure whenever he had a dream about monsters, or fire, or the unfathomable free-fall of death. Once, on the *Amazon-Maru*, Ramon had told me about a recurrent nightmare in which he was stabbed by masked assassins disguised as dancing girls; "My *Black Orpheus* dream," he called it, for he apparently had his nightmares as neatly catalogued as his spools of colored thread. I turned and started to tiptoe from the room when an alarm clock went off. I froze, cursing my own bad timing; C. J. had seen me when she reached up to shut the alarm off, and now I would have to stay.

At C. J.'s drowsy suggestion, I brewed a pot of *bancha* tea in the big, sunny kitchen, and when I brought it into the bedroom Arasuke was awake too. No one seemed to be in a hurry to get out of bed, so I distributed the cups and then sat on the bare floor and sipped my tea. C. J. was sitting up, hugging the lilac-colored futon to her chest like a strapless, quilted prom dress; Arasuke, looking like a rumpled medieval hit man, was leaning on one elbow, drinking his tea, and Ramon was apparently still asleep. There didn't seem to be much to talk about; I didn't think anyone would be interested in my story about sipping gruel at the Sodo, and I felt so awkward about my inconsiderate, ill-timed intrusion that I just wanted to finish my tea and go far, far away.

I was looking out the window at the cherry blossoms when I became aware of a flurry of peripheral movement: the futon had dropped from C. J.'s bare chest, and she gathered it up again, giggling. "Oops," she said. "Don't say 'oops,'" said Arasuke. "You know I love your hairy nipples." And then, from under the futon came the sleepy rain-forest voice of Ramon, saying: "I do, too."

A hot-and-cold flash of shock and embarrassment ran through my body, and then, forgetting about the ritual of tea and the etiquette of leave-taking, I stood up and rushed from the room, ran down the stairs, leaped on my borrowed bicycle, and pedaled furiously away. "It serves you right," I told myself as I rode blindly under the canopy of cherry blossoms, oblivious to anything but the distressing scene being replayed over and over in my memory. "You shouldn't have dropped in without calling first." But the telephone at the house on Cherry Blossom Lane had been out of order for days and besides, everyone in Japan drops in on everyone else at the most ungodly hours, without calling first. Still, I vowed that I would never again pop in on anyone uninvited, or unannounced.

In those days I thought of myself as a well-traveled woman of the world; I had seen the phrase *ménage à trois* often enough to know which way the accents pointed, but I had never thought about the grim, greasy, unhygienic reality of a woman having sex with two men at the same time, in the same bed. What of the emotional havoc, the jealousy, the inadvertent voyeurism, the soggy sheets?

And then I remembered that Ramon was bisexual; was it then a *ménage à quatre*, with Ramon as designated switch hitter? I knew it was none of my business, but I couldn't stop thinking about the morality, and the logistics.

* * *

Yukio was due to arrive in Kyoto that afternoon, and by the time he picked me up in his parents' white sedan I had come to terms with the morning's events. It helped to think of C. J.'s sexual activity as just another expression of the feelings that made it possible for me to want to be physically close to two men at the same time (though never simultaneously). It was just a difference of degree, and risk, and choreography. Call before you visit, knock before you enter, sympathize before you judge: those were my conclusions after several hours of troubled thought. But I couldn't help feeling that there was something fundamentally unnatural about what I had seen and heard in the house on Cherry Blossom Lane, and I was not looking forward to seeing C. J. Holcomb and her bookend-lovers again.

It was a rare treat, in those days, to go for a ride in a car. Mostly we walked, or else we took streetcars, or subways, or buses, or trains, or if we were very flush, or disastrously late, an occasional taxi. Japanese public transportation is highly advanced (although I considered the phasing-out of the old streetcars, with their mellow wood and artichoke-green velvet seats and proud, dapper-uniformed conductors, a giant step backward), but it is just that—public, and when you are a foreigner in Japan, being out in public means never being allowed to forget for an instant that you are a very conspicuous curiosity.

So, quite aside from the romantic frisson I felt at the sight of Yukio's lively face and long, lean gaucho's body, and at the realization that I was the first person he had chosen to visit in Kyoto, I was excited when he said, "Where would you like to go? I'll drive you anywhere, as long as I can have the car back by six."

"Well," I said, "I've been wanting to go to the Gandhi Center."

"The Gandhi Center? I know where that is, but why?"

"There's a woman there, an Indian, who gives lessons in Bharata Natyam."

"What's that?" asked Yukio.

"It's some sort of classical Indian dancing," I said. "I don't really know much about it, but I met an American woman about a year ago who was absolutely mad about the dancing, and the teacher, and when she demonstrated a few steps I had a strong feeling that it was something I was meant to do."

"Say no more," said Yukio, but happiness had made me garrulous, and I said a great deal more. I babbled on about Zenzenji, and the tofu-man, and the monks, and the Maeda family, and serendipity, and spring in Kyoto, and cherry blossoms, and children carrying garlands of bright paper rings. I chose not to mention what had happened that morning with C. J., though, for I kept remembering, with a self-renewing shock, that she knew what it was like to have sex with Yukio Yanagida, the present-moment love of my life.

* * *

The Gandhi Center was housed in a modern building in one of Kyoto's many student districts, near Doshisha University, and the dance studio was on the ground floor. When we walked in, the teacher, a tall woman with a knee-length black braid, was up on a raised stage, demonstrating a *mudra* (symbolic hand-gesture) to a man in a blue serge business suit. After a moment, the man hopped down off the stage, put on his shoes and socks, greeted us, and went out the door. I watched through the window as he walked down the street: a completely average-looking Japanese businessman with a thoughtful expression on his face and his right hand curled into a graceful, ancient mudra.

"May I be of some help to you?" said the teacher, in the dry, slightly British accents of a well-educated East Indian. She was still standing on the stage, doing some stretching exercises. Her body gave an impression of roundness, and of compression, like a well-stuffed sausage, but her smooth dark skin was stretched over muscle, not the oleaginous curds of cellulite. She had an oval face, with strikingly horizontal features (long almond eyes, a wide mouth shaped like an archer's bow, cantilevered cheekbones), and she was dressed in a tank top and billowy harem pants of red and black silk batik. She wore bells on her ankles, and when I said that I wanted to take lessons the dancer stepped off the stage, came jingling towards us, and handed me a red-bordered business card which read, simply, *Vasanthamala*.

"Why do you want to study Bharata Natyam?" Vasanthamala asked, as we sipped sheeny rose-petal tea from porcelain cups. I told her about the former pupil I had met. "Ah, yes, Shirley," she said. "Two left feet, but a heart of gold." I wondered briefly what she would say about me someday—"two left feet and a heart of lead," perhaps—and then dismissed the thought as Western folly.

"There's another thing," I said. "I hadn't thought of it until now, but when I went to dances in college, people used to tell me that my movements reminded them of Indian dancing. So maybe that's why I responded so strongly to Shirley's demonstration."

"Hmm," said Vasanthamala, rubbing a coffee-colored finger over her rosy naked mouth, "that's very interesting. Do you by any chance believe in the transmigration of souls?"

"I believe in everything," I said agreeably. I hadn't yet come across the wet-blanket epigram that states: "A person who believes in nothing is a fool, but so is a person who believes in everything."

After leaving Vasanthamala's dance studio, Yukio and I strolled around the neighborhood. We stopped at a teahouse, where we sat on bamboo stools with red cushions and drank foamy green tea and ate roasted mochi in a dark, tangy sauce. Afterwards we crossed the street to explore a small neighborhood shrine. There were racks of *ema*—antique, weather-beaten votive tablets, one side decorated with paintings of white-plumed cocks and gold-hatted courtiers and ghostly maidens, the other covered with earnest prayers for peace, prosperity, healthy progeny, automotive safety, and passing grades. A disheveled old man with a tangled gray beard, rumpled brown kimono, and faded black split-toe socks was sleeping under a stone lantern. Our conversation must have wakened him, for he sat up, bleary-eyed and blinking, as if from a century-long nap.

"Imagine if we fell asleep right here, right now, and didn't wake up for a hundred years," said Yukio. The idea of falling asleep together anywhere, for any length of time, seemed very appealing, but I was too shy to say so. Instead, I sang a few *sotto voce* bars of "Wouldn't It Be Nice," confident that the audacious implications would pass undetected.

Yukio was very alert, imaginative, and observant, and his conversation was full of surprises. "The gauchos used to sit around at night and tell stories and drink *maté* tea—bitter, strong, and green—from a communal gourd, through a silver straw called a *bombilla*," he said dreamily, when we stopped to inhale the verdant aromas at a loose-tea shop. I was happy to discover, as we meandered through the time-warp streets behind the shrine, pausing to chat with children, cats, and dogs, that Yukio too enjoyed unstructured venturing, and took delight in small tableaus and modest microcosms.

Yukio had to pick up his mother at a flower-arranging show, so he drove me back to Kaiko-in. *Home to the gate and a very sweet sudden goodbye,* says my typically cryptic journal entry. I know there was a brief, promising kiss, and I remember wondering, a bit jealously, whether he had practiced on any gaucho-girls.

After Yukio dropped me off I went out to shop for dinner. About a block from Zenzenji there was an alfresco market—that is, it had tent-like ceilings, but no walls between the stalls—and I frequently went there to buy miso paste displayed in volcanic mounds (ivory, amber, deep adobe-red), and sugared beans like frosted jewels (jade and onyx and topaz), and vivid pyramids of fresh fruit and vegetables from farms outside Kyoto.

Less frequently, I would visit the small specialty shops on a nearby street which slanted down toward the river, to buy soybeans (scooped out with an old-fashioned wooden box-measure), or seaweed (thick ribbons, spiky branches, gossamer shreds), or sesame seeds (for myself, and for the birds), or brown rice. No one ate brown rice in Japan in those days—not even at Zen monasteries—except as gruel to be choked down in time of illness. Every time I went to buy a pound of brown rice the proprietor (to whom I had explained, several times, about being a vegetarian) would say, solicitously, "Guai demo warui no?" ("Is there something wrong with you?")

Slowly and laboriously, for I had only a rice-cooker and a single hot plate, I prepared a meal of brown rice mixed with green peas, cloudy *misoshiru* soup with trailing clouds of *konbu* seaweed and elfin forest mushrooms, a tofu-and-squash sauté, and fresh seasonal-fruit compote, and then I went next door to the Sodo. I had seen Toku-san that morning when I was out sweeping in front of Kaiko-in; after I apologized for having missed zazen the night before, he smiled and said, "That's all right; we were going to sit anyway. Just come whenever you can, and when you can't come, don't worry about it." And off he went in his wooden clogs and patched blue koromo, whistling an old Japanese brothel-tune, with Shiro at his heels.

When I reached the Sodo, the long-legged, broad-shouldered young monk was still sitting in front of the Gateless Gate with his head bowed over his baggage. I had consulted *The Training of the Zen Buddhist Monk*, and I now knew that he was requesting admission to the Sodo as a novice, for a minimum period of two years. The admission ritual involved sitting in front of the gate for two days and one night, after being ostensibly turned away, then sitting in a room in extended solitary meditation for three additional days, before finally being accepted into the life of the monastery. Poor guy, I thought automatically, and then my pity turned to envy. No, I thought, *lucky* guy. He's going to have the real Zen experience, from A to Z (or from "ah" to "un"), while I'm being allowed to sneak in by the side door to sip the watered-down tea of layman's Zen.

A very young monk with a face like a Chinese cherub showed me to the Zendo; I was early, for a change, so I decided to assume the position (lotus-legs, overlapping palms, downcast eyes) ahead of time. I also thought that this would be a way of avoiding eye contact when the monks entered the hall, for I didn't know the proper etiquette. Should I smile at my acquaintances? (But would that appear frivolous?) Or should I be solemn and straight-faced? (But would that seem stuck-up?)

I heard the sound of sixty slipper-shod feet shuffling up the hall, and as they filed past me and into the Zendo proper I wondered if it was sacrilegious, or rude, to have started to meditate already. (But how trivial and strangulated-with-selfhood were the subjects of my 'meditation'!). Suddenly I heard a loud voice, directly in front of me, saying, "No, no, not that way!" and I raised my eyes to see a tall, emaciated, red-faced monk with protuberant eyes and gigantic ears, standing with feet apart and frog-like hands on bony hips, glaring at me.

"I beg your pardon?" I said meekly. The scary-looking monk reached out, grabbed my shoulders, and roughly rearranged my posture.

"Your shoulders are uneven," he said, and I noticed that his thin-lipped mouth was filled with a jumble of crooked yellow teeth, like a pile of deerhorn dice in an antique shop. "All your energy will be trapped in your muscles, and they'll be so tense that you won't be able to meditate properly now, or sleep properly later. And look at your hands! Don't you know by now that it's left over right?" I looked down, and sure enough, my right hand was on top of the left again. So much for mnemonic devices, I thought.

My entire body seemed to be blushing, and my skin felt prickly all over, as if I had fallen into a blackberry patch. "I'm sorry," I said, and then added, with an attempt at self-mocking charm, "I'm just an embryonic meditator, you know." That modular line ("I'm just an embryonic something-or-other," with the blank filled in to suit the occasion) had always disarmed people in the past, but the ruddy-faced monk just glowered at me and said, "Now concentrate! This isn't a game!" and walked away. I may be an embryo, but he's a hard-boiled egg, I thought defiantly, but I was close to tears. I tried to clear my mind and think about the new koan I had assigned to myself ("Hyotan Namazu"; how did the catfish get inside the narrow-mouthed gourd?) but I couldn't shake the feelings of humiliation and disgrace, for I was certain that everyone had been listening, and watching, and judging me.

It was very warm in the Zendo, and at one point I felt myself becoming drowsy. Remembering my painful encounter with the *keisaku* ("discipline stick"), I propped my eyelids open with imaginary toothpicks, like Malcolm McDowell in *A Clockwork Orange*, and tried to concentrate on the obstinate opacity of the koan. I was relieved when the bell rang to signal the end of meditation, and after making the requisite bows toward the altar I hurried home without talking to anyone.

That's it, I thought, I'm never going to zazen again. I'll just meditate by myself. The only thing I could find to feel cheerful about was that I had managed to stay awake, and although the bespectacled *jikijitsu* had paused in front of me once or twice, he hadn't given me the bow of doom, or flogged me with his stick.

* * *

"My mother doesn't approve of my consorting with foreigners," said Yukio when he picked me up the next morning, wearing a white shirt and matching shorts, "so I had to tell her I was going to play tennis."

"Well, whatever the reason, your foreign consort thinks you look very dashing all dressed in white," I said boldly, and we laughed.

"Today," said Yukio as he headed out of town, "I am going to be an autocrat, a dictator, a despot. Yesterday I was your chauffeur, but today I am your kidnapper."

"That's fine," I said. "I just hope no one comes up with the ransom." It was exciting to be able to say such unambiguously romantic things to someone so irresistible, and to know that he would reply in kind.

Sure enough: "Don't worry," Yukio said. "I wrote the ransom note in lemon juice." The clouds, too, seemed to have been drawn with invisible ink, and as we rode along through deep green forests, the sky grew clearer and bluer by the minute. By the time we arrived at the pastoral village of Takao, the low clouds of morning were just a memory, like Mugen's kiss in the graveyard and everything else that had ever happened.

Yukio had chosen a famous treehouse-restaurant set in a frothy grove of white-flowered mountain cherries above a rushing river. We sat outside on a balcony and ate an exquisite country lunch: cherry-blossom soup, with variegated pink petals floating on top of the thin sour broth, like butterfly wings; gingery steamed tofu; and all sorts of savory mountain delicacies—ferns, and roots, and nuts. I was alarmed by the prices on the menu, but Yukio said, "Don't worry, my father gave me money."

"Does he know you're, um, consorting with a foreigner?" I asked.

Yukio laughed. "I just told him I was taking the woman of my dreams to lunch, and he said, 'Have a good time, and don't be home too early!' Don't worry about my parents; my dad's open-minded, and my mother just hates all non-Japanese because her favorite aunt was jilted by an

American G.I., and it ruined her life, and her reputation. But I'm an adult, and I'll make my own decisions, and live my own life." I was impressed by Yukio's proclamation of independence, and I said so. The truth was, it struck me as refreshingly un-Japanese, but I kept that thought to myself.

Over tea and grayish-fuchsia rice cakes flavored with the pungent leaves of the *shiso* mint, Yukio told me about his life as a gaucho in Patagonia. "I herded sheep, not cattle," he said. "As a Japanese, I am not accustomed to grand vistas of unpopulated space, and I was overwhelmed by the vastness of the pampas. There were great expanses of rolling rust-colored hills, suddenly dropping off into huge, craggy powder-blue glaciers, still unthawed after a million years of sunshine. The surrounding sea was a deeper blue, the overarching sky was deeper still, and it was all just blindingly beautiful. The work was hard," he went on, "but the men I worked with—two Argentineans, a Peruvian Indian, and a third-generation Scottish foreman who still wore a kilt to parties— were so kind, in their rough way, and so patient with me, and so unerringly true to themselves, and to the land, that every day was a joy. Sometimes, for fun, we would go off on horseback and hunt rheas with *boliadoras*—leather thongs with stones at each end—and on very special occasions everyone would get dressed up, the men and their wives and children and girlfriends, and sing the gaucho songs and dance the gaucho dances that have been passed down for centuries. During the two years I was in Patagonia I grew two inches and gained fifteen pounds, but the thing that grew the most was my heart, and my love for this vulnerable earth, and its bumbling, conscientious inhabitants."

If I hadn't already been utterly enraptured with Yukio, that touching speech would surely have turned the tide. I was so moved that I actually had tears in my eyes, but I blinked them away and said casually, "What about your hat? Is that a souvenir of the Patagonian pampas?" Yukio nodded. He took off his putty-colored suede hat, with its pentimento sweat stains, floppy brim, and bolo-band, and placed it on my head.

"There," he said, "now you're a gauchita." And then, in front of an entire roomful of his judgmental countrymen, Yukio did a very brave and daring thing: he leaned across the cherry-blossom-sprinkled table and gave me a sweet, chaste gaucho kiss.

After lunch we wandered through a fragrant forest of evergreen cedar until we came upon a large stone into which were carved two gigantic footprints, with the natural swirls and whorls of a human foot transmogrified into an elaborate rococo design. "According to legend, these are the footprints of the Buddha," the sign declared. I was transfixed. "Did you bring a camera?" I asked.

"No," Yukio said wryly, "just a tennis racket."

"Well, do you mind if I make a quick sketch of these footprints?" I asked. "I love the patterns."

"Not at all," said Yukio. "I'll be down there, reading my book." He held up a paperback copy of *The Age of Discontinuity*, in English, and then walked down the stone steps.

After I finished my drawing, I ran down the steps. One of them was loose, and I tripped and fell down, twisting my ankle quite badly. After lying on the ground for a few moments, alternately moaning and cursing my clumsiness, I stood up and slowly limped the rest of the way in a fair amount of pain.

Yukio had fallen asleep on a long, flat, sun-dappled stone with *The Age of Discontinuity* (which I assumed was a book of social commentary) lying open on his white-shirted chest, his long brown legs akimbo, his arms flung over his head in an almost balletic position. I thought of trying a Sleeping Beauty role-reversal, but even though we were obviously involved in an enthusiastic reciprocal courtship, I didn't feel confident enough to waken him with a kiss. So I amused myself by gazing dreamily at Yukio's secret sleeping face and watching with morbid fascination as my increasingly zaftig ankle began to turn a lovely Ice-Age blue.

THE SAGE WITH
THE *SANPAKU* EYES

The window opens like an orange
The lovely fruit of light

Guillaume Apollinaire
"Les Fenêtres"

—KYOTO

Whenever a conversation with a new acquaintance lagged in those days, I had a couple of restorative gambits up my sleeve. One was a variation of "Desert Island Discs," wherein I would ask which records, books, and works of art they would choose to pack for a lifetime's banishment to a sandy, uninhabited speck in some uncharted archipelago. I knew it was a difficult and even sadistic question, but the answers (squeezed out slowly, like tofu through cheesecloth) were always so interesting that I couldn't stop asking.

The other silence-subverting stratagem was to say: "If you had to give up one of your five senses, which would you choose to relinquish?" (My answer: touch.) This question would usually provoke a lively discussion of the essential role of the senses in the pursuit of pleasure. While I was living at Zenzenji, I thought a lot about the five (or six, or seven) senses, and whether they were meant to be transcended, or simply enjoyed. Sensualism versus asceticism was surely one of the most ancient of ideological tugs-of-war, and it often struck me as ironic that the Sodo, a place dedicated to Spartan living in the pursuit of enlightenment, offered a constant, voluptuous treat for the senses.

For the eyes, there was the green velour of mossy gardens, in or out of bloom; the clean geometry of half-timbered buildings, shiitake-brown on Mykonos white; the soft citric light through rice-papered windows shaped like bells, or tulips; the swoop and luster of dark-tiled roofs; the occasional glimpse of an ancient, witty scroll; and the work-of-art monks themselves, with their ambient glow, fine faces, and timeless costumes. (Would I have loved Zen if it hadn't been beautiful? Of course not.)

For the nose, there was the heady scent of incense, which had the same effect on my lungs as falling in love at first sight. There were the mellow leguminous cooking aromas, the earthy bouquet of old walls baking in the sun, and the fresh green smells of garden and vegetable plot. For the mouth (if it was lucky), there were the hearty flavors of simple food, lovingly prepared. For the fingertips, the soles of the feet, and other touch-receptors, there was the warmth of saffron plaster infused with summer, the glossy grain of tatami, the coolness of satinwood floors. (I still maintain that touch is the most dispensable of the senses unless you place a premium on sexual sybaritism, or earn your living with a Ouija board.)

Finally, the ears: If, to turn the game around, I were sent to visit a Zen monastery with only one functioning sense, I think I would choose the auditory. Just as music is more powerful and immediate an evoker of emotion than words or visual images, so the sounds of the Sodo thrilled me more than all the other sensations put together. The delicate plink of brass bells, the sharp rap of ebony clappers, the reverberant percussion of the wooden fish, the calm good-humored voices of the monks, the poetic plop of frogs in the lily-pond, the staccato bark of a Zen-dog, the ominous medieval instrumentation of the roshi's lectures; these sounds seemed to bypass the analytical mind and play directly on my heart. But the music that really moved my marrow was the archival, revolutionary chanting.

A year after I had first walked past the Sodo wall and heard the undulant waves of sound ("Namu-kara-tan-no-tora-ya-ya") I was still overcome with joy, envy, and longing every time I heard the monks chanting in chorus. I was fascinated by the texts of the sutras (the Daihishin Dharani quoted above contains such pagan-sounding lines as "Hail to the blue-necked one"), but it was the cadence that I found mesmerizing, and transforming. "Sa-bo sa-bo mo-ra mo-ra mo-ki mo-ki ri-to-in ku-ryo ku-ryo ke-mo to-ryo to-ryo ho-ja ya-chi mo-ko ho-ja ya-chi to-ra to-ra chi-ri-ni." The syllables seemed to follow one another with mystic inevitability, with the rapturous momentum of a great symphony, or a mad romance.

* * *

Quill pen, India ink, rough gray paper; I was sitting in my little room, drawing small pictures, when there was a knock on the door. "I just wanted to tell you that the bath is ready, if you're in the mood," said Mrs. Maeda, known to everyone as Okusan.

I had hobbled up to the bath house when it opened at two p.m. to soak my ankle, so I said, "Not today, thanks."

"What's that you're drawing?" the Okusan asked, looking down at my sketch book.

"Oh, can't you tell?" I was disappointed, for the subject should have been obvious. "It's Daruma-san."

"Why, of course it is, I see that now," Okusan said, and a faint smile appeared on her sweet, weary face. The smile grew larger and larger, and she quickly excused herself and left the room. I could hear her out in the hall, laughing in the breathless, spluttering way of someone who has tried desperately to keep a straight face and now is trying to muffle an uncontrollable outburst of hilarity. I looked down at my drawing.

"Well, I think it looks like him," I muttered, but my feelings were hurt and my confidence undermined, and I spent the next hour drawing subjects of which I felt more certain: sensuous snake-women and lute-playing angels and fabulous birds with double-lidded eyes.

Bodhidharma (known in Japanese as Daruma or, more respectfully, Daruma-san) is the patron saint of Zen Buddhism. He is frequently depicted in portraits as a cross between a wino and a visionary: a sort of oracular derelict. Because of his intimate and seminal connection with Zen, Daruma has long been a favorite subject for ink paintings, both in China (where he emigrated from his native India) and in Japan, where he may or may not have spent some time. The eccentric philosopher/sage is generally portrayed as a long-faced, dome-headed, scraggly-browed, scruffy-bearded man with a flat nose and flamboyantly-flared nostrils, a small hoop earring in one elongated, fleshy-lobed ear, and an expression of bemusement or disgruntlement on his wide, down-curved mouth—a refreshing change from the blank mask of serene enlightenment worn by most Japanese saints. Daruma's most striking features are his eyes: startlingly *sanpaku*, with huge hooded lids, they resemble a couple of fried ostrich eggs with undersized yolks. According to legend, Daruma cut his eyelids off when they began to droop during a nine-year marathon of meditation in a cave at the Shao-Lin temple in China (also known as the birthplace of kung fu, and scene of innumerable badly-dubbed martial arts movies).

Another legend says that when Daruma finally emerged from the cave his legs had atrophied completely; hence the limbless red Daruma dolls seen everywhere in Japan. Because they will always right themselves when knocked over ("Fall down seven times, get up eight," says the proverb) they are considered symbols of resiliency and general good luck, and one of the most widespread folk rituals in Japan involves buying a Daruma doll, painting in one eye when you make a wish or set a goal, and then (often with great ceremony) painting in the other eye when the wish comes true or the goal is attained. Everyone practices this lively bit of superstition, from turnip farmers to Prime Ministers.

The best paintings of Daruma, in my opinion, are those by Zen priests. I had seen one by Hakuin (the same master who said "Both music and dancing are voices of the way"), and I was so captivated that I had been trying to capture its essence—the wild eyes, the arabesque features, the air of manic omniscience—ever since. Evidently, I hadn't come close. I had just slammed my sketchbook shut when there was another knock at my door. "Come in," I said.

It was the Okusan again, this time bearing a tray with a tiny teapot, a matching cup, and a plate containing two spongy pink rice-flour confections wrapped in cherry leaves. "I know you must have heard me laughing just now, and I'm sorry," she said. "It's just that your picture of Daruma was so amusing, and so unusual, that I just couldn't help it." I suspected that amusing was a kindly euphemism for ludicrous, but I gladly accepted the apology, and the snack. Even now, I'm not sure what the Okusan found so hilarious about my drawing, but that experience crystallized my awareness that I was, and would always be, a myopic outsider peering through a very small hole in a very dark glass at a culture I would never fully understand.

"By the way," the Okusan said when I returned the tray, "I forgot to tell you that the rent is usually due on the first of the month."

"Oh, I'm sorry," I said. "How much is it?"

"Three thousand yen a month."

That was less than ten dollars, in those halcyon days when the dollar was worth three hundred sixty yen, and there were still travel books titled, unsatirically, *Japan on Five Dollars a Day*. Transportation was cheap, groceries cost a pittance, atmosphere was free, and I was able to live comfortably in Kyoto on my earnings from teaching English conversation four or five times a week, at a thousand yen per student, per hour. I had automatically inherited Toozie's six pupils: two shy salarymen, a potter's apprentice, a *shacho* (company president), and two small girls who were the granddaughters of a calligraphy-class friend of the Okusan's.

Aside from the trip to the bath house, I had spent the past two days in my room, reading and writing and drawing, with my injured ankle enshrined on a pile of pillows like some dowager's pampered Pomeranian. The swelling was down and the bruises had faded, so I decided to go for a slow diagnostic walk. I had no sooner ducked through the Kaiko-in gate than a friendly voice said, "Hello! We thought you had gone back to America!"

It was Zo-san, smiling broadly and carrying a basket filled with lacy-leafed carrots, for he was the official cook of the Sodo. "You won't get rid of me that easily," I said. "I just sprained my ankle looking at the Buddha's footprint." Zo-san nodded gravely, as if such looking-glass statements were a staple of ordinary conversation.

He took off his white kerchief and mopped his sweaty shaven head, and then he said, "When you have recovered, please come again to zazen."

"I'd love to," I said, forgetting my oft-repeated vow of Never Again, "but I'm so ashamed about what happened with that frightening monk."

"Oh, that's just Do-san. Don't mind him. It's his job to keep the novice monks in line, and he takes his work very seriously. It was nothing personal." Zo-san smiled reassuringly, that incandescent smile. His skin was a warm Gauguin gold, like oil-rubbed wood from a warm climate, and his face and head were shadowed with dense stubble. I remembered reading that the monks only shaved on days containing the digits four or nine, and this day was an eight.

"But I felt like such a fool," I said, realizing as I spoke that such dead-horse beating was the antithesis of true Zen discourse. "Wasn't everyone laughing at me?"

"No one was laughing at you, or even thinking about you. Everyone was worrying about their own problems, and thinking about their koan, and wishing they could take a nap instead of doing zazen," Zo-san said. I found his words very soothing, and I craved another dose.

"So you really don't think my presence is a nuisance or a distraction?" I said, jumping up and down, now, on the poor horse's grave.

"Not at all," Zo-san replied patiently. "But let me ask you something. Are you seriously interested in zazen?"

"Yes," I said. I hadn't precisely enjoyed my first two sessions, but I was definitely interested in learning how to be wise and serene, like the Obaasan of Kaiko-in, and if zazen was the way, then I was seriously interested in zazen.

"In that case, you should come to the next O-Zesshin," he said. "The next time you see Toku-san, ask him if it would be all right—we've never had a foreign guest before, but I'm sure he'll say yes." I had read about Sesshin (O-Zesshin just means Big Sesshin), the semi-annual sessions of intensive meditation during which the disciplines become more rigorous and all the monks go without sleep and concentrate on solving their koan, but I had never dreamed that I might be permitted to participate. My mind raced. Maybe I would even be given a koan to ponder, and a scary, transmogrifying audience with the roshi!

"Telephone!" called the voice of Musashi, the middle son of Kaiko-in. "Were you and Zo-san speaking English?" Musashi asked when I came inside.

"No," I said, "I've never heard him speak a word of English."

"Oh, he speaks fluently, you know," Musashi said, and then he vanished into his room.

I took the phone call in the kitchen; it was Nashiko, the apprentice to a colleague of the potter with whom Toozie had worked, wondering whether she could change her first English-conversation lesson to that day, instead of the next. "Sure," I said, "come on over." Nashiko turned out to be a petite, intelligent, animated young woman with a long ponytail and an *ukiyo e* face. She wore a stylish trouser-suit of heliotrope linen, but there was clay under her fingernails and there was a dab of dried slip on her forehead, like a free-form caste mark. "Did you come from the studio?" I asked, and she nodded.

"Sometimes I think I'll never get all the clay off," she said. "I even dream about clay."

We hit it off immediately, for we both liked art and craft and atmosphere. Nashiko was rhapsodic over my little room, with its view of the morning-glory wall beyond the garden, and I found her an ideal pupil. Her English was quite advanced, so instead of doing the usual "pattern drills," we acted out little fantasy-dramas in which she was the stern interviewer and I was a nervous job applicant, or I was the traffic-court judge and she was a glamorous jet-setter, caught speeding on the Paris-Marseilles Highway in her Lotus Elan. Then we played Desert Island Diversions (Nashiko chose Beethoven's Seventh Symphony, *Snow Country*, and a plate—any plate—by Shoji Hamada). The hour passed very quickly, and I felt a bit guilty about being paid for having such a good time.

The next morning I went out to buy some raisins and red-skinned Spanish peanuts from a broom closet–sized shop on the corner. The proprietor, a minuscule old woman with the high, piping voice of a child, sat all day on a stool surrounded by her wares: forty or fifty clear-glass apothecary jars filled with nuts, seeds, ginger pastilles, green-tea jawbreakers, dried mushrooms, fish shreds, sweet beans, shrimp chips, and other mysterious snacks. While I waited for the shopkeeper to wrap my purchases (she insisted, even though I explained that I was planning to eat them as soon as I got home), I mused about the Japanese work ethic. One of the things that impressed me most about the Japanese people was the concentration and devotion they brought to their work. Itinerant noodle-vendors, floor-moppers, emptiers of bedpans; no matter how unglamorous the task, there was almost always a sense that the worker believed his job had meaning, and value.

The keepers of small neighborhood specialty shops seemed to me to be the apotheosis of this exemplary attitude toward work, and commerce. They were sometimes so ancient that every shuffling step seemed a miracle of effort, but they were so touchingly solicitous, and so grateful for my measly business, that I often left their shops with tears in my eyes. How, I used to wonder as I bowed out with fifty yen's worth of seaweed or a hundred-yen bag of soybeans, can these dear old people survive?

All the shops I patronized around Zenzenji had living quarters in the back, and sometimes when the proprietor emerged from behind a curtain in response to my call of "Gomen kudasai," I would catch a glimpse of dark-wood apothecary chests, antique folk toys (Daruma dolls, straw horses, waving cats), and the remains of an interrupted meal laid out on a low table: rice, pickles, the calligraphic skeleton of a single grilled sardine. It struck me as slightly obscene that I probably received more for an enjoyable hour or two of English-conversation teaching, for which my primary qualification was having been born in the USA, than those hard-working old people made in an entire week.

On the way back to Kaiko-in with my carefully-wrapped package, I met the monk with the black-framed glasses—the jikijitsu—who had hit me with a stick. I was going to nod and keep walking, but to my surprise he stopped and said, "Oh, I've been wanting to talk to you!"

"To me?" I said, with a sinking feeling. Was he going to criticize my sitting posture, or tell me that it was obvious that my mind was wandering and I should just give up on zazen?

To my surprise and relief he said, "I hear that you play the shakuhachi."

"I don't really *play*," I said. "I only know three or four songs."

"But you can read the Japanese sheet music, and when you blow into the flute some sound comes out?" I nodded. There was a myth that it took the average person three months to coax any sound at all from the shakuhachi, but all the students I knew had been playing audible (if squeaky) scales by the end of the first week.

"Good!" said the monk. "Then we can practice together sometime. If you're free now, I'll show you the place." Without waiting for my reply, he marched down the slope past the Sodo, around the corner, through the gate of one of the many sub temples of Zenzenji, and into one of the most amazing Japanese gardens I had ever seen: velvety moss and flaming azaleas and polished-zinc reflecting ponds, like medieval mirrors.

On the way back, we were in the midst of an odd conversation ("I like your black-rimmed glasses. Are you a Buddy Holly fan?" "I don't know. What is Budji Horii?") when I thought I heard a faint mewing sound, coming from the bushes at the bottom of the Sodo slope. "Did you hear that?" I asked Den-san, for that was the jikijitsu's name.

"Oh, it's just those little birds—you know, sparrows."

"Are you sure?" I said dubiously. "It sounds more like a cat to me."

"Oh, look," Den-san said, pointing toward the top of the hill, where Migaku was standing, waving a Ping-Pong paddle and jumping up and down. "I think you're being paged."

We quickened our pace, and as we approached, Migaku shouted, "*Kuso!* I was playing *pin-pon* and then you got a phone call and I had to come and get you, *kono yaro!*"

"I'm sorry," I said, but Migaku was already gone, slashing at the air with his Ping-Pong paddle, long legs flying in all directions.

The call was from Yukio, saying he was back from Tokyo and suggesting that we get together with some friends from the ship and do something "fun and superficial."

"I was sort of thinking of going to zazen," I said.

"No, no, you mustn't put any pressure on your ankle," Yukio said, adopting a lofty medical tone. "Wait a few more days."

"All right," I said. I hadn't spoken to anyone from Cherry Blossom Lane since the three-peas-in-a-futon incident, but they were still my friends, and I knew I couldn't avoid them forever.

* * *

That day in the woods at Takao, when Yukio had awakened to find me sitting on a log with my swollen ankle elevated on a rock, he had been amazingly kind and sympathetic. "I'll take you to my house," he said, as he carried me to the car, ignoring my protestations that I was perfectly able to hobble by myself. "Besides, I've been wanting to introduce you to my dogs." (Aha! I thought, for meeting the dogs is the ultimate vote of confidence from an animal lover.) The next day, while I convalesced in my little room, I made a watercolor illustration of that scene: the gorgeous Japanese gaucho carrying the pale, swooning damsel through the woods, gallantly pausing every few yards to untangle a trailing rope of maiden-hair from a rapacious shrub or tree branch.

I was slightly nonplussed when Yukio pulled up in front of a non-residential building with leaded windows and a sign that read, "Mersey Beat Coffee Shop: All Beatles, Only Beatles, Beatles Forever." ("Don't worry," he said, "I don't live here!") Appropriately, "Help!" was playing as we walked in; Yukio got me settled in a Malaga-leather booth, ordered a cup of "Liverpuddle Tea" for me, and then left, saying, "I'll be back as soon as the coast is clear." The coast, I gathered, was his house, and the offshore shark, or barracuda, was his xenophobic mother. I was nursing my second cup of Liverpuddle Tea (strong black brew with thick cream and treacle) when Yukio returned.

"It worked out perfectly," he said. "My mother was there when I came in, but I talked her into going to visit her sister in Osaka, since my dad's away on business. Sorry I'm so late—I decided to drive her to the train station and wave goodbye, just to be safe!"

The rest of that afternoon is a vague but lovely memory, perceived as it was through a vertiginous haze of pain, caffeine, and romantic infatuation. Yukio doctored my ankle with ice, heat, Chinese-herb liniment, and blue-and-white polka-dotted cloth bandages; he fed me green tea and almond cookies and he showed me his Patagonian photo album (flaming sunsets, opalescent dawns). Most significantly, he introduced me to his dogs: Chikamatsu, a frisky black-and-white terrier in the "His Master's Voice" mold, and Hime ("Princess"), an ancient, half-blind, multiparous spaniel whose pendulous udders were trampled obliviously underfoot every time she lumbered off in pursuit of a disintegrating tennis ball.

Yukio showed me his room, too. It was furnished in Western style, with a bunk bed, desk, and rocking chair, and it had the slightly melancholy aura of a space which has been outgrown and abandoned by its occupant. There were posters of Tierra del Fuego, Charles Darwin, and John Lennon on the wall, and on the blue-coverleted bed was an old stuffed duck-doll with a red pom-pommed sailor hat and big, round, sanpaku eyes. The room reminded me of a man I once knew in Cambridge, who told me that his major erotic fantasy was to make "wild, noisy love" to the woman of his dreams on the top bunk of his childhood bed, while his mother baked oatmeal cookies downstairs. "Well," I said politely, stifling the obvious Betty-Crocker-meets-Freud quip, "I certainly hope you'll find the woman of your dreams someday."

"I think I've found her," said the man, and he gave me one of those soulful, searing laser-looks, the sort of gaze that sends shudders down the spines of virgins and courtesans alike when it emanates from the eyes of a man they wouldn't want for a lambada partner, much less a wild and noisy lover.

I wondered if C. J. (even with an ankle that was throbbing like a transplanted heart) would have seduced Yukio right there on his narrow bed, while the duck—which I had eventually recognized as *the* duck: Disney's Donald, or Donarudo Dakku, as he is known in Japan—looked on in wide-eyed horror, or excitement. Of course she would have, just as she wouldn't have hesitated to waken Yukio from his *Age of Discontinuity*-nap in the forest with a kiss, or with some bolder, more intimate gesture.

After rehearsing several opening gambits, I settled on self-mocking self-deprecation, prefaced by a sincere apology for my bad manners. C. J. responded with a casual "Hey, no big deal," and she was enthusiastic about my suggestion that we get together for a shipmates' reunion. "Let's do, by all means," she said. "I have a surprise for you, anyway."

"Uh-oh," I said in what I hoped was a light, playful tone. "I'm still recovering from the last one."

C. J.'s surprise turned out to be the unexpected presence of Elijah Ruskin and Lewison Lear, who had completed their love-hotel reconnaissance tour of southern Japan and were stopping over in Kyoto before heading north. We met in the little park outside Popeye, and as everyone exchanged greetings I realized that I felt slightly uncomfortable with every person there. With C. J., Arasuke, and Ramon, for obvious reasons; with Lui and Elijah and Ramon because I had once rebuffed their advances, and even with Yukio, who was rapidly becoming one of my favorite people on earth, because he had been physically intimate with C. J., and because I couldn't help wondering if seeing her again (for she did look very fetching in her red dress, with a matching carnation behind one ear) might rekindle that spark.

While the other six were playing on the swings and climbing up the slide, I limped slowly down the canal, looking at the flickering fish just beneath the surface of the gray-green water, and letting the late cherry blossoms fall on my head like a benediction. I found a fresh white chrysanthemum in a trash barrel, and took it as an omen, or a semiotic shout. Ahead of me, going through another can of trash, was an old gypsy-man, dressed in layer upon layer of eclectic antique clothing in shades of nicotine and charcoal, with his treasures wrapped in a soiled green fan-patterned furoshiki. His back was turned, and I watched as he took a drink from a frosted polar-blue bottle. (Water? Saké? Elixir of madness?)

The vagabond's back looked tense and angry, but when he turned and began walking toward me his face was calm and pleasant, almost radiant, beneath the sunburn and the grime. When the man came closer I saw that he had remarkable features, with the fried-egg eyes, the wide, mournful mouth, and the flaring nostrils of a classic Daruma-drawing. Impulsively, I held out my white chrysanthemum; he accepted it with dignity, and thanked me in polite Nagoya-accented Japanese. When I looked back the gypsy-man was standing silhouetted against the canal smelling the flower, like the Buddha at the moment when he "invented" Zen.

"Where have you been?" Lui asked, when I returned to the playground.

"On desolation row," I said, quoting without attribution, for we had all committed every oracular word of "Blonde on Blonde" to memory. "Or maybe on exaltation row."

Lui gave me a quizzical look, and then said, half-jokingly, "Why do you always have to be so damned metaphysical?" I resisted the urge to retort, "I don't know; why do you always have to be so damned *physical*?" Instead, I went over and joined Yukio on the swings. A few minutes later, after milling around like drunken paramecia, the group formed an uneasy queue and shuffled into the red-lit rock and roll inferno, where my old travel consultant, Jim Morrison (who was still out there somewhere, slouching toward a bathtub in Paris), was singing "Come on, baby, light my fire."

A slightly awkward hour later, as I sat looking around at the familiar faces, made mythic by the diffuse red light, it occurred to me that I had a choice. I could continue to feel alienated from C. J., Arasuke, Ramon, Elijah, and Lui just because their desires and mores didn't correspond exactly with mine. Or I could take the munificent evolutionary view and dismiss our differences as bilgewater under the bridge of friendship. "It's worth a try," I said out loud, confident that I wouldn't be heard above the music ("Magic Carpet Ride," full volume).

"Did you say something?" C. J. asked.

"Yes," I improvised, "I said, 'It's really a treat to see all these faces together again.'" And then I looked around the table and smiled at everyone, one at a time, not just with the teeth but with the eyes, and everyone smiled back. Maybe it was my imagination, but there seemed to be a subtle change in the atmosphere after that, as if a cloud of communal doubt and resentment and regret had been lifted. Just then, by uncanny coincidence, "Let It Bleed" began to play: "'We all need someone we can lean on/And if you want it, well you can lean on me ...'"

"Let's all go out and dance, just like old times!" said Elijah, and so we did. Or rather, they did. My ankle was still too tender to bounce around on, so I just stood in one place and waved my arms in the air, like a late-night TV evangelist in the throes of a major revelation.

MAD MONKS IN LOVE

I have the taste to be a monk but,
alas, not the character.

Hugh Walpole
Rogue Herries

—KYOTO

Ah, that cherry-blossom spring; oh, that starflower summer. I used to waken every morning to the sound of the Sodo drum and realize, with a sense of infinite wealth and wonder, that there were 2,500 other temples and shrines in Kyoto, each with its own history, mystery, magic, and drums, just waiting to be explored. One sunny afternoon I set out by bus to visit an ancient shrine on the outskirts of town where, I had heard, there was a row of charming canal-side teahouses serving hand-made soba, artistic Japanese sweets, and the best green tea in town. It was a long trip, so I was disappointed to find all the teahouses silent and shuttered. (CLOSED MONDAYS, said the signs.) I cheered myself up with a pleasant ramble around the cypress-shaded shrine, with its antique buildings of dolphin-colored wood, and then I headed back to the bus stop.

The bus only ran once an hour, and I deduced from the lingering smell of exhaust that I had just missed it. I sat on a bench under a big old *sakura*, well past its blooming prime but still the loveliest of trees, and began reading a Penguin paperback copy of *Through the Looking-Glass* (sent by my Oscar Wilde–look-alike friend Corin, who shared my fanatical fondness for Lewis Carroll). "The rule is, jam to-morrow and jam yesterday—but never jam to-day," I read, and then I paused to reflect that while many religions are preoccupied with "jam to-morrow" (that is, an afterlife), Zen concentrates on jam today: the precious, vivid present.

After a few minutes I heard footsteps, and I glanced up from my book. Walking down the country lane was a tall Zen monk in a short blue robe. He had a broad, prominent-boned face, and he was carrying a single shiny-leafed camellia branch with three perfect, ruffly-petaled red flowers. It was such a striking picture that I couldn't help staring, but the monk seemed unaware of my presence as he marched purposefully by.

The hour passed quickly, and eventually the old green bus came wheezing up the lane and stopped to disgorge two middle-aged women wearing beauty-parlor coiffures and fancy kimono. I climbed aboard the bus and went to the very back, where the air was cooler and the legroom more expansive. As I turned to watch the cherry trees receding from sight, I saw the same wide-faced monk, retracing his steps. This time the flowers were gone, and his empty hands were clasped across his abdomen. I thought I detected a subtle difference in his expression, too: a romantic shine in the eyes, the shadow of a secret smile.

I wonder who he gave the flowers to, I thought. Probably a tea ceremony teacher, or a patron of the temple, or maybe even to his own mother, living nearby in a tumble-down cottage surrounded by bush clover. But I couldn't help thinking: What if he took them to a woman, a lovely nervous poetess in pale kimono whom he loves but can't be with until his training is completed? I could see them, sitting in eloquent silence and staring longingly at each other, with the vase of blood-colored camellias between them like a barrier, and a bond.

For some reason, my fantasy about the camellia-monk made me think of Fuji Mugen. I opened my journal to record my thoughts and it fell open to the page on which I had described our most recent encounter, unplanned as usual, a few days earlier. *We walked up "our hill," through a wonderful lost green forest of enormous trees cloaked in shaggy, sentient moss, to drink mountain water from the dragon's mouth, to watch the sun setting in a sky brocaded with mauve and violet clouds, and to salute the Ah-Un Nio (huge muscular temple-gate guardian sculptures, one with open mouth, the other with lips closed, their hands arranged in corresponding mudras). We discovered a funny-dog street where every dog had some comical idiosyncrasy, then stopped at a roadside teahouse to drink thick bitter tea and eat elaborate crumbly sugar-cakes shaped like green-and-fuchsia squash blossoms. Mugen drew a circle on his napkin, and said: "A snake begins to nibble on its own tail; it eats all the*

way up to the head and not until it's dying does it notice what it has done."
"The Worm Ouroboros," I said, and I tried to describe that fantastical, lap-
idary book. Down the hill, trading foolish esoteric jokes; ours is a rare
togetherness (okay: love) which seems to thrive on separation and sudden-
ness. Back to the Sodo, an amazing sight through an open door: all the
monks naked in the bath-house, shaving one another's heads with long-
handled straight razors. P.S. I love Yukio, too. Later, as I walked to Zenzenji from the bus stop, I thought about all the things I hadn't said a
month or so before when Mugen and I were walking in the graveyard,
things that now seemed to need to be said. I also wanted to ask Mugen
if he thought it was possible to feel romantic love for more than one person at the same time, and I wanted to ask him if the roshi had given him
a koan.

I went in the side gate of the Sodo, behind the tool shed, and headed
toward the guest house where Mugen always stayed. In the courtyard
where Toku-san had first said, "I want to introduce our isoro," I met a
cement-spattered workman carrying a shovel. "Do you by any chance
know whether Mr. Fuji is still here?" I asked.

"What do you want with that freeloader?" said the workman, with a
familiarity I found offensive. "He's crazy, you know. He likes this—" he
mimed draining a glass of saké "—and *this*." He dropped his shovel and
made a grotesque koochie-koo gesture with his dirty, nicotine-stained
fingers.

The man leered at me, and I caught a rank whiff of unfiltered-
tobacco breath. "Is that phony monk your boyfriend?" he asked.

"Um, not exactly," I said.

"That's good, because I'm available!" The workman illustrated this
repellent remark with the same salacious-*shiatsu* gesture, and I fled,
flinging an assortment of incongruously polite exit lines over my shoulder. It was a distinctly unpleasant experience, and an hour or two later it
occurred to me that I had violated my still-fresh vow not to go visiting
unannounced, and had paid the price, in spades.

The next morning, I went to a Bharata Natyam lesson. I couldn't
dance because of my wobbly ankle, so Vasanthamala concentrated on
teaching me the mudras for "wisdom," and "desire," and "repose." The
Bharata Natyam lessons had turned out to be everything I hoped they
would be. Vasanthamala was a wry, patient teacher, and as the steps and
the accompanying chants grew more complex, she always made sure

that I had grasped one sequence (stamp right, stamp left, stamp right, then turn; "te-jun-ta-ha, te-jun-ta-ta") before going on to the next.

I loved to watch her large, flat, beautiful feet; they seemed to have a kind of autonomous divinity, and I half-expected to see ornate spiral designs on the soles, like the "Buddha's footprints" in the forest at Takao. Vasanthamala's feet seemed to be in elemental touch with the earth; she was obviously born to dance Bharata Natyam. I used to look at my abnormally high arches and despair, for I knew I would never be able to produce that reverberant sound, the lusty fishmonger's slap of foot-flesh meeting solid ground.

On our breaks, a half-joking ritual had evolved: I would ask when I might be allowed to dance with bells on my ankles, as Vasanthamala did, and she would reply, "When you are ready." Then we would talk about Indian food, and E. M. Forster, and past lives (I couldn't recall any, but Vasanthamala was fairly certain that she had been a favored consort of Gautama Buddha during his hedonistic sex-monster phase), all the while sipping thick, slippery tea made from cinnamon or cardamom or sassafras, for Vasanthamala believed that caffeine was hazardous to the human nervous system.

Exhilarated by my new knowledge, I returned to Zenzenji to meet C. J. We had agreed to have lunch together, since we hadn't really talked privately since my arrival in Kyoto, and there was, C. J. said on the telephone, "a passel of stuff to discuss." C. J. had grown up in Fort Worth, and although she had gotten rid of her accent by hiring a dialect-reversal coach, she hadn't entirely purged the rustic Texasisms ("He's all hat and no cattle," "That old dog won't hunt," and the occasional auto-genetic you-all) from her vocabulary.

"Where shall we go?" C. J. asked as we walked past the Sodo. "I don't know," I said, "let's just walk until we find someplace irresistible." That is one of the addictive things about Japan, even now: in any city or large town, almost every non-residential block contains an elegant little sushiya or a folk-art noodle shop or an aromatic tempura specialty house. It's no wonder that peripatetic visitors (and peckish natives) often end up eating six or seven meals in a single day.

"How's the dancing going?" C. J. asked. "Oh, I absolutely love it," I said. "My teacher is really magnificent; she's like a many-armed goddess, or an earth mother, very mystical and intelligent. She told me she was a temple dancer in a former incarnation, and she thinks I may have been one too, based on what she calls 'a certain conflict in your aura.' I can believe it, about her at least."

"Maybe that's why you're so repressed now, because you're doing penance for having been a temple trollop in another life," C. J. said gleefully.

"Very funny. And I'm not repressed, I just have my own beliefs and standards of behavior, bizarre as that may seem."

"It does," said C. J., with a grin. We had emerged from one of the lower gates of Zenzenji and were walking along beside the high peachy-saffron tile-topped wall.

"This is it," I said, stopping in front of a child-sized arch, no more than four feet high; it was, quite literally, a hole in the temple wall. An ivory-on-cocoa calligraphic banner reading "Menrui" (Noodles) hung beside the door. C. J. had been across the alley, buying a big bouquet of star-shaped purple and white balloon flowers ("For my tokonoma," she explained), but now she joined me.

"Wow," she said, "a magic door."

We ducked under the arch and found ourselves in a leafy courtyard filled with wooden tables. All the tables were full, and the clientele was a colorful cross-section of the neighborhood: black-robed priests, workmen in their distinctive, flamboyant costumes, flashily-dressed love hotel proprietors of both sexes, elegant older women in subdued kimono who might be teachers of the arts, or geisha-house owners. "Rats, it's full," said C. J., but as we turned to leave, a woman in a white kerchief emerged from a small building, carrying a tray of steaming noodles in dark brown *Tanba-yaki* bowls.

"Oideyasu," she said, treating us to the Kyoto-dialect version of the welcoming chorus heard all over Japan, usually in some variation on "Irasshaimase!" We went through the door the woman had indicated and found ourselves in a dim cool room with reproductions of the gilded illustrations for *The Tale of Genji* on the wall, several antique *maneki-neko* ("waving cats") on the shelves, and a lacquer-leafed branch of white camellias in the tokonoma, under a scroll-painting of a boldly-calligraphed circle.

We ordered *zaru-soba*—cold buckwheat noodles topped with shredded seaweed and sesame seeds, then dipped, bite by bite, into a dark broth enlivened with a vivid-flavored mix of pulverized spices, chopped scallions, and a dollop of potent sinus-clearing *wasabi* (horseradish)

paste. We spent a few moments marveling at our good fortune in finding such an atmospheric place ("Through the looking glass, indeed," I
said, pulling the eponymous book from my bag) and then, as I knew she
would, C. J. got down to business. "About the other day," she said,
twirling a sidelock of strawberry-blonde hair around her index finger.

"I've forgotten all about it," I fibbed, for I really wasn't in the mood
for a weighty conversation.

"No, you haven't, and neither have I. You were obviously upset at
finding me in bed with two men, but I'm not sure why. Were you jealous?"

"God, no."

"I didn't think so—I mean after all, you're the one who ended up
with the sexy gaucho."

"I guess I was just surprised," I said, "but it served me right for dropping in uninvited. Can we talk about something else, please?"

"Sure," said C. J. "Uh—what's your sign?"

"Vertigo," I said, recycling an old joke. "What's yours?"

"Venus," said C. J. We laughed, and that seemed to clear the air
much better than a mediated discussion would have done. Between
bites of cool, chewy, earthy-tasting soba and sips of roasted-barley tea,
C. J. told me how she had come to be involved with Arasuke and Ramon
simultaneously. Uncannily, my wild surmise was correct: Ramon had
his "*Black Orpheus* dream" one night and crawled in next to C. J., "just
to snuggle." She found his proximity unexpectedly exciting, and one
thing led to another; then Arasuke woke up and said sleepily that he
didn't care what C. J. and Ramon did, as long as he didn't have to watch,
or participate, and as long as it was understood that he was still the
alpha male in their little jungle.

The arrangement didn't sound terribly harmonious to me, but it
wasn't as wanton as I had imagined. "So you just, um, do it with one at a
time, not both at once?" I asked. "I sort of pictured a big slimy pile, like
slugs on a dead rodent. I used to see that in my garden sometimes," I
added apologetically.

"Gee, I'm flattered," said C. J., not quite managing a smile. "But I
always prefer to think of myself as a *live* rodent, somehow." I decided it
was time to change the subject, or at least the object. "Do you really
think I would be happier if I had a hyperactive sex life, like you do?" I
asked.

"It isn't about happiness," said C. J., shaking her head at my obtuseness. "It's about pleasure."

* * *

I was ready for a dose of innocence that afternoon, and it was almost too perfect, when I returned to Kaiko-in, to find two adorable little girls waiting outside my room with their well-dressed mothers. My new pupils! I had totally forgotten they were coming, but fortunately I was only five minutes late. The women (Mrs. Menjo and Mrs. Shibui) were sisters, and their daughters, Chika-chan and Kiko-chan, were cousins, though they looked more like fraternal twins. They both had tea-bowl haircuts (ear-length bob, thick fringe of bangs) and *kokeshi*-doll faces with large bright eyes, rosy cheeks, and tiny pouting-parabola mouths.

It didn't take long to figure out that Mrs. Menjo and Mrs. Shibui were archetypal examples of a sociocultural phenomenon known as *kyoiku mama* ("education mother"): that is, mothers whose driving force and primary goal in life is to get their children onto the idealized educational continuum that begins with the "right" nursery school (preferably one patronized by royalty) and ends at Tokyo University, or Waseda, or Keio, springboards to a prestigious job-for-life at a first-class corporation (or in those days, for a woman, to marriage to an "elite"). While their American counterparts might have talked about the importance of communication or the joy of learning, the kyoiku mamas, their daughters only a year or two out of diapers, were already worrying about the English-language entrance requirements for exclusive high schools. "We feel so fortunate to have found a native speaker to teach our girls," said Mrs. Shibui. "Japanese people don't know how to teach English at all."

"Please be patient," added Mrs. Menjo. "As you know, we Japanese are hopelessly bad at languages." I recognized those statements as two of the staples of Japanese low self-esteem, along with shortness of stature, lack of nasal elevation (the "low-nose" complex), uniformity of hair color, and the absurd myth that Japanese are a "yellow race." We had our lesson in the big tatami room at the end of the hall, with its splendid peacock-painted doors, so it wasn't until the little girls had left (after piping the newly-learned phrase "See you soon!" at least fifteen times apiece) that I went into my room and saw the vase containing three artfully-arranged purple starflowers.

"Oh, they aren't from me; your friend came by and asked me to put these in your room, as a surprise," said the Okusan when I thanked her for the flowers. "She brought me some too; wasn't that nice?" Venus: goddess of beauty and blossom, protectress of gardens, laureate of love. "Very nice," I said.

That night, since my ankle was completely back to normal, I went to zazen. I had been practicing in my room, and to my relief it paid off: Den-san didn't hit me with the stick, and the dour Do-san didn't even speak to me, much less pummel me as he had the other time. After a few minutes of polluted-stream-of-consciousness ramblings, I found myself in a state of relaxed awareness; not awareness of my immediate environment, but a free-floating sense of what I could only call "being and somethingness."

This was a great improvement over my past attempts at meditation, and I was enjoying the feeling of organic cognizance verging on catalepsy when I was brought back to reality by the tinkle of a bell. In the dimness, I could see the monks climbing down from their perches and slipping into their zoris, and I decided that it must be time to go home. I started to disentangle my legs from the lotus position, but the man next to me (a late arrival whom I hadn't noticed before) motioned to me to stay as I was.

One by one the monks got down from the platform and shuffled out of the meditation hall, until there was no one left but Toku-san. From the hallway I heard the sound of muffled undersea bells, and of voices raised in what sounded like anger. I heard stranger, more ominous sounds as well; the sound of blows being struck, the crash of breaking crockery. I found it impossible to return to my trance, for after a moment of bewilderment I had deduced that I was having my first indirect encounter with the essential Zen ritual known as sanzen, and I was mystified, agitated, and intrigued. I was also very envious of the monks who went off to rendezvous with the roshi and returned to the Zendo, sometimes limping or with oddly crumpled faces, as if they were holding back tears or curses, and I wondered whether I would ever be permitted to confront this thrilling mystery first-hand.

After the session was over, the other guest, a diminutive young man with a stubbly shaved head, dressed in a shimmery kimono of khaki silk with a plum-colored obi, introduced himself as Mr. Saba. His features were flat and fluid, as if a heavy clinging cloth had been laid over a face of more prominent proportions, and he had short, high, calligraphic eyebrows above narrow-lidded brown eyes. Saba-san told me that he was apprenticed to a master bamboo-brush maker in nearby Nara, and he looked a bit taken aback when I pointed at his shaved head and said, "Are you a phony monk, too?" (I would never have said that in English.)

"I guess so, if you put it that way," he said. Obviously, he wished I hadn't. "By the way, are you going to O-Zesshin?"

"Yes," I said. "I'm really looking forward to it, but I'm a bit nervous."

I had paid a ceremonial visit to Toku-san in his office the day before, armed with a box of pastel confections in the shape of clematis flowers, and he had said, "By all means, do come. But wear something comfortable, because we'll be sitting a lot." He indicated my knee-length paisley dress, and I nodded. What I needed for O-Zesshin, I thought, was a long skirt, or some hakama, the traditional Japanese equivalent of culottes.

"Are you sure you don't want to give me your koromo?" I asked teasingly. The blue monk's robe was hanging on the wall looking sheer and iridescent, like a Brazilian butterfly.

"I'm very sure," said Toku-san, with his trademark twinkle.

The next morning I heard the drums at five a.m., as usual. I decided to be decadent and sleep in until six, so it was foreordained that there would be a knock on my door at five-thirty. "Are you up?" said the humorous, slightly hoarse voice of the Osho-san, the priest of Kaiko-in, just outside my door. "You have a visitor." Not wanting to admit that I hadn't risen to greet the paling moon, I quickly scrambled into my clothes and brushed my hair, wondering who would be coming to visit me so early in the morning.

To my surprise, it was the new monk, the one I had seen slumped over his baggage in front of the gate. He had been introduced to me, after passing his admission-tests, as Saku-san. He was a large young man in his early twenties, with an oversized head and features to match; he was built like a temple-guardian statue, or a rugby player, and he seemed to fill the entire genkan with his primal, hulking presence. "I hope I didn't wake you," he said, in a rough north-country dialect.

"Oh no," I lied, for no human being ever wants to admit that he is so weak as to require rest, even during those dark and silent hours that are traditionally set aside for sleeping. I had been staring at Saku-san's animated massive-featured face and his shapely blue-veined forearms, but now I noticed that he was holding something.

"I found these when I was sweeping, and somebody said that you like cats," he said, placing a small, rectangular cardboard box in my hands.

I looked inside and there, on a bed of uncooked white rice, were two dirty, wild, marble-eyed gray kittens, scrawny and frightened and hissing like gargoyles. "Where did you find these?" I asked, and when he told me I realized that it must have been their little mews I had heard the other day when I was with Den-san. (Sparrows, indeed!) It was a wonder they had survived this long.

"Will you keep them?" Saku-san asked.

"What if I didn't?" I asked.

"Then they would be left to die, or to be found by someone else if they were lucky."

"But why doesn't the Sodo adopt them?"

"Because then we would become a dumping ground for every unwanted cat in town, and they would tear up the tatami. Besides, some monks have allergies."

'But what about the vow you take every day, to save all sentient beings?"

"It's a nice idea, but not very practical," said Saku-san with a wide-shouldered shrug.

So I took the tiny kittens, and made them a softer bed with a couple of folded bandannas, and tried to calm them down by stroking their fur and singing "Ragtime Cowboy Joe" and "Jerusalem." After a while, I put them in their box and went into the alfresco hall to get them some water. Later, when the shops opened, I would buy a couple of doll-sized baby bottles, and a half-pint of milk.

As usual I glanced into the misty garden on my way to the sink, to see what was in bloom, and to check on the progress of the seeds I had planted: *hyotan* gourds and tangy shiso mint. In the far corner of the garden I saw the Osho-san, dressed in a blue suit, bending over to smell a deep carmine rose. I thought he was going to break off a bud and stick it in his buttonhole, but he didn't; he just took another sniff of the rosy perfume, sighed, picked up his briefcase, and vanished around the corner of the house.

I was very touched by this incident, not just because the Osho-san didn't pick the rose, but because I knew that he hated going to work every day in an office in Osaka, and that he only did it because Kaiko-in was such a poor temple, without patrons or endowment. I thought, as I often had before, what a mistake it is to judge anyone by their appearance, or costume. If I had seen the Osho-san on the commuter train in his commuter-suit, would I have had the vision to see the priest, and the noble, magnificent man, beneath the blue serge surface?

I named the kittens Kanzan and Jittoku, after the eccentric Chinese sages of Cold Mountain. I knew I couldn't keep them, because the Oku-san was allergic to cat-fur, and they couldn't stay cooped up forever in my tiny room. The Maedas were all very sympathetic and supportive; they told me not to worry, that a good home would surely turn up. And if not, well ... But I couldn't bear to think about what might lie beyond that ominous ellipsis.

The next day, after bottle-feeding my little charges, I turned the *kotatsu* (a low table with a built-in heating device on the underside) on low, for warmth, set an alarm clock nearby to replicate their absent mother's heartbeat, and went off to visit the famous priest of an even more famous Zen temple. I had first met him when I was sixteen years old, traveling around the world with my older sister; we wandered into his temple on February third and had the rare treat of witnessing the *setsubun* ceremony, in which dried soybeans are tossed into the four corners of a room and a refrain of "Out with demons/In with good fortune!" is chanted over and over. My sister and I were so captivated by this display, and by the witty, lively English-speaking priest, that we lost track of the time and missed our ship from Osaka to Tokyo. We had to catch up with it by train since we only had shore passes instead of proper visas, and we were shadowed all the way by an apologetic police escort who kept plying us with dried, shredded eels, evidently to make up for his inability to speak a word of comprehensible English.

I had returned to the temple (which was much larger and wealthier than Zenzenji) five years later, with a friend who presented the antic priest with a package of steak, saying, with a vaudevillian wink, "This is for your dog." I was shocked by the changes since my first visit. The classic rock-and-gravel garden from which the temple's fame derived was now wired with loudspeakers, blaring forth an incessant din of Japanese and English and making it impossible to sit in silence and appreciate the symbolic stones. The "garden of meditation" was overrun by throngs of giggling schoolchildren, tour-group lemmings, and loud-voiced foreign visitors; the souvenir stand had been expanded, and I thought the priest looked a bit plumper than when I had first met him. Perhaps it was a result of consuming all the meat my friend Claudia had given him over the years, for she had told me that the priest did not, in fact, own a dog.

When I went back alone, on my third visit to the temple, the garden was even more crowded, and the loudspeakers seemed to have been cranked up to Coney-Island level. I didn't expect the priest to remember me, but I hoped to use our previous encounters as an excuse to engage him in a conversation about various Zen conundrums. To my surprise he detached himself from a group of German tourists (he was a well-known amateur polyglot) and greeted me by name.

"How is Claudia?" he asked when we had finished our long-time-no-see bows. "She's still in Tokyo going to school," I said. "How's your carnivorous dog?"

"Fine," said the priest, rubbing his convex stomach. Just then a burly Frenchman in a striped fisherman's jersey came up and asked if he might be photographed "*avec le prêtre.*"

"*Con molto piacere,*" said the priest, mixing up his Latinian languages a bit, and then, to me, "Can you wait a few minutes?"

"I'd better go," I said, "but I'll be back. The next time we meet, I'd like to talk to you about Zen."

"The next time we meet," said the famous priest of a famous temple, "I'd like to talk to you about love."

THE CIRCLES
OF THE STORMY MOON

The beautiful antique attire that no maiden or wife may wear

Lafcadio Hearn
Kokoro

—KYOTO

*S*he was an alarmist, a pessimist, a duenna of death. When she looked out the window late at night and saw a light on the bay, her first surmise wasn't "crab-catchers'" or "octopus pots"; it was "A child has drowned, the sharks are near, the body will never be found." Those melodramatic lines had appeared unbidden in my notebook, in my handwriting, the purple ink still wet. I didn't write fiction in those days, and I was trying to figure out where the lines had come from, and what I ought to do with them, when Mondo knocked on my door. "There's someone outside to see you," he said gruffly.

"Thanks," I called, opening the door just in time to see him shambling across the textured expanse of yellow-green tatami and disappearing back into his room, grunting softly like a winter-logged bear.

I slipped on my geta and went out into the sun-dappled courtyard. "Den-san!" I said. The jikijitsu—solemn supervisor of zazen sessions and wielder of the salutary keisaku-stick—was standing beside a dwarf pine tree, dressed in his gray homespun work clothes. There was a white kerchief over his shaved head and his black-rimmed glasses were glazed gold by reflected sunlight. "You look wonderful," I said, and then I noticed that he was holding something wrapped in an orange furoshiki. "Oh, not more kittens!" I said, and then we laughed at the absurdity of that response, for the package was shaped more like a sword than a cat.

"No," he said, untying the loose knots that held the furoshiki together, "I just wanted to show you my flute." He held out a beautiful shakuhachi made from a single piece of dark gold bamboo, lacquered inside in British racing green. While I admired the stylish flute, Den-san said, "Are you busy tomorrow night?"

"I was going to go to zazen," I said.

"There's no zazen for the rest of this week," Den-san said. "Most of the monks have gone to Tokyo on takuhatsu. Anyway, if you're not busy, I thought we could go to the secret garden and practice 'Kurokami' together." ("Kurokami," or "Black Hair," is the title of a plaintive, haunting, relatively simple-to-play Japanese love song.)

"I'd like that," I said, and we set a time. It wasn't until after Den-san had ducked through the Kaiko-in gate and disappeared around the corner calling "Don't forget to bring your flute!" that I realized I didn't have a flute to bring.

My primary priority for the day was to find homes for the kittens. I had given them sponge baths and dried them with towels and brushed their fur, and they were looking considerably more appealing than when I had first seen them. They seemed to be a bit plumper, and they were definitely more contented. I had covered their little box with olive-and-fuchsia folk paper, and I placed them in it, atop a purple furoshiki (in Japan, presentation is paramount). Then I went down to the little playground at the bottom of the Sodo slope where there were always a few children playing, while their magazine-reading mothers or tea-cosy crocheting grandmothers looked on.

"Would anyone like to adopt a cat?" I asked the multi-generational crowd at the playground. One woman ignored me, several shook their heads no, and two or three murmured apologetic demurrals, but all the children shouted, in uncanny unison, "Yes!" One little girl peered into the box of kittens and said, "Oh, they're so cute, and so tiny! And my mother said I could have some cats."

My heart leaped. "And do you like these cats?"

"Oh, I love them!" said the little girl. "I'll name one Neko-chan ('Kitty-cat') and I'll name the other one Neko-chan, too."

"Do you think I could talk to your mother?" I asked. This was too good to be true, finding a home for both kittens together, and with such a sweet little girl to cherish them and call them by name. (I was sure the kittens wouldn't mind sharing a name.) "Is she here?"

"No, my mommy went to Shikoku." My heart slumped.

"But my granny is here!" announced the little girl triumphantly, pulling me by the hand toward an elderly, sour-faced woman with tightly marcelled matte-black hair.

My hopes were dashed as quickly as they had been resurrected. The grandmother said curtly that there was no way they would adopt even one kitten; there was a new baby in the house and everyone knew that cats were evil creatures who sucked the breath of babies. (I knew better than to argue with such an ancient canard, and I was momentarily annoyed with Goethe for claiming that superstition is the poetry of life.) When I mentioned the mother's purported two-cat promise, the older woman said, "Oh, she must have meant a stuffed cat." I had a brief, horrific vision of my dear little kittens, murdered, disemboweled, and reconstituted by the taxidermist's grisly art into stiff-limbed statues with glass eyes and spiky fur, but then I realized that the grandmother was talking about soft toys.

I trudged home and fed my still-homeless kittens, to whom I was becoming more attached by the moment. ("It's always a mistake to name them," the Obaasan had told me, and I sensed that she might have some poignant stray-cat stories in her files, too.) I felt in dire need of some cheering up, so I made sure that Kanzan and Jittoku were asleep, and that their bed was dry. Then I set off for the antique-bazaar where Arasuke and Ramon had bought their colorful used kimono.

The bazaar, which was held on the twenty-fifth of each month, took place at one of the largest temples in Kyoto, a vast compound of tile-roofed buildings and white-gravel walkways as broad as a Parisian boulevard. Along these tree-lined corridors hundreds of merchants had set up canopied wooden stands or had spread their eclectic treasures (scrolls, ceramics, statuettes) on straw mats. There were food vendors, too, selling the usual open-air fare: chopped-octopus dumplings, fish-shaped waffles filled with sweetened adzuki-bean paste, bestiamorphic lollipops in transparent colors (moonstone and garnet and amber), along with such folk-medicine exotica as pulverized snakemeat and extract of Monkey Island aloe.

There were some contemporary products for sale—shoddy shoes and cheesy handbags and Tom & Jerry satchels—but the majority of the vendors dealt in antique bric-a-brac, or used clothing. For a thousand yen apiece I bought two gorgeous, well-preserved silk kimono. The fabrics were so harmonious that they seemed to have been made to be worn together, but the elderly merchant, his walnut-shell face peering out through a richly-textured forest of cotton and silk and brocade, told me that the two garments were not related in any way. One kimono was a double-thickness robe with a contemporary-looking pattern of red and purple cross-hatched squares on a gray background, lined with watery beet-colored silk. The other was one of the most striking works of textile art I had ever seen: sinuous royal-purple leaves and crimson cherries on gilded branches, against an ivory sky. I also bought a long, wide rectangle of indigo-dyed cotton, more black than blue, with an arabesque floral design against a pointillist galaxy of tiny off-white dots, and a handful of sashes, at a hundred yen apiece: one in shades of dusk and amethyst, one in rusty earth tones, one in delicate Necco-wafer pastels, and several solid pinks, reds, and purples.

My visit to the temple fair hadn't merely cheered me up, it had made me positively euphoric, and I rushed home, eager to try on my new regalia. I put on the cherry-motif kimono first, and belted it with three bright silk sashes. I wore the double-layered kimono on top, flapping open like a long overcoat; I put my hair up in a Gibson Girl pompadour and slipped into my black lacquer geta with the red velvet straps. Since the only mirror in my section of Kaiko-in was an octagonal fragment above the sink where the Maeda sons and the boarders washed their faces and brushed their teeth, I could only guess at how I looked in my glorious new outfit. Pretty spiffy, I suspected, and I decided to celebrate with a trip to the seaweed store.

I was used to being stared at, gawked at, even photographed by strangers, but the response on this day was different. The first woman I passed, a housewife with a basket full of long white daikon radishes, glanced at me, then did a double take that would have embarrassed a burlesque comedian. Her jaw fell open, her eyes popped, and she clapped her hand over her mouth, though not in time to muffle an apoplectic splutter. After encountering two or three similar reactions, I began to feel self-conscious, and I decided to abort my seaweed-mission. On the way back to Kaiko-in I met Mondo, who was heading for the university on his red moped, with a matching bookbag slung over his shoulder. When his jaw dropped, I knew something was seriously wrong, for Mondo had known a number of foreigners and should have been inured to our eccentricities.

"Where did you get those clothes?" he asked. I told him. "They're very nice," he said. "But—"

"Oh," I interrupted, "did I tie the belts wrong or something, or do I have the lapels overlapped like a death shroud? I always forget which side goes on top." One of the most common mistakes non-Japanese make when dressing in kimono is to put the left side under the right, a style favored only by corpses.

"It's not that," said Mondo, and then, surprisingly, he began to giggle. "You see," he said, "those robes are a type which are associated with, uh, courtesans."

"Courtesans? Oh, that's good!" I said. I liked the archaic sound of the word, the connotations of flair and style and accomplishment.

"No, actually, what I mean is—prostitutes. So it is very shocking for Japanese people to see someone, particularly a foreigner, wearing such clothing out on the street. It doesn't really reflect well on our temple, either, so perhaps you might just want to wear them in your room, for now. They *are* quite beautiful, though, and very becoming," he added comfortingly, and then he was gone in a cloud of carbon monoxide. I picked up the gaudy skirts of my socially unacceptable finery and ran down the alley to Kaiko-in as fast as my clogs would carry me, praying (for once) that I wouldn't meet a monk on the way.

After I had bottle-fed the kittens, changed their box, and stroked them off to sleep again, I unwrapped my piece of indigo-dyed, peony-printed *aizome* fabric. I wanted to display it somewhere so I could enjoy it all the time, but three of the four walls of my tiny room were taken up by cupboards and sliding doors, and the fourth was already covered with art posters and postcards (Botticelli, Munakata, Tomioka Tessai). Then I remembered that I needed a long summer-weight skirt to wear to O-Zesshin. That's it, I thought. A traveling exhibition! I threaded my needle with red thread and sewed a long, full skirt with a drawstring waist, tied with a purple cord.

Sometimes the loveliest hours are the quietest ones; sitting alone in my cozy little room with no appointments to keep, listening to the sudden spring rain on the garden, the kittens safely asleep and all my problems and shortcomings temporarily forgotten, I felt, as I watched the reasonably straight line of small red stitches grow longer and longer, that this was the ultimate in tranquillity. I felt in elemental touch with time, and place, and being. Maybe I should have been a tailor, I thought;

seamstress, dreamstress, *sartor resartus* of the red thread of fate.

I don't know when the note was slipped under my door, but it was there when I stood up to try on my new skirt. *Nashiko called,* it said in the Okusan's spidery calligraphy. *She says that if you go to this address, the woman who lives there—they call her the Cat Auntie—might give your cats a home.* I was jubilant, yet sad, at this news, but even in my state of tumultuous ambivalence I took the time to notice that Nashiko's name was written with the character for *mu,* the term, used frequently in Zen, for "nothingness." For a moment I envied Nashiko the profundity of her name—"Child of the Void"—and then I realized that what I really envied was her Japaneseness.

The Cat Auntie lived about ten minutes away, behind a tall gate overgrown with morning glories. I rang the doorbell, and she appeared with an almond-colored cat on one shoulder, like a benign familiar. She was a tall woman in her sixties, with wiry gray hair in an untidy bun, sharp features, and gentle eyes. "Do they have names?" she asked.

"I've been calling them Kanzan and Jittoku," I said, hoping she would be impressed by my erudition.

"Those are pretty fancy names for such ordinary cats," said the Cat Auntie brusquely. "I shall call them"—she thought for a moment—"Kumo (Cloud) and Hagi (Bush Clover)." I had to admit that those were very good names, and after telling the Cat Auntie about how and when the kittens liked their milk ("Don't worry, I know how to take care of cats," she said with a tolerant smile) I thanked her and headed home.

I should have been rejoicing, for I had accomplished my goal for the day. But I had grown to love the kittens, and to enjoy the structure which being a mother-figure imposed on my life. I felt hurt that the Cat Auntie hadn't even considered using the names I had chosen, and I thought it was snobbish of her to call the cats ordinary, as if they could help having been born to an alley cat and not to an Abyssinian. I was once again in need of cheering up, and by the time I got home, I had thought of the perfect antidote to my attack of feline-separation angst.

I first read about Gordon Coyne in the *Japan Times;* an American columnist, herself a legend, described him as "the legendary gentleman antique-dealer who writes like an angel, and looks like a god." I was intrigued, and when my Sophia classmate Claudia Kimmel (she who used to take gifts of raw meat to the famous priest of the loudspeaker-temple) caught up with me in the hall one day after a "Yeats and the

Noh" seminar and said, "What are you doing for the three-day weekend? Would you like to go down to Ashiya and meet a 'legendary gentleman?'" I knew that the fates had once again deigned to dabble in my social life.

I hit it off immediately with Gordon Coyne, who was tall, pale, Apollonian, and astonishingly smart. I got along very well with his motherly, musical housekeeper, Ayame Tanbo, too, and I had visited them several times since, on my own. Gordon lived in a house that had once belonged to a *daimyo* (feudal lord), and every element of the structure, and of the decor, was truly exquisite. I had never seen such an elegant, effortless, sophisticated way of living, and I was in such awe of Gordon's accomplishments as playwright and art connoisseur and unpretentious *beau vivant* (not to be confused with *bon*, for while he did enjoy eating well, that was never as important as living beautifully) that I tended to behave in his presence like a starstruck acolyte. He in turn treated me as an interesting equal, and it was a very pleasant and, for me, instructive symbiosis.

I had planned to telephone just to say hello, but when I finished telling Gordon that I was feeling more lonesome than liberated after giving up my cats, he said, "Why don't you come down for the night?" So I got on the train and rode through the rice-fields and rustic villages, past vermilion-gated shrines and copper-roofed temples, to the little town of Ashiya. I walked from the station to Gordon's mansion under a chiaroscuro ceiling of catfish-shaped rainclouds, and as usual, when I stepped through the brass-trimmed wooden gate I felt as if I had entered another dimension: the realm of impeccable taste, adventurous thought, and atmospheric perfection.

A recording of *Turandot* was playing as I stood in the genkan, calling out "Hello!" Gordon appeared at once, looking cool and blond and solvent in a white silk shirt and a navy blue blazer. "Oh," he said, looking at my new indigo-print skirt. "I knew it was just a matter of time before someone would think of using those scraps to sew something to wear."

"Do you like it?" I asked.

"On you, it works," he said, and I took that as a yes.

I slipped off my shoes, then peered around the entry hall in mock suspicion. "Are you sure there are no celebrities here?" I asked. Gordon Coyne knew an astounding variety of people; once I had come down from Tokyo and had found Gordon, a retired American torch singer, and a famous Swedish avant-garde composer sitting around eating Godiva chocolates and listening to Scriabin.

"Not a one," said Gordon, and then he added matter-of-factly, "but you just missed David Bowie and two monks from Lhasa."

Part of the delight of visiting Gordon at home was the constantly evolving decor. He used to say that the only thing in his house that was not for sale was a Tibetan time-mandala, and while the basic furniture (couches, tables, chairs) seemed to remain the same, there was frequent turnover among statuary, paintings, rugs, scrolls, and stone and ceramic pieces. I wish I remembered the Tibetan mandala well enough to describe it, but all I recall are some colors (black, blue, salmon, violet, mauve), some cherubic homunculi, a whimsical-whiskered fish, and my own reactions: *I feel I have glimpsed the secret at the bottom of the well of eternity*, I wrote in my always-understated journal. Later, Gordon told me that when the Swedish composer first saw the time-mandala he said, "*Min Gud*, it's the basis of mathematics, and thus of music."

The living room was a veritable museum filled with rare and valuable works of art, but Gordon was so completely at ease with the artistic splendor around him that his guests ended up feeling comfortable, too. "Oh, good, nobody bought the Bodhisattva," I said, running my hand over the smooth, fragrant surface of an ethereal life-sized sandalwood statue of a Buddhist demigod riding on a sea-dragon, the graceful elongated hands forming two of the mudras I had learned at my last Bharata Natyam lesson.

"Nobody had five million yen," Gordon said with a mock-mercenary smirk, but I suspected that he too had fallen in love with the statue, and had decided not to part with it at any price.

Hanging in the tokonoma of the vast pale-carpeted living room was a scroll I hadn't seen before: a long, brocade-bound piece of parchment-colored rice paper, decorated only with a bold snaky circle in grayish-black ink, a few lines of calligraphy, and several red-ink *hanko* (stamps) of various sizes, round and square and oval. "Oh, there's that circle again!" I said.

I told Gordon about the similar scroll I had seen at the little noodle-shop, and he said, "I know that place. There's a marvelous, manic auction at the temple around the corner, once or twice a month; you should go there sometime." Then he explained that the flamboyant *enso* is one of the staples of Zen-inspired art, and that the single-brush-stroke circle is an all-purpose symbol of completion, sequence, regeneration, and life.

"I love that image," I said. "It always reminds me of the Worm Ouroboros."

"I love it too," said Gordon. "It always reminds me of itself."

We had talked before about the circular cycles of life, and how you often don't realize that a circle is in progress until it has been completed. And then (in what Koestler calls the "AHA reaction") the pattern suddenly becomes clear, and everything seems to make perfect sense. I was about to say something along those lines—nothing new, just a reprise of old revelations—when Gordon, evidently reading my mind, began to hum "May the Circle Be Unbroken." I began to sing along, he joined in, and it wouldn't have surprised me to have heard a swelling orchestra of zithers and sitars in the background. What we heard, instead, was the ringing of a Tibetan lamasery-bell, as Ayame Tanbo called us to the massive antique-zebrawood table for dinner.

Ayame had prepared a delicious meal of cold "scattered sushi"—bits of cooked vegetables and shrimp (which I fed surreptitiously to a glossy black cat named Kurokami) and shiitake mushrooms tossed with slightly sweet, vinegary rice. "I love my little room at the temple," I said, "but no matter where I'm staying, when I come here I realize I'm living in a hovel."

"I have always lived in beautiful places," Gordon said reflectively, and then he added kindly, "At your age, it doesn't matter where you live, because your mind is a palace, and you furnish it with dreams. But I—I need my space, and my Bodhisattvas, and my Klipsch speakers."

I mentioned that I was planning to attend the upcoming O-Zesshin at Zenzenji, and Gordon said, "Oh, I recently heard about an interesting one-week retreat. I'm not certain what sect of Buddhism it is, but the monastery is deep in the mountains, miles from the nearest pachinko parlor. Evidently the aim is to open the eyes of the spirit by focusing on one sense at a time. On the first day, they concentrate on colors. On the second day, they concentrate on sounds. On the third day, smells. Fourth day, tastes. Fifth day, sensations. On the sixth day, they try to open the third eye and experience the sixth sense. And on the seventh day, they concentrate on 'Ahhhhh.'"

"'Ahhhhh,'" I echoed, knowing Gordon would appreciate the histrionic Sanskrit sigh. "That sounds wonderful. I wish we could go there right now, tonight!"

"Not before dessert," said Ayame, appearing in the door with a tall dark-chocolate cake wittily decorated with an eighteenth-century netsuke carving of Fukurokuju, the ithyphallic god of good fortune.

There was a huge grotto-like bathroom in my wing of the house, with gas lamps and piped-in music (Monteverdi madrigals, "El Amor Brujo," Lotte Lenya, the Who; Gordon's tastes were nothing if not eclectic). After I turned the taps off the sound of falling water continued, and I realized it was raining. I thought of trying zero-gravity zazen in the hot bath, but I was feeling too languid for anything so ambitious. Instead, I imagined that I was the passionate consort of the feudal lord who had once lived in the house. When this line of fantasy proved too stimulating, I decided it might be more appropriate to be the daimyo's ascetic sister (a Zen nun and secret novelist), but that didn't feel right, either. In the end I compromised: I closed my eyes and listened to the rain and pretended to be my very fortunate self.

After a very long bath I went off to my antique-filled Western-style room, feeling like the Little Princess. I climbed into the four-poster bed and listened to the rain falling, harder now, on the aristocratic antique roof, and then I noticed an old book (left behind, perhaps, by a previous guest) on the many-drawered apothecary chest that served as a bedside table. The title was *Hindu Ceremonies*, and it was an outraged but obviously titillated account of "pagan absurdities" by an elderly French cleric, a wheezing self-righteous cenobite who had visited India in the early nineteenth century. About the devadasis he wrote: "The temple dancers are unspeakably lewd; their attitudes are lascivious and their gestures indecorous." I yawned and turned the page, and then I felt the galvanic shock of the completed circle, for at the top of the page were these words: "This licentious dancing is of course the source of Bharata Natyam"!

I had never made that obvious connection, and I was delighted, for I had always felt a certain ambivalent kinship with the devadasis. *Linear rain, circular revelations*, I wrote in my journal. *Being here amid so much rich antiquity, I realize that the only real dynasty is now.* As I drifted off to sleep with Kurokami-the-cat lying warm and heavy on my feet, I heard the poignant strains of the eponymous song: "I think about your long black hair, and tears begin to fall ..." Ayame Tanbo had finished tending her magnificent hearth, and now she was playing the *koto*.

As I was preparing to leave the palace of dreams the next afternoon,

Gordon said casually, "There's some rejected pottery out back, in front of the shed. If you see anything you like, feel free to take it." There was a huge jumble of unbroken cups, bowls, plates, and vases; hundreds of irresistible ceramic pieces, in all my favorite blue-and-white patterns of fish and flowers and Chinese cherubim. I took only what I could fit in my furoshiki, but it was a large furoshiki, and I must have staggered away with twenty or thirty pounds of distinctive pottery.

As I was saying my grateful farewells in the genkan, I noticed a two-foot-long envelope of antique brocade, with something in it, lying on a T'ang dynasty chest that was used as a shoe cupboard. "What's that, a short sword?" I asked.

"No," said Gordon, sticking the brocade-encased object in my Mexican bag. "That's your new flute."

* * *

The afternoon was at its most golden as I walked up the hill toward the Sodo. Behind me, I heard the tofu-man's horn, and I wondered what Henry Purcell would have thought of that odd Oriental wind instrument. (Gordon had treated me, during an opulent English-style breakfast, to the playing of the trumpet concerto.) "Welcome home!" said a voice behind me, and I turned to see the shining face of Zo-san. "Where have you been?" he asked, leaning on his bamboo rake. I told him. "And what's in that big furoshiki?"

"It's pottery; would you like to see it?"

"Yes," said Zo-san, with that extra-luminescent smile, "I'm quite interested in old ceramics."

I spread out the cloth on the sunbaked cobblestones, and together we examined my haul. "If you see anything you like, please take it," I said, and without any of the usual civilized circumlocutions ("Oh, I couldn't possibly; well, okay, if you insist, but are you sure it's all right?") Zo-san selected a simple heather-green vase, said "Thank you very much," and walked away. At the top of the hill he raised his vase in an exuberant toast, and I raised my empty right hand (curved, automatically, around an invisible goblet) in response.

As I was gathering up my wares, feeling a bit like a peddler at the antique bazaar, a woman came by carrying a piece of tofu in a little brass bucket. She picked up a white plate with a splashy orange-and-green floral design and said, "How much for this?"

"Oh, it's not for sale," I said. "These are presents for my friends—I was just showing them to one of the monks." The woman put the plate back, obviously disappointed, so I said, "Oh, go ahead and take it, I have plenty."

Just then several other women came by carrying their dinner ingredients: sloshing tofu, leafy vegetables, fan-tailed fish. "Look," the first woman said, "she let me have this for free!" and a minor feeding frenzy erupted as the other three women began to fight over the pieces they wanted. This wasn't what I had had in mind, but when I thought about it, it seemed a very enlightened, Buddhistic thing to surrender your possessions to strangers—and to rather unappealing strangers whom you had no expectation of seeing again, and no desire to impress. I still had enough pieces to share with my friends, but there wasn't much left for my own cupboard: just two small teacups, blurry blue irises on web-cracked white porcelain.

As I was congratulating myself on my generosity, nobility, and non-materialism, I heard one of the women say, "Yappari, hen na gaijin!" ("Just as I thought, a strange foreigner!").

Her companion, who had grabbed my favorite fish-patterned blue-and-white platter, replied, "Kurutte'ru ja arahenka?" ("She must be crazy!"). I felt sick and betrayed, and for a moment I was overcome with a feeling which any Westerner who has lived in Japan will surely recognize. I hate this country, I thought. I don't belong here. I want to go back to the United States, right now! Then I remembered that I had an appointment with a musical monk, and I ran home to fetch my sheet music.

Because of my fondness for anticipation and ritual unveilings, I didn't unwrap my new shakuhachi until I met Den-san in the secret garden. "Oh, good, you brought your flute," he said. He examined the lacquer finish (black outside, with a scarlet lining, like the Sodo bowls) and then said, "This is quite old; do you know who made it?"

"No, I don't," I said, and then I told him how I had acquired it. "It was fate," I concluded.

"It was coincidence," said the pragmatic Den-san. "But a very nice coincidence."

Den-san and I played "Kurokami" several times, with a gradual decrease in missed notes and a corresponding increase in harmony, and

I couldn't help wishing Ayame Tanbo had been there to accompany us on her koto. A light rain began to fall, and we agreed to call it a night. As we walked past one of Zenzenji's sub-temples, I glanced inside the half-open door and was not at all surprised to see an enso-circle scroll hanging in the tokonoma, above an antique camphorwood carving of Bodhidharma seated in the lotus position, wild eyes closed, indignant mouth in calm curmudgeonly repose. Den-san had an errand to run, so I started up the hill alone, trying, with limited success, to pick out "Will the Circle Be Unbroken" on my fateful new flute.

The rain had stopped, and there was a misty aureole around the moon. It looks like a snake, or an enso, or the Worm, I thought. Then I recalled Gordon Coyne's comment: "It always reminds me of itself," and I remembered that one of the tenets of Zen was to see and appreciate things in, of, as, and for themselves.

"What a lovely ring around the moon," I said out loud. I felt suddenly more awake, and aware, as if I had peeped through the barred windows of my self-imposed prison of simile and metaphor, of wishful analogy and sodden thought, and had caught a glimpse of the simple, subtle, infinitely real world beyond. And as I followed the friendly haloed moon up that beloved slope toward my tiny temple room, I knew it would take more than a couple of crude, ungrateful fishwives to curdle my love for Japan.

MISTRESS OF NONE

Tagei wa mugei.
Many arts = No art.
Japanese proverb

—KYOTO

The two-headed macaque was crouched beside a turquoise stream, each head gobbling one oblong half of a vivid waxy-skinned fruit: bright flamingo-pink on the outside, with neon-purple flesh and apple-green seeds.

Just then Mondo started up the raspy motor of his moped, and I woke up. I marveled for a moment at the inventive bestiary and the vibrant palette of the mind asleep, and then I stumbled over to the closet. Sleepily, I pulled out the first clothes that engaged my eye: a purple sundress and a woven cotton belt striped in pink and purple and turquoise and yellow-green. There was no mirror in my room, and it wasn't until later in the morning, when I caught sight of my colorful reflection in an incense-shop window, that I realized that my outfit echoed the colors of my monkey dream: the unconscious as valet, or lady-in-waiting.

"That's an interesting costume," said Toku-san, just after lunch. He was out walking with Shiro, and they passed by Kaiko-in just as I was dragging Mondo's bicycle through the small door beside the gate. "Where are you going, to an Indian-dancing lesson?"

"No, I'm—"

"To a woodblock-printing lesson?" I was studying with a famous printmaker, a friend of Nashiko's family, who had, by amazing coincidence, provided the illustrations for *Zen Flesh, Zen Bones.*

"No, I'm—"

"To practice shakuhachi with Den-san?"

"No, I was just—"

"Perhaps to write some verses, or to draw pictures of Daruma-san?"

Oh, no, I thought; he must have been talking to the Okusan. I wondered what else she had told him. "No, not today. I was just going—"

"Why do you have so many hobbies, anyway?" Toku-san asked.

"They aren't hobbies," I said indignantly. "They're pursuits." Toku-san looked skeptical.

"But what are you going to do with your life?" If we had been speaking English I might have said that I wanted to be a transcendental hygienist (a dreadful contrivance which I occasionally used, in jest, to convey my desire for a pure, dreamy, constructive life), but I had long since learned that no English pun can survive translation into Japanese. The truth was that I had tentatively decided to go to graduate school and become a teacher and translator of Japanese, but that goal suddenly struck me as too presumptuous to share with a native speaker, and too commonplace to share with an enlightened being. Also, I was worrying a lot at that time about the Zen emphasis on "vertical wisdom"—that is, a penetrating non-intellectual insight—versus "horizontal wisdom," defined in one book as "knowing all *about* something."

Fortunately, Toku-san was ready with another question. "Which of your 'pursuits' do you enjoy most?"

"Art, and writing, and dance," I said, "but I don't think I could make a living at any of those things. I just have a lot of diversified interests, and I'm hoping that if I pursue them all faithfully I'll eventually become a Renaissance woman, by default."

"That's just Western vanity," Toku-san said sternly. "You should choose one road (*ipponmichi*) and follow it to the end. You'll never get anywhere if you run off to explore every phantom path through the woods." Oh no, I thought, he obviously sees me as a total dilettante, and he doesn't even know about all the other arts and crafts I studied in Tokyo: the copper-plate etching, the loom-weaving, the calligraphy, the Noh, the classical ballet.

In those days a naturally polite gaijin living in Japan was almost forced into dilettantism, although I admit I didn't require much persuading. A typical example: one night in Tokyo I was riding home on the subway after a bamboo-flute lesson, when a group of bright-faced girls, all dressed in pastel kimono, struck up a conversation with me. After the usual diagnostic pleasantries, they asked what I thought of Noh. I replied that I found it fascinating and mysterious, and a week later there I was, wearing my brand-new white tabi, holding a borrowed purple fan, chanting, a bit croakily, "Tera wa katsura no-oh" and gliding, more or less, across a highly polished cryptomeria floor in the elegant suburban mansion of a young fifth-generation teacher of Noh.

The "Noh walk" was not easy to master; it involved moving forward, heel to toe, very slowly and fluidly, never lifting the moving part of the foot more than an eighth of an inch off the floor. Once I got the hang of it, I found the slow-motion precision very relaxing, and even today when I find myself alone in a room with a glossy wood floor, I sometimes slip off my shoes and try a few furtive steps. In the 1980s, when every city street corner featured at least one breakdancer spinning on his sacrum or walking backward-in-place, I often thought that the Noh-glide might have been an esoteric precursor, or an artistic presentiment, of that illusory moonwalk.

I felt chastened by my encounter with Toku-san, but I was relieved that I hadn't had to tell him where I *was* going, for I was certain he wouldn't approve of that, either. It was the week before O-Zesshin, and I was in a panic. The night before, Saba-san, the brushmaker's apprentice, who often stopped by Kaiko-in to say hello, had asked me if I had memorized all the chants I would have to recite during O-Zesshin. "No," I said, "I haven't even thought about it. All the monks said that no preparation was necessary. Why, have you?"

"I'm about halfway through—I may have to read from the *kyo-hon* (sutra book) for the longer chants, but I've got the mealtime chants and the Hannya Shingyo down already." The Hannya Shingyo, known in English as the Heart of Great Wisdom Sutra, is the centerpiece chant of Zen, and is used by several other branches of Buddhism as well.

"Oh dear!" This was an unforeseen complication. "Where can I get a kyo-hon, quick?"

"Right here," Saba-san said with a smile, pulling a little rectangular accordion-folded book, about the size of a Washington State ferry schedule, from the sleeve of his persimmon-colored kimono. Despite his shaved head and his appetite for asceticism, Saba-san was a rather flashy dresser. "I bought one for you, too," he said. The sutras were written entirely in Chinese characters (without the usual cursive word-endings found in contemporary Japanese), and I wouldn't have been able to decipher a single word if not for the *furigana*, microscopic phonetic readings written in *hiragana* script, to the left of each character.

After memorizing the first few lines of the Hannya Shingyo ("MA-KA HAN-NYA HA-RA-MI-TA SHIN-GYO: Kan-ji-zai bo-sa gyo jin han-nya ha-ra-mi-ta ji sho-ken go-un kai ku do is-sai ku-yaku …") I began to wonder what the hypnotic sound-sequence meant. I was aware that my curiosity was very Western, and probably contrary to the no-written-transmission tenet of Zen, but I couldn't help it; I wanted to know what I was chanting. There was a library of English-language books about Zen at a sub-temple of one of Kyoto's great Zen temples, and that was where I was heading when I encountered Toku-san (the stern sibyl of the Zen-zenji crossroads) and was called upon to defend my diversification of interests.

* * *

Aside from some minor anxieties, the week before O-Zesshin was a time of happy anticipation, for I was certain that something life-changing would happen during the week of intensive meditation. In the mean-time Yukio and I were exchanging metaphysical mash notes while he was away in Tokyo (for we had both declared it, in every language we could think of: we were in love), and sharing riverside rambles and soul-stirring kisses whenever he returned to Kyoto. Everywhere we went, people stared and whispered, and I could feel them reducing us to the classic nativistic equation: *Nihonjin to gaijin*, The Japanese and the For-eigner. I knew that the women, especially, saw me as a potential mud-dier of genes, diluter of traditions, subverter of racial purity, a Black Ship Barbarella trying to steal one of their living national treasures: a tall healthy handsome fertile man.

I had more friends that spring in Kyoto than ever before in my life—far too many to introduce here. There were potters, poets, weavers of cloth, spinners of tales, embryonic scholars of folklore and literature, apprentices in arcane arts and crafts. Almost every evening three or four people would drop by, bringing boxes of sweets or bags of rice crackers, and I would brew a pot of *senna*, a confectionary elixir made from licorice root, anise seed, and some unidentified sweet-tasting herbs, which I purchased by the bag at a dark, aromatic Chinese apothecary shop. The herbalist's windows were filled with jugged snakes and pale, muscular ginseng roots so huge and so sentient-looking that (I used to joke) I didn't know whether to worship them or cook them for dinner.

We would sip our "absinthe tea" and talk and laugh until Migaku banged on my door and shouted, "*Kuso! Chikusho!* How the hell am I supposed to get my beauty sleep with all this goddamn racket going on?" and then everyone would slip on their shoes and say goodnight. I enjoyed the stream of visitors, and although I sometimes wished for a bit more solitude, I felt it was my obligation, as a person who had the good fortune to be living in a picturesque temple, to share the atmospheric wealth. After all, when the rice cakes were eaten and the teapot was empty, most of my friends (Japanese and foreign alike) went home to cramped characterless lodgings—the house on Cherry Blossom Lane and Karen's country cottage were the shining exceptions—while I got to stay behind in my own cramped but character-rich lodgings and fall asleep to the faint aroma of incense from the nearby altar, and wake up to the sound of a monastery drum.

I have always loved libraries, and the roomful of English-language books on Japanese religion (with an emphasis on Zen) had a peculiar musty charm. I had visited it several times before, and I always made some interesting discovery, or rediscovery, in the water-spotted, mildewy, hyperallergenic pages of books by Suzuki, Humphreys, Ponsonby-Fane, Puini, Percival Lowell, et al. Entrance to the reading room was free, but the price I paid for my academic revelations was having to listen to foreign aficionados of Zen pontificate about the religion in arid, humorless terms that seemed to have no connection with the lively, beautiful way of life I observed and envied every day. *Dreary overheard Zen-talk*, I groused in my journal. *There are many names for the same road, but the idea of practicing public zazen with a bunch of blue-eyed bores does not appeal at all. I marvel anew at the serpentine twists (and shouts) of Fate that conspired to drop me on the enchanted doorstep of Zenzenji.*

On this visit to the library I learned something new: that the "preliminary focusing" which precedes total concentration in zazen is called *jidori*. I made a list of the Eight Worldly Winds, and noted that the three requirements for enlightenment were great faith, great doubt, and great perseverance. (Well, I thought, at least I've got the *doubt*.) I also came across the phrase "nature mystic" in an essay about Zen gardens, and I experienced an intense "AHA reaction." Aha, I thought, maybe that's what I am, a nature mystic ("Hullo clouds, hullo sky"), and maybe that explains my soul's-core affinity for the organic atmospherics of Zen.

As a bonus, I rediscovered one of my favorite Zen parables: *Three monks were traveling together when they became lost in the mountains. It was growing dark, and just as they were beginning to wonder whether they might have to sleep under the stars, a cabbage leaf came floating down the stream. "Look!" said one monk. "There must be someone living farther up the stream." "Perhaps so," said the second monk, "but I would rather sleep outside than seek lodging with a person who would waste a precious vegetable leaf." "Don't be so quick to jump to conclusions," said the third monk, pointing at the opposite bank of the stream, where a woman, carrying a long-handled hook, was running along in pursuit of the fugitive leaf.* (My revised, if not revisionist, rendition of the original all-male tale.)

I still find that story more satisfying than many novels; it seems amazing that a six-line anecdote can incorporate suspense, conflict, character development, moral issues, and a surprise ending. More personally (and isn't everyone a solipsist at heart?) I can identify with the purist snobbery of the second monk, with the third monk's support for the benefit of the doubt, and with the earnest conservationism of the woman with the hook.

There was a small bookshop attached to the library where, on this day, I found a useful book of Roman-letter transliterations and English translations of all the chants I would be hearing during Sesshin. As I waited in line to pay for the book, I overheard a tall bearded American saying to a Grace Slick look-alike, "Yeah, I'm heavy into meditation now. I've got to reach satori by Christmas, 'cause that's when my visa runs out."

"Yeah," the girl said, "I really dig zazen too. It's so much hipper than TM—I mean, no offense to the Beach Boys or anything, but after a few years it was like 'Om mani padme *ho*-hum,' you know what I mean?"

The man smiled, a quick flash of gray flannel gums and yellowish teeth. "So, like, are you gonna sit tonight? I missed you last time," he said in a lower voice.

The girl nodded, and the bearded man moved closer. "Maybe we could grab a soda or something after zazen," he murmured, toying with a strand of the evil-eye beads she wore around her neck. The girl nodded again, and tossed her long black bangs. "That could be cool," she said. Zen and the art of the pickup line; it shouldn't have bothered me, but it did, for the irrational, exclusionary possessiveness I felt about the Sodo had extended itself to include Zen Buddhism in general. I rushed back to Zenzenji feeling oddly sullied by my contact with American Zen, as if I had just visited a pornographic bookstore, or attended a meeting of the John Birch Society.

I stopped at the open market to buy some red miso, and on my way out I saw Toku-san, leaning on the counter of a cold-drink stall and sipping a bottle of chocolate milk. I was shocked at what I perceived as a flagrant public violation of monastic dietary rules, but I composed my face and said hello. "Where have you been?" Toku-san asked. He seemed to be in a particularly jolly mood.

"Um, at the library," I said. Toku-san shook his finger at me in mock-disapproval.

"You've been reading books again," he said, and then he smiled, a benevolent, tolerant, milk-ringed smile.

At that moment all my uncharitable feelings dropped away, and I understood, temporarily at least, that self-affirmation through exclusion is no affirmation at all. (*I looked in the mirror/And what did I see?/That the blue-eyed bore/Was me.*) When I glanced back from the market entrance, Toku-san was still smiling. He caught my eye and raised his bottle of chocolate milk in a mock-courtly toast, and then I saw his lips move. "Kanpai," he said. "Cheers."

* * *

The following day I went looking for the hole-in-the-wall noodle shop I had visited with C. J. I followed the same route we had taken (at least it looked the same) but the wall was unbroken by doors, and no banners flapped in the wind. I had tried to find the elusive noodle shop on other occasions, twice with a friend in tow, without success; evidently, as I explained to my disappointed companions, the H. G. Wells "Magic Shop" syndrome ("Here tomorrow, gone today") must have been at work.

On this day, I stumbled upon an exciting compensation for my thwarted noodle-quest: the temple auction Gordon Coyne had described, with absolute accuracy, as "marvelous, and manic." In a large tatami-matted room, a bald-headed man in an eggplant-colored robe was calling out a litany of indecipherable staccato syllables. When he turned, I recognized his ivory-ringed surplice: the priest as auctioneer. A rowdy crowd of antique dealers—all men, except for one slender gray-haired woman with a long brown cigarette in a tortoise-shell holder—were shouting, gesturing, and quarreling as the procession of rich-patinaed objects was offered for bidding.

There were tall gilded-lacquer screens, tiny cloisonné dragon-beads, brass teakettles and bronze incense braziers, tinkly silver hair ornaments and vermiculate cast-iron sword-hilts, hundred-drawered apothecary chests and thousand-ribbed suits of bamboo armor, delicate ink-paintings and bold calligraphy, bolts of brocade and indigo and *soie sauvage*, ceramics rough and smooth, Noh masks and kabuki kites, netsuke and saké jugs: eloquent, silent repositories of history and memory and dreams. Later, I was raving to Inaka Hakamune (my fellow boarder) about the auction. "Did you see anything you wanted?" he asked.

"Everything," I said.

"And what did you buy?"

"Nothing," I said proudly.

I emerged from the auction by a different door and discovered I was lost. The temple wall was in front of me, so I decided to follow it, for I knew that it would eventually be punctuated by a gate, and I was familiar with all of the gates of Zenzenji. I walked along for a half a block or so, turned a corner, and there it was: the arched dwarf-door, the brown-and-cream banner, the smell of roses. It was early afternoon, and I was able to get a table outdoors.

As I waited for my favorite warm weather lunch of zaru-soba, or chilled buckwheat noodles, I wrote in the journal which I carried everywhere, along with a bottle of colored ink (on this day, a deep magenta) and a blunt-tipped quill pen. As I scribbled my impressions of the temple auction, I became aware that two men at the next table were watching me. I assumed they were antique dealers, for I had heard them discussing Shanghai snuff bottles. "Look," said one, pointing his triangular chin in my direction. "She doesn't have the face of a Hindu, but she seems to be writing Sanskrit. It certainly doesn't look like English." I pretended not to have heard this critique of my penmanship, but I couldn't stifle a smile as I recorded the comment and added, *Just another devadasi on her lunch break.*

When I got up to leave, the two antique dealers, who were evidently indulging in a three-*tokkuri* lunch (a "tokkuri" is a small carafe of saké), stared at me. "Look," said the one with the pointy chin, "she's wearing a mattress cover for a skirt! Only a strange foreigner would think of that!" The two men leered at me and then began to laugh, and I ducked through the miniature door in such haste that I banged my forehead on the top of the elfin arch.

The comment about my skirt was a shock, and a new source of anxiety. I had never stopped to wonder what the piles of indigo-print material at the temple bazaars and antique shops had been used for originally, but "mattress-cover" did seem to explain the long rectangular shape of many of the pieces. I had no objection to wearing a recycled futon-cover on the street, for to me it was just a piece of beautiful cloth, but I didn't feel that an article of bedding would be a suitable costume to wear to O-Zesshin. I was already self-conscious about being the first foreigner ever to attend a Sesshin at the Zenzenji Sodo, and the possibility that someone, anyone, might free-associate mattress/bed/sex, or that they might think I wanted to provoke such a thought-sequence, made me realize that my priority for that afternoon was not spiritual but sartorial. I needed to find a long, comfortable, leg-covering garment that wouldn't conjure up images of the bedchamber, or visions of fertile flesh.

As I was pondering this problem, I found myself in front of a curious-looking shop. The windows were filled with a dusty jumble of broken grave-horses and tattered fans and unraveling brocade, while the space above the door was occupied by a large Victorian clock-face adorned with anthropomorphic, rosy-cheeked suns and moons; a Betsy-Wetsy doll with blonde hair and a drawn-on caste mark on her forehead, wrapped in a sari made from a scrap of red, white, and pink Girls' Day kimono silk; and a stone lion with its mouth open wide in the "ah" position associated with root canals and Sanskrit semiotics.

I wasn't looking for anything in particular, but when I found a pair of dark indigo hakama trousers at the bottom of a pile of antique haori jackets, and when I learned that their price, after negotiation, was five hundred yen, I knew I had found my new costume. "Do you think it would be suitable for a woman to wear these hakama to a Zen Sesshin?" I asked the silver-toothed, gold-spectacled proprietor.

"Well, it might be a trifle strange, even for a foreigner," he said, stuffing my five-hundred-yen bill into the drawer of his antique brass cash register and slamming it closed. ALL SALES FINAL, said a sign above his head. "But you can easily make them into a skirt. It's so easy you could do it before breakfast." "Asameshi mae" ("before breakfast") is a Japanese idiom meaning "easy as pie," "a piece of cake," "like taking candy from a baby." (And isn't it an odd coincidence that so many of the equivalent idioms in English deal with sweets?)

* * *

An hour or so later, I was riding Mondo's bicycle through the Zenzenji compound after a quick trip to the dry goods store to buy some indigo thread. As I rode past the gate of the sub-temple where Den-san and I had practiced shakuhachi, I was seized by a desire to peek into the secret garden. I leaned my bicycle up against a sparse-leafed sapling and started to go inside, but then I heard an alarming noise: the whoosh and twang of an arrow slicing through the air and hitting its target.

I peered around the gate and saw a familiar-looking monk, dressed in gray work-trousers and matching jacket, with a white kerchief tied around his massive head, standing on a stone slab under a violet-flowered tree, shooting at a round straw target set up against the disintegrating saffron wall. Next to the monk was a bucket and a bamboo rake, from which evidence I deduced that he was meant to be off with the others, cleaning up the temple grounds. The archer-monk was muscular, stocky, and medium-tall, with a distinctive broad-featured, slightly bellicose face; with his hulking build and fearsome mien, he reminded me of Benkei, the legendary swordsman and faithful sidekick of the folk hero Minamoto Yoshitsune. After a moment, I remembered where I had seen the monk before: he was the Ouroborous-obliterator, the intimidating unsui who had scuffed his feet on my show-off sketch in the sand of the Sodo's rear courtyard, one cold December day.

The monk took an arrow from his quiver and threaded it into his bow with infinite grace, and focus. At the instant of release, just as I was thinking, "Now *this* is a classic Zen tableau!" there was a loud metallic crash as my untethered bicycle toppled over. The archer was obviously startled by the sudden percussion, for the arrow went wide of the target and lodged in the trunk of a maple tree. I fled in embarrassment, hoping that my presence hadn't been detected. Just outside the gate I thought I heard a faint whimpering sound, but I didn't stop to investigate.

As I wheeled my bicycle past the Sodo, I cast my usual longing glance through the gateless gate. To my surprise, Ryu-san, whom I always thought of as the Motown monk, was lurking just inside the gate, beckoning frantically for me to join him. "How are you?" I asked.

"Fine," he said hastily, "but I wanted to ask you a favor."

"Ask away," I said.

Ryu-san looked around nervously, and then said in a very low voice, "When you're in your room next door and you hear the bell that signals the beginning of zazen, could you please play some music?"

"What do you mean?" I asked. I thought he wanted me to play my flute or to beat the Kaiko-in altar drum, but I couldn't imagine why.

"Well," said Ryu-san, almost whispering now, "I was just hoping you could play 'Mustang Sally,' 'Try a Little Tenderness,' or 'The Oogum Boogum Song.'"

"Oh, I see!" I said, barely managing not to laugh. "*That* kind of music. The problem is, I don't have a record player, and in any case I left all my records in the United States."

"Shucks," said Ryu-san. "That's the thing I hate most about being a monk: living without soul music."

I was confused. "I thought everyone was here voluntarily, because they wanted to become enlightened and to learn how to live beautifully and simply, by the ancient precepts of Zen," I said.

Ryu-san laughed. "There are a few like that, serious old style monks; Toku-san, and Zo-san, and Také-san, and Nu-san, and Do-san, and Den-san, and Mon-san, among others," he said. "But a lot of us, especially the younger ones, are just here because this is where our parents want us to be, and in Japan you don't say no to your parents. Some of the younger guys are training to take over their fathers' temples when the old men die; in my case, though, it's pure parental blackmail. My dad's a priest, and even though my older brother has agreed to take over the temple, my parents won't send me to college in America unless I prove I can stick out two years in a monastery."

"How much time do you have left to, um, serve?"

Ryu-san looked at his wrist, then mimed surprise at the discovery that he wasn't wearing a watch. "Seven months, fourteen days, six hours, thirty-three minutes, and eleven seconds," he joked. "And then: Apollo Theater, here I come! Uh-oh," he added as Nu-san appeared in the door of the Sodo with a quizzical look on his face, "I'd better get back to work." And off he went, singing "When a Man Loves a Woman" under his breath.

"The man at the antique shop said this would be easy," I said to Nashiko an hour later, through a mouthful of pins, and she burst into laughter. She had come for a lesson (I pretended to be a nouveau riche American art collector, and she was an imperious Ginza gallery-owner) and afterward she offered to help me with my hakama-conversion project. Now, as we sat on the floor of my room, surrounded by scraps and shreds of the dismembered garment, I could see that I had made two terrible mistakes: buying the hakama in the first place, and then tearing them apart. Before breakfast? Perhaps, but only if you possessed super-human tailoring skills and a magic needle, and worked all night.

One problem was that the hakama were older, and the fabric less sturdy, than I had thought: when we ripped open the waistband we discovered that it was lined with partially-disintegrated newspapers which bore the startling date of October 8, 1886. We should have stopped there, but instead we tore out all the seams, and then I realized that the hakama were destroyed forever, and there was no way the pieces could ever be made into a skirt. "I feel like the goddess of destruction," I said to Nashiko. "I've ruined something beautiful, and stolen its history, for my own selfish, superficial purposes."

It was a bleak moment, and I welcomed the distraction of a telephone call from my friend Karen McKie. An hour later, Nashiko and Karen and I were riding in a luxurious driver-car sent by our hostess to take us to a high-class suburb of Kyoto. "Tell me again what this is all about," I said to Karen. "It sounded surrealistic when you described it on the phone."

"Well," said Karen, "you've heard of *Raku-yaki* pottery, of course, and you know that it's named after a long line of master potters named Raku."

"Of course."

"Yes, I have heard also," said Nashiko. We were speaking English, and she seemed to be nervously thrilled both by this real-life language exercise and by the prospect of visiting the famous Raku estate, for pottery was the most important thing in Nashiko's life.

"Well," Karen went on, "Raku-sensei—he's the seventh generation, I believe—is a friend of the potter I studied with when I first came to Kyoto, remember?"

"I remember," I said.

"I do not remember," said Nashiko, valiantly keeping up her end of the conversation.

"That's okay," said Karen. "Anyway, it seems that Raku-sensei bought the Okusan—his wife—a Western-style range complete with oven, and she wants to learn how to bake chocolate chip cookies! Apparently she ate them in California some years ago, and she's been craving them ever since."

"So they called in an expert?" Karen's fondness for sweets was well-known.

"Well, Mrs. Raku bought all the ingredients at one of the imported-food stores in Tokyo, and there's a recipe on the side of the chocolate-chip package, so how hard can it be? My mouth is watering already; I can't remember the last time I had a chocolate chip cookie!"

When we arrived at the vast compound of airy Japanese-style rooms cantilevered over a maze of classical gardens, we discovered that we had come on a very busy day. The seventh-generation pottery master and his assistants (I counted fourteen, all male, all dressed in willow-green *happi* coats with beige calligraphy) were in the midst of the semi-annual firing. We were only permitted to observe the process from a distance, but even then it was fascinating and dramatic: an elemental ritual of creation, from earth through fire, and water.

The clay, made of ground-up Kamogawa River stones from Kibune, had already been shaped into the rare rough shapes that have inspired tea masters and thrilled collectors for over four hundred years. The bowls were heated in an open kiln to a lava-glow, then immersed in a concoction of wood ash and straw which acted as a sort of dry glaze, and finally plunged into a vat of water with a serpentine sizzle and hiss. The result, when the ashy residue was wiped away: a deeply-pockmarked teabowl, a grail of rough perfection, glazed in matte-yet-glossy black undershot with green and gold and gray.

"What a magical process," I said.

"It certainly is," said Karen. "I'd love to see it close up."

"I don't think that is possible," said Nashiko, but Karen marched purposefully off to ask whether we might be allowed to stand in the ring of artistic activity with the other (male) observers. She came back a moment later, looking annoyed. "They told me that women are never allowed in the firing area because they're unclean," she said.

"Unclean?" I said, looking at my ink-stained knuckles.

"You know," Karen said, "because we *menstruate*! I mean, like, welcome to the Dark Ages!" Just then Mrs. Raku, a petite, energetic woman wearing a red Minnie Mouse apron over an expensive kimono of pearlescent gray silk, summoned us to the kitchen.

There, amid much hilarity and snitching of dough, we demonstrated the proper way to combine the ingredients and prepare the pans. Just as we had finished dropping the first batch onto the shiny new cookie tins, Mrs. Raku was called away to welcome some important guests. ("I hope they didn't bring their polluted wives," Karen said bitterly.) We put the tins in the oven and then wandered outside, where we became so engrossed in watching the mystical alchemy of earth, fire, and water that, inevitably, we forgot all about the cookies until we smelled them burning.

Karen and Nashiko and I scrubbed the circles of carbon off the cookie tins, and when Mrs. Raku returned to the kitchen, expecting to see fresh-baked piles of her favorite cookies, she found us starting over, from scratch. The second batch was flawless, and when we served them to the potters and visitors with cups of cold barley tea it created almost as much of a sensation as the firing spectacle itself.

"Doesn't that seem like a perfect microcosm of Japan's male-dominated society?" I said in the driver-car on the way back to town. "The women baking cookies while the men are creating glorious eternal works of art."

"The women *burning* cookies," said Karen, and we all laughed. "No, seriously," she said, "you're right. At times like this I wonder if I've made a major mistake, falling in love with a Japanese man. I mean Tatsuya's wonderful, but in the end he's still incurably male, and irrevocably Japanese."

"Oh dear, is your boyfriend have some disease?" Nashiko asked with real concern. Karen and I hid our smiles and apologized for having inadvertently excluded Nashiko from the conversation, and we spent the rest of the ride talking about the wonders of ceramics, and fantasizing about opening a chocolate-chip cookie stand on the banks of the Kamo River.

That evening I went out to buy a bottle of India ink. As I walked, I pondered my most immediate problem: O-Zesshin started in thirty-six hours, and I didn't have a thing to wear. I'll just have to wear my rose-colored wool skirt, I thought. But then I began to worry that, aside from my personal discomfort, the unseasonal wearing of wool would be a major solecism, an affront to the highly developed Japanese awareness of the subtleties of seasonal etiquette.

Just outside the south gate of Zenzenji I saw something unusual lying beside the curb: a flash of indigo bordering on lapis lazuli. I leaned down and there, among a pile of mildewed magazines and umbrella-skeletons, was a neatly folded piece of delphinium-blue silk. Toku-san's koromo! I thought, but of course it wasn't. It was a long, wide piece of aged silk moiré, soft and sheer but not transparent, in the loveliest shade of blue I had ever seen. (Shades, actually, for there were several gradations of color from fading, and wear.) There were a few neatly-sewn patches, which enhanced the charm of the cloth, and the resemblance to Toku-san's oft-coveted monk's robe was uncanny.

I raced home, my errand forgotten, and proceeded to hand-sew an ankle-length gathered skirt, slightly bell-shaped, with an attached waistband whose trailing ends could be tied in a bow. I thought it was the perfect thing to wear to a Sesshin, and I felt blessed, chosen, and very relieved. When I was finished I tried on my new skirt and then dashed off a note to my mother, thanking her for having taught me the basic survival skills: cookie-baking, an appreciation of small miracles, and the running cross-stitch. I thought of enclosing a bit of doggerel I had written earlier that day, on heavy dark-gold paper: Jill of all trades/Mistress of none/Courtesan, charlatan/Dilettante, nun/Sly scribe of reams/Of eidetic lists/Lassoer of mists/Procuress of dreams.

In the end I decided the rhyme was too gloomy, and too true, to share with a worry-prone parent, so I settled instead on a wood-block proof-print of a red-bibbed *Jizo* (Japanese patron saint of children and travelers). Finally, I sealed the bulky letter, put on my nightgown, lit a chunk of piñon incense, and turned out the light. It had been a long, strange, delightfully diversified day, and I was very happy to hit the One Road of sleep.

❖

NAKED IN THE RAIN

❖

If sex were all, then every trembling hand
Could make us squeak, like dolls,
The wished-for words.

Wallace Stevens
"Le Monocle de Mon Oncle"

—KYOTO

*D*esire is the death of delicacy; I'm afraid I have devoted far too much of my post-pubescent life to proving the terrible truth of that phrase. My months at Zenzenji were a time of especially harrowing insights into the awkward waltz of the outsider, the gangling larcenies of longing. When you don't want anything desperately, it's easy to be rational and self-possessed; but when you're madly in love with a person or a place or a phenomenon, your desire to invade that existential air-pocket transforms you into a giant anemone of need, totally devoid of pride or decorum or self-awareness, with thousands of tiny tentacles waving pathetically in the air while you shriek: "*Like* me! *Love* me! Let me in!"

The Sodo seemed to me to be a sort of cosmic cookie jar, filled with everything I wanted in those days: beauty, serenity, simplicity, wisdom, ritual, mystery, style, and the company of fascinating men. As if it weren't enough of a treat to have access to this repository of wonders, I was always pushing at the borders and grasping at the ungraspable, like a goat trying to swallow a pear-shaped shadow. Afterwards, as a delicate moment lay shattered or soiled, I would despise myself for my wanton wanting, my craven craving, my inelegant earthly appetite for the intoxicating atmosphere of Zen.

Toku-san was my usual victim, for I saw him more often than anyone else, and we always stopped to talk. We would have a brief jolly exchange of greetings, and then he would continue on his way with (I was sure) a clear, unruffled mind. I, too, would begin to walk away, my mind awhirl with queries and quandaries and desires, and, inevitably, I would call after him, "Oh, by the way ..." Then I would ask some arcane pedantic question about Zen ("Isn't Suzuki's description of *prajna* as 'the fundamental noetic principle whereby a synthetic apprehension of the whole becomes possible' a tortuous intellectualization of a visceral, non-verbal rapport with reality, and isn't such horizontal thought contrary to the basic teachings of Zen?"), or request a favor ("Are you going to sit zazen tonight? May I come?"), and while Toku-san's replies were invariably courteous and encouraging, I always felt that a perfect moment had been spoiled.

The day before O-Zesshin was to begin, I was on my way home from a dancing lesson when I met Toku-san, looking inscrutably medieval in a short black robe and a big mushroom-shaped hat of woven bamboo, at the main gate of Zenzenji. "Hooo!" he said, with his usual good humor; we commented on the ominous weather (eggdrop sun in a surly sulphuric sky), and then we said good- bye.

Ten seconds later, without thinking, I called after his picturesque departing back, "Oh, Toku-san! May I come to zazen this evening?"

"There will be no zazen this evening," Toku-san said, without turning around, and I realized that I had done it again.

It had been a typical morning, including the social infelicity. I woke up at four a.m., went for a walk, made some tea and ate some peanuts and raisins and a banana, practiced writing kanji for the time it took a stick of incense to burn down, studied my book of chants, practiced dancing in the Kaiko-in garden, went to a wood-block print lesson and worked on a triptych of secular angels with flutes and lutes, went to a Bharata Natyam lesson and learned two new mudras, and then rode Mondo's bicycle back to Zenzenji, where I met Toku-san at the gate and had the death-of-delicacy exchange previously reported.

As I rode through the temple compound, I noticed Mon-san, the fearsome-looking archer-monk, crouched by the side of the wide path, pulling weeds. I had never spoken to him before, and I was surprised when he looked up and said, "Come here for a minute." I leaned my bicycle against a sturdy tree and joined Mon-san with some trepidation, expecting a lecture or a reprimand, but he merely pointed at the mound of dirt in front of him and said, "Look." Lying on the rusty soil was a large pinkish-brown earthworm, coiled into a circle, head to tail.

So many metaphorical thoughts sprang to mind—of snakes, of enso, of circles 'round the moon—that I had to remind myself, sternly, that I was looking at a curled-up earthworm; not at a sign, or a symbol, or fodder for some Byzantine simile. Still, I couldn't help marveling at the coincidence of being shown, by the Obliterator himself, the same image that had been erased from that dusty courtyard some months before, and I wondered whether the monk appreciated the sheer circular symmetry of the moment. "Is it eating its tail?" I asked.

"It isn't eating anything," said Mon-san matter-of-factly. "It's dead."

"Oh dear," I said. "I don't deal well with death."

"I'll tell you a secret," said Mon-san, carefully burying the earthworm under an azalea bush. "Neither do I."

Mon-san invited me to help him pull some weeds, and I soon discovered that, contrary to his warrior-like appearance, he was gentle, and sensitive, and very funny. We became involved in a philosophical discussion of what constitutes a weed, and whether an unattractive wild-growing plant should have as much right to live as a cultivated flower; this led to my trotting out the "But would you love him if he wasn't beautiful?" story. Then Mon-san told me about learning archery from a ninety-year-old master of the art, and about his dreams of traveling to India and China, to retrace the steps of Daruma, the patron saint of Zen.

In the midst of a discussion of the Daruma-related proverb, "Fall down seven times, get up eight," I suddenly realized that I was late for an English-teaching appointment, so I stood up, vertebrae creaking, and brushed the dirt from my skirt. "Oh, look," I said, pointing at a patch of grass. "A four-leaf clover! In America, it's considered good luck to find one of those."

"Is that so?" said Mon-san, looking up at me with his deceptively ferocious-looking face. "Well, I think it's good luck to find a *three*-leaf clover."

* * *

I rode home as fast as I could, pondering the practical-Zen ramifications of Mon-san's three-leaf–clover remark on the way. As I passed the Sodo gate I peeked in and caught my first glimpse of the roshi of Zenzenji. The petite, elderly Zen master, whom Mon-san had told me was famous for his calligraphy, was cultivating the soil around a bed of lavender irises, while his attendant, the tall lithe Také-san, stood beside him, deflecting the sun with a bamboo umbrella.

Back in my room, I found a note saying that both my English conversation students had called to cancel their lessons; Nashiko because she had to help unload the kiln, Mr. Onda (one of the salarymen) because he had a cold—which, in the case of a salaryman, is usually a euphemism for a work-related hangover. This was a pleasant surprise, for much as I enjoyed teaching, it was always a treat to have a sudden transfusion of freedom. I considered my options—twenty-five hundred temples and shrines to explore, fifteen people to whom I owed letters, numerous chants and hundreds of kanji to memorize—and I decided to take the rest of the day off and pay a visit to Karen McKie.

"Well, it's seriously rustic," Karen had said when I asked her to describe the cottage that she and Tatsuya had been fortunate enough to rent through one of those convoluted *on*-and-*giri* machinations so common in Japan, land of formalized gratitude and ritualized moral responses. (As I recall, Tatsuya's law-school mentor had done some minor bureaucratic favor for a nephew or cousin of the landlord, twenty years before.) "It's like a Mother-Goose cottage," Karen continued, "and there's a temple nearby, and everything is incredibly green."

Well put, Karen, I thought when I stepped off the wheezing city bus at a village ten or twelve miles outside Kyoto. There were tall trees overhead and flowering vines growing along the bamboo fences, and there was a lushness to the foliage, and a yellow-green richness to the light, that I wasn't used to seeing in the gravel-and-cobblestone heart of the city. An unpaved country lane led to Karen's shady, secluded cottage; it was an idyllic setting, and even though I was madly in love with my urban temple, I felt a twinge of biophilic envy, and a sudden urge to rusticate.

The four-room house was furnished sparsely but comfortably with recycled treasures, rescued from the weekly trash truck. Karen collected teapots and Tatsuya collected hand-painted kites, and these items were attractively displayed along with their joint collection of hand-made folk toys of wood, straw, bamboo, and paper. There was a thick-walled granary behind the house which they had converted into a studio, and the shelves were stacked with ceramics from their own kiln. Karen favored simple shapes and pale, nacreous glazes, while Tatsuya, who had courageously disobeyed his parents and left law school to pursue a career as a potter, used hand-building techniques to make large, geometrical pieces which he glazed in metallic silver, gold, and bronze.

"Uh-oh," Karen said we sat sipping oolong tea and nibbling on the almond cookies I had brought, "I forgot." She jumped up and went out to the kitchen and began opening and closing cupboards. "Shit!" she said, as she passed through the living room. She went into the bedroom and banged around, and then she went into the bathroom. "Shit!" she said again, more loudly. A moment later Tatsuya came in, looking fetchingly un-lawyerlike in a blue beret and clay-covered overalls.

"What's wrong?" he asked.

"I can't find my pills," said Karen.

"Not again," said Tatsuya, with a calm, loving smile. "Don't worry, we'll find them."

I leafed through an illustrated book of Bernard Leach's ceramics, while the sounds of domestic archaeology continued. "Did you look under the magazines?"

"Of course."

"What about the hamper? They were in the hamper once, remember."

"I remember."

I thought they were making an awfully big fuss over a bottle of vitamins, and it wasn't until Karen cried, "Here they are, in my purse, of all places!" and emerged from the bedroom carrying a little beige plastic compact that I realized that the frantic search had been for her birth control pills.

Tatsuya followed her to the kitchen, and while she pried the tiny pastel disc from its place in the tantric wheel, he filled a glass with water from the tap. Standing there at the window, against a vivid primary-color backdrop of flowers, trees, and sky, the two of them looked so handsome, so loving, so complicit, that I felt a rush of envy. I suddenly saw all my supposed true loves as immature infatuations, and I felt intimidated by my ignorance of the "midnight mysteries": the cabalistic congruence of people in serious living-together love.

As I sat there, feeling more and more like an intruder, I began thinking about the metaphorical moats that separate initiates from outsiders.

In religion, there is the sudden satori of Zen and its Occidental counterpart, the epiphanic conversion. In linguistics there is the rapturous moment when you finally get the hang of the unconscious intonation of a foreign language and are mistaken on the phone or in person for a native speaker. There's the great barrier reef of puberty, which turns dreamy children into single-minded predators enslaved by their prehistoric mating instincts. And then there's the mysterious threshold of the orgasm—or rather of the elusive female climax, for the male version is evidently not so much a mystery as an ineluctable physiological response.

In Western society we have the luxury of being experiential perfectionists, and many a romantic relationship has run aground on the issue of the female's pre-orgasmic state. I must have heard (or overheard) twenty proud-warrior stories about how some guy masterfully initiated a glacial girlfriend, or another man's unfulfilled wife, into the molten Nirvana of sexual release. ("I never dreamed it could be like this," the grateful women always sigh.) Those contemporary locker-room stories are just variations on an ancient oral tradition: the epic saga of the male as studly avatar of sexual satori—not to be confused with enlightenment, or love.

I remembered that Toozie had once talked about the "erotic groove of collaborative contraception"; it had been one of her more shockingly-detailed revelations, but I thought now that I understood what she meant. The devices were different—she had been talking about condoms—but the principle was the same. Contraception was obviously the unglamorous cousin (or chaperone) of rapturous lovemaking but I sensed, that day in the country cottage, that there could be something touchingly romantic about the process when both partners were equally involved in its execution, and when their hearts were warmed by long-term tenderness, not just engorged by late-night lust.

Karen and Tatsuya returned to the living room and we resumed our conversation about Leach, Hamada, and *Mashiko-yaki*, but I sensed something different in the atmosphere. Once before, in Cambridge, I had been in a room with a man and a woman who were so filled with desire for one another that they gave off a sort of pheromonal incense (I remember thinking it was a grilled-cheese sandwich, burning in the skillet), but I hadn't had the sense to catch the hint, and take my leave. This time, I was quicker to recognize the aura of conjugal desire; I invented an urgent reason for returning to Kyoto, and said goodbye. When I glanced back at the cottage I saw Karen and Tatsuya standing in the living room window, engaged in a long, backlit kiss. I turned away just as they began to succumb to hormonal gravity, and when I looked back one last time, the window was empty.

I was happy to be in the country, and I had no reason to rush back to Kyoto, so I decided to explore a nearby temple on the way to the bus stop. The temple, which belonged to one of the more mystical sects of Buddhism, was known for its Peking-style grounds, and on this perfectly clement day I seemed to have the famous garden all to myself. There were bamboo groves and carp-ponds dotted with turtle-shaped rocks, there was a circular stand of flame-colored azaleas and a vermilion bridge, and the effect—dramatic, yet tranquil—reminded me of a dream-landscape in a ten-volume Chinese novel.

As I perched on a cushion of pooltable-green moss, watching the carp swimming through a reflected forest of azaleas, seven athletic-looking young men with shaved heads and solemn expressions, dressed in white cotton under-kimono (the traditional costume for committing ritual suicide, though they didn't look *that* solemn), marched purposefully across the scarlet bridge. It was a stunning sight, and as I sat savoring the afterimage, I heard the sound of sutra-chanting from off in the forest. I crept along until I came within sight of a chilly-looking waterfall, crashing over a gold-veined gray stone into a clear, knee-deep pool below. I crouched behind a bush aflame with crimson flowers and then I saw the monks' wide-sleeved white robes, fluttering on the branches of a hickory tree like gigantic newborn butterflies.

I could hear the voices of the monks, murmuring sutras from the pool behind the waterfall. A moment later they emerged—seven strong young men in epidermal shades of pink and white and brown—to stand naked under the chilly waterfall, and my entire body erupted in goosebumps when they began chanting, with a tremulous lingering vibrato, the familiar syllables of the Heart of Great Wisdom Sutra. "MA-KA HAN-NYA HA-RA-MI-TA SHIN-GYO: Kan-ji-zai bo-sa …" After the first shudder of recognition, I began to chant along with them, *sotto voce*, beneath the burning bush. I was transfixed and ecstatic, and not until the doxology had died away with a trailing yodel of the final word ("Shin-gyooooo") which sounded uncannily like the call of an itinerant goldfish vendor ("Kin-gyooooo"), did I realize that I had been drenched, all unaware, by a sudden waterfall of soft spring rain.

On the way home, I mused (sacrilegiously, I feared) about the parallels between the mysteries of sex and Zen: both were paradoxical, both potentially addictive, both involved what Borges calls a "climactic moment." Stimulated by my day in the country, and by the infinitely tender and erotic sight of that empty cottage window, I began to rethink my positions on non-procreational sex, and birth control. Those seven strapping young men, singing naked in the rain, had inspired a thrilling fantasy-image of myself and Yukio chanting together under a slightly more temperate waterfall, then dropping slowly out of sight onto a Chinese-novel bed of velvet moss and crimson petals.

* * *

When I walked into Kaiko-in, Mondo was just coming back from the family living quarters.

"What are you up to?" I said.

"Oh, my mom went to her calligraphy class so I had to make dinner for my grandmother."

"How is the Obaasan?" I asked. "I haven't seen her in ages; maybe I'll go and say hello."

"She's asleep now," said Mondo. "She never goes out anymore; she's like an old dry bone, stretched out down there all day." He illustrated this shocking statement with a jocular taffy-pulling gesture. I must have looked horrified, because Mondo patted me on the shoulder and said, "It's a joke, it's a joke."

The next morning I went out for my usual morning walk. As I strode around the corner I almost collided with Zan-san, the treasurer of the monastery, whom I had first met in Tokyo. Our conversations since then had been limited to the exchange of greetings, so I was surprised when he stopped and said, "Where are you going?"

"Just for a walk," I said.

"It must be nice to have so much free time," said Zan-san, flashing his gold-capped canines. It sounded like a snide remark, but I believed that all Zen monks were perfectly beneficent beings, so I figured I must have misinterpreted his tone of voice. The permanent sardonic set of Zan-san's mouth and the mischievous glitter in his eyes made everything he said sound slightly mocking, or combative.

After a few moments of unmemorable banter, the monk said, "See you later," and sauntered off. I walked a few steps and then I was seized by the inevitable afterthought.

"Zan-san," I called after him, "may I ask you something?"

"You can ask," he said when I caught up with him, as if to imply, *But I might not answer.*

"Well," I said, "I've been wondering for quite some time why all the monks have such short names." It occurred to me even as I spoke that Zan-san was probably wondering why I hadn't just asked one of the Maedas. He answered very courteously, though, explaining that a monk's monastery-name is taken from the reading of the final character in his given name. He told me that his first name was Kazan, an unusual name taken from a surname with literary and historic overtones, meaning "volcano"; and Zo-san's full name was Sozo. "Oh, like *sozo* (imagination)?" I asked.

"No," Zan-san said with a laugh, "the characters are totally different. You should ask Zo-san to explain what his name means—he speaks fluent English, you know."

In response to my shameless prodding, Zan-san also revealed that Toku-san's name was Antoku, after the ill-fated infant emperor. (Aha, I thought, he was pulling my leg that day when he told me his name meant "Buddhist salvation!") Den-san's name was Raiden, Jun-san's name was simply Jun, Také-san's name was Hirotake, Nu-san's name was Kasanu, Saku-san's name was Junsaku, Ryu-san's name was Toryu, Mon-san's name was Shibuemon, and the sinister Do-san was named after another emperor: Tsuchimikado. "Thank you so much; it's been very instructive," I said as we parted for the second time. Zan-san said "Don't mention it," but I thought I detected a note of weariness in his voice.

* * *

Zenzenji had a number of entrances, and exits. Some were great wooden gates, others mere slots in the wall. Under the gate that led to the shrine-dotted shopping street between the river and the temple walls, there lived an old mouse-colored man. He was brownish-gray in his entirety: clothes, skin, hair, whiskers, even his cigarette holder (wood and pewter), and he blended with the grayed brown of the weathered gate like a Tahitian lizard on a dried mango leaf. The old man was quite spry, and he seemed to spend most of his waking hours scavenging; I had seen him down by the river, poking through piles of trash, and sometimes, when he was away, I would leave a little gift in his nest of rags and papers: a hundred yen, a tangerine, a box of fancy matches.

On this day, after my educational encounter with Zan-san, I went to a fruit stand and bought two spotless, firm-fleshed bananas; I ate one myself, and gave the other one to the old man under the gate, who appeared to have just awakened from a siesta. I felt pleasure in sharing my relative wealth, in seeing his tobacco-colored face crease in a check-ered smile of surprise; but even as the banana passed from my hand to his I had a vision of myself saying to some generic glowing monk: "I bought two bananas and gave one to the old man under the gate," and of the monk responding with an expression of admiration, or affection. I knew that a generous gesture should be its own reward, but I seemed to be afflicted with a sort of compulsive auto-telescopy: a need to see myself as others saw me, and to try to nudge that perception in my favor.

"Big sister!" I looked down at the small doll-face, the eyes half-cov-ered by a thick wedge of black bangs under a white beret, the red velvet pinafore and white lace socks splattered with the mud of joyous play. After a moment I recognized the face: it was the little girl whose super-stitious grandmother had refused to permit a "demon cat" in the house. "Big sister!" the little girl repeated, addressing me by the standard term for waitresses and for unrelated women who are older than the speaker, but not quite old enough to be called "Auntie." She took my hand and pulled me toward the playground, where another little girl with green-ribboned pigtails stood holding a paper bag. Uh-oh, I thought, cats. Sure enough, as we approached I heard the familiar mewing sound, and in a sudden flash of philological insight I understood the origin of the phrase, "to let the cat out of the bag."

The kittens were identical: three tiny, blind ginger-and-white triplets no bigger than tiger prawns, stuffed into an empty bag from "Pâtisserie Kyoto Station" and tossed under a bush (the same bush I had passed in my flight from the secret garden) by some lip-service Buddhist who blithely assumed that a temple is an SPCA with incense. I took them home, and after I had bathed and dried their puny, shivering bodies and suckled them with a doll-sized bottle filled with warm milk, I gave them names. I know, you should never name an animal which isn't yours to keep, or which you intend to eat, but even though I couldn't tell them apart, I felt better knowing they had some individual identity, for a name is a proof of a welcomed birth, and of a future. I called them Kachina, Kabuki, and Kiranosuke, more for the sound than the sense, and while they slept under the heated kotatsu-table I went and placed a call to the Cat Auntie.

* * *

Toku-san had told me to come to the Sodo at seven p.m.; there would be a session of zazen meditation with a number of guests, and then O-Zesshin would begin officially at 3:30 the following morning. I had once introduced Toku-san to Yukio, and they had chatted about zazen, but I was surprised when Toku-san said, "Please bring your veterinarian friend, if he's free." I was uneasy about combining the woman-in-love aspect of my life with the seeker-of-spiritual-serenity part, but I felt obliged to tell Yukio of the invitation.

To my alarm he said, "Oh, I'd like to go. I've been too busy to do zazen in Tokyo, and I've missed it."

Yukio arrived from Tokyo on a mid-afternoon train, and he showed up at Kaiko-in a bit later in his mother's car, borrowed for some ficti-tious errand. He was dressed in one of his equatorial sunset-shirts, and he looked incredibly appealing. "There's someplace I want to take you," he said.

"Wait," I said, "I have to feed the kittens first." Yukio came in and helped me warm the milk and fill the bottles and then very gently, like some gigantic god-father, he held the minuscule cats in his palm and fed them their milk. I was always very touched to see how much he loved animals, and my experience the day before at Karen's had turned my heart into a roiling cauldron of strong and scary romantic feelings for this smart, complex, compassionate, worthwhile man.

"Why here, and why today?" I asked when we parked outside the gates of a rambling Shinto shrine associated since antiquity with fertil-ity, and horses.

"You'll see," said Yukio, and he led the way (he seldom held my hand in public, but when we were alone he never let it go) through the tall gray-wood gates and up a gravel path to the main building with its antique Noh stage and gilded eaves, past the gift shop with its brocade amulets and paper fortunes and wooden votive tablets painted with black and white horses, through a grove of rosy maples, up a winding path, to a grassy hilltop beside a pellucid stream. Through the tall cryptomeria trees, I could see the towers of downtown Kyoto, and the misty seaweed-colored mountains beyond.

"This is one of my favorite spots," Yukio said, "and I wanted to share it with you." He sat down on the grass and began to unpack his knapsack. He spread a straw mat on the ground, and then laid out a picnic of crisp rice-flour cookies in the shape of horses, pale gold *nashi* (Japanese pears), and a thermos of brown-rice tea. "I remembered that you liked brown rice," he said.

After devouring Yukio's thoughtful little feast, we reclined on the blanket and, between epic warm-fusion kisses, we talked about Zen. "I remember the first time I saw you," I said, and we reminisced about doing zazen (though never together) on the *Amazon Maru*, about flying fish and phosphorescent light, about cows in the hold and bold women in the showers.

"I just wish I had found you sooner," Yukio said. "I'm still ashamed about behaving like such a randy beast with—with that woman."

"Her name is C. J.," I said magnanimously, "and it doesn't matter. After all, the red thread of fate doesn't always follow a straight line."

"You know, I never could draw a straight line," Yukio said playfully. "Look, I'll show you." And while I watched, he took his long healer's forefinger and drew an invisible, electrifying line from my mouth, down my throat ("*Hakucho*," he murmured. "White bird?" I guessed, translating the syllables literally. "No, swan," Yukio said in English, and I swallowed), down the road between my ribs. I held my breath when he paused at my sternum, but he smiled and said, "No detours," and I swallowed again, the involuntary gulp of ardent anticipation.

As Yukio's finger continued its journey down my long skirt to my feet and then slowly back up again, this time beneath the fabric, he never stopped talking. (I was busy listening, and trembling, and trying to breathe.) "My parents are unquestioning believers in the Pure Land sect," he said, "but even as a child I preferred Zen. I liked the atmosphere, I liked the art, I liked the faces of the monks—wise and humorous and humble—and I liked the fact that Zen doesn't take itself too seriously. I liked the idea of living life to the fullest—in a spiritual, not a hedonistic, sense—through your own power, rather than just biding your time on earth, chanting nonsense and never really thinking anything through, in the hopes that you'll go to some fantasy heaven when you die. I do believe in God, or gods; I think there's some sort of brilliant divinity with unimaginable creative powers, though I don't think human beings are that deity's most polished inventions. And I think ..."

While Yukio rambled on, I was holding tightly to the hand that wasn't drawing the not-quite-straight line, and I was thinking, This man is practically my psychic double. I love him madly, I desire him with all my heart, and I would be happy to have his child, any day, any year—even nine months from this very moment. At the same time, another part of my mind was saying, "Um, listen, that's probably not such a terrific idea," to which my vibrating body replied, "Trust me, sweetheart. Would I give you bad advice?"

Being touched by Yukio, my red-thread soulmate, would have been almost unbearably thrilling under any circumstances, but our contact seemed much more profound (and more erotic, too) because he was speaking about intimate, ultimate topics instead of crooning the standard catechism of seduction: *I want you, I need you, you've really got a hold on me.* By the time Yukio stopped talking and bent to kiss me, I had been reduced to a puddle of let-me-be-your-mistress mush. I had only one thought, or feeling, at that instant: I wanted to go somewhere lovely and private with Yukio Yanagida, some deep-mountain hotspring inn where we could lie down for a week or two with a "Do Not Disturb" sign on the rational lobes of our brains. I felt like a cabbage leaf on a rushing river: powerless to stop the romantic momentum, even if I had wanted to.

And then, just as I was ready to say "Ravish me now, I'm yours forever"; ready to let the woods be our inn and the hilltop our bed; ready to give up zazen, O-Zesshin, graduate school, my citizenship, my self; precisely then, in that climactic moment of mindless hormonic possession, Yukio suddenly stood up. He walked over to the stream and very slowly, like a doctor (or a veterinarian) preparing for surgery, he washed his hands and face. Then he turned to me and said, with his gentle Japanese-gaucho's smile, "Well, we know our bodies are awake. Now let's go work on our souls."

THE HEART LIKES
BITTER THINGS

*He just sat with his mind empty, and when his thoughts, which were
mainly ignoble, flowed back into it they had a pleasant freshness.*

E. M. Forster
A Passage to India

—KYOTO

A bsent-minded, forgetful, scatterbrained; I have never taken
offense at those epithets, although I prefer the more genial
"head in the clouds" or "lost in a dream." I must have spent a
thousand hours searching for misplaced keys and essential documents
(unlisted telephone numbers scribbled on cat-food coupons, passports
accidentally misfiled under "Recipes to Try Someday") or retracing my
steps to find a treasured address book left atop a big-city pay phone.
And on innumerable monsoon season days I have discovered, when the
sporadic rain began to fall again, that I have left my umbrella somewhere very far away. On the brass luggage-rack of an outbound train,
perhaps, or hanging on the back of a bentwood chair at some smoky
café, or in a bamboo cylinder in the entry hall of a temple or a sumo stable.

The annals of Zen contain an uncannily relevant parable: *A monk
who considered himself enlightened went to visit the priest of another temple. It was a rainy day, and as they were sipping ceremonial tea, the priest
said casually, "Oh, by the way, on which side of the genkan did you leave
your umbrella?" "I don't remember," said the arrogant monk. "Then you
are not yet enlightened," said the priest.*

One of my hopes, as I slid open the door of the Sodo at 3:30 a.m. on the first full day of O-Zesshin, was that I would emerge at the end of the week of intensive zazen with a somewhat clearer idea of where I had left my metaphysical umbrella. Of course, I hoped to be struck with the galvanic thunderbolt of satori, too, but that seemed an unlikely, even presumptuous goal. Much as I loved the aesthetics and atmosphere and austerities of Zen, I was by no means a full-time, one-road devotee; indeed, after my picnic on the horse-shrine grass with Yukio, I was more intrigued than ever by the realm of romantic rapture. Still, while I didn't really expect to become officially enlightened, I did hope to be clarified, focused, and improved.

I remember that first endless, confusing day as a montage of nervousness, menial labor, poetic images, and embarrassing moments: a slow-drip-irrigation dose of ignominy and discomfiture. There were a great many ritualistic details to keep track of, and, inevitably, I made a number of gaffes, errors, and faux pas. Each mistake made me even more nervous, and thus more inclined to commit another blunder.

Nu-san had taken me aside two days before O-Zesshin began. After presenting me with my own set of sturdy wooden chopsticks and a nest of worn black lacquer bowls lined with red (all loaners, alas), he had patiently demonstrated the complex choreography of mealtime: how to ask for seconds, when to bow your head, how to clean out your bowls with hot water after the meal, how many grains of rice to set aside for the hungry ghosts. It all seemed quite simple in the abstract, and I felt confident that at the dining table, at least, I would be an unobtrusive guest.

The first day's breakfast went smoothly enough. It was just thin rice gruel and pickles and tea, and I muddled through with the helpful Nu-san at my elbow, prompting me with gestures and nodding his approval. By lunchtime we had sat zazen for a couple of hours, and had spent the rest of the morning in physical labor, so I was ravenous. The lunch menu was more complex: white rice cooked with barley (unmitigated white rice was a rare and luxurious treat); miso soup with dice-sized squares of tofu and ribbons of konbu submerged in the high-protein silt; steamed turnips and carrots with soy sauce; the Sodo's trademark takuan pickles; and weak tea the color of daffodils. Nu-san (my mentor, my training wheels, my cultural crutch) had returned to his usual place at the head of the table with the other senior monks, leaving me sandwiched between two aloof-seeming young unsui to whom I had never spoken before.

This was the basic mealtime ritual: first we would chant (I managed to keep up, though I frequently had to peek at the sutra-book spread out in my blue silk lap like an accordion-pleated napkin). Then we held our hands in *gassho* position (Dürer style: palm to palm, fingers pointed toward the sky) until the serving monks stopped before us with their wooden buckets of barley-rice, their cast-iron vats of miso soup, their brass pots of tea and hot water. Bows would be exchanged, we would proffer the appropriate bowl, they would fill it and return it to us, we would bow again, and so on down the line.

We would use our long chopsticks to pick up seven grains of rice for the *segaki*—"hungry ghosts"—and make a little pyramid on the outer edge of the table. (The serving monks scraped these donations onto a dish at the end of the meal and then threw them to the hungry pigeons, or the ghostly silver carp.) Then we would begin to eat, in silence. No talking was allowed, and the occasional click of chopsticks, the chants, the ping of a bell, and the clack of wooden clappers to signify the beginning and end of the meal were the only sounds heard in the dining room. After a time the servers would come down the line again, offering seconds, and almost everyone would request another serving of a given dish by holding up their hands in gassho. If we didn't want any more, we bent our heads low over the table as the monks passed.

At that first lunch, I mistook the miso vat for the rice bucket. There was an awkward moment as I held out my rice bowl to a bewildered-looking monk who was offering me a brimming ladleful of soup, and I remember the feeling of flustered humiliation as I put my bowl down and bowed my head, for I didn't want more soup, and it was strictly forbidden to leave even a trace of food uneaten. Finally the rice came along; I asked for a second helping, and ate it, but I was still hungry. I had been running all day on a dish of gruel; I had scrubbed floors and toilets, and done several hours of zazen, which, although sedentary, does require effort, concentration, and the expenditure of nervous energy.

When I saw the rice bucket coming down the line for the third time I thought, Oh, good, and put my hands up in supplication. Then I saw that all the monks on my left were falling like dominoes trampled by a bear, bowing their shaved, shining heads over the table. For a moment I was mesmerized by the musical progression of the row of black-robed backs, but then I realized that I was the only discordant note in the concerto: the only person asking for thirds. (Twenty-plus years later, I still feel a flash of mortification as I re-experience that awful moment.) I started to put my bowl down and bow my head, too, but it was too late: the serving monk had stopped in front of me, and he was filling my bowl.

I picked up my overflowing rice bowl and began to eat, while the lines of monks on both sides sat motionless and silent, hands folded in their laps, staring straight ahead. I was aflame with self-consciousness; every bite was torture, each rice grain looked as large as a meteorite, my chewing seemed to echo from the rafters, and no matter how fast I shoveled the rice into my mouth, the bowl seemed to remain full, like one of those self-replenishing milk jugs in the Biblical parables. Finally I finished the last grain, and as I wiped out my bowls I felt certain that I had been branded for life as a greedy gaijin. Then I remembered the proverb: "Only a freeloader asks for a third helping of rice," and I blushed as red as the lining of my lovely lacquer bowl.

Later that day, at the end of an hour of cleaning floors on my hands and knees, I went into one of the outdoor stall-toilets next to the Zendo. No one had seen me enter, so I was startled to hear an angry voice calling my name. I emerged to find Do-san, toadish hands on protruding hipbones, glaring at me with red-rimmed eyes. "How did you know I was in there?" I asked. He pointed at my gray rubber zori, a touching surprise-gift from Toku-san, the evening before. I had shed the zori when I clambered into the stall where, since Japan is the land of specialized footwear, a pair of red vinyl "toilet slippers" was waiting.

My new rubber sandals were in never-the-twain position: one pointing east, one pointing west. Do-san reached down and very gingerly, as if he were handling radioactive offal, turned my duck-foot zori so that they were side by side, pointing outward, ready to step into. "That's the way to do it," he said.

"Thank you," I said. "Is that how you knew I was in here, because my slippers were pointing the wrong way?"

"No," he said—gleefully, I thought, although his face remained severe. "I knew it was you because your slippers are larger than anyone else's." (I wear a size 8, but Japanese men, to their eternal chagrin, tend to have very small feet.)

And then (speaking of feet) there was the *kinhin* fiasco. Zen training is ascetic, but not sadistic; hence the ritual known as kinhin, a walking-break in which the monks are allowed to get up and march rapidly around the Zendo in single file, while continuing to meditate. No one had told me about kinhin, and the first time Den-san gave the signal and everyone clambered down from their cushions, I had no idea what was going on. Saba-san, who was sitting next to me, got down and joined the line of walking monks—I couldn't help thinking of Musical Chairs— while motioning to me to follow him. But when I tried to get up I discovered that my feet were solidly asleep, and I knew they wouldn't support my weight.

My feet and legs often fell asleep during the extended zazen sessions; I figured that was part of the pain in which there was, I hoped, some progress. The sensation would return after a couple of minutes of surreptitious post-zazen massage, but I thought it would be indecorous to rub my petrified feet in full view of the parading monks. The hell with it, I thought. I'll just go on sitting. After all, I'm a foreigner; what do I know?

That evening as I was leaving the Sodo I overheard Saba-san talking to Mr. Otsuka, a tailor specializing in monks' robes whom I had seen at zazen a couple of times. "She's really *erai* (noble)," Mr. Otsuka was saying. "I mean, she was meditating so deeply that she didn't even get up for kinhin!" And so the die was cast, and for the rest of the week, much as I would have loved to stretch my legs, I remained sitting on my perch while everyone else marched around the hall, for I was still in the thrall of "perception is all," and I didn't want to disillusion Mr. Otsuka, or anyone else who might think that my prolonged sitting was due to a formidably focused mind, and not to comatose feet.

All in all, it was a chastening, stressful seventeen and a half hours. During that first day I often found myself thinking about the seven-day deep-mountain sense-intensification retreat Gordon Coyne had described, and wondering how it would differ from a Zen Sesshin. Perhaps that is why my mosaic memories of that week seem to fall into categories of sense, rather than of sensibility.

On the first day, they concentrate on colors … The deep red of a rice bowl, the gauzy pink of an azalea, the empyrean blue of a patched koromo. The satiny sparrow-brown of weathered wood, the bitter-chocolate brown of bell-shaped window frames, the young-grass green of bamboo mats. The lordly purple of the roshi's robe, the lustrous aubergine of eggplants, the chrome-yellow of takuan pickles.

Not just colors, but images. Shadow warriors on the front lines of Zen: the outline of benevolent threat, looming on the wall. I knew the jikijitsu-patrollers were my pals Den-san and Mon-san, but the mythicizing dimness transformed them into the dual personifications of Manjusri, the sword-bearing Bodhisattva who rides a grinning lion, and I held my breath until they passed.

Another dramatic sight: the diminutive yet imposing roshi of Zenzenji, preceded by the Chinese-cherub monk carrying an oil lamp, walking through the Zendo during the long evening meditation-session. He paused in front of me for what seemed like several minutes, and I felt as if every cell in my body were electrified. I concentrated on rhythmic breathing, and when I heard the footsteps shuffle off toward the main hall I opened my eyes slightly and saw the Zen master's big-sleeved shadow projected on the opposite wall, monstrous and bat-like; I was disoriented from so little sleep and so much zazen, and I almost cried out in wonder, and fear.

Not just images, but visions: the fascinating faces of thirty monks, moving through light and shadow. When I saw them all together, at mealtime or in walking meditation, I always marveled at the sheer physiognomic variety. The faces were a festival of geometric shapes: round, square, oblong, triangular. At least half of the ten nose-types identified by Leonardo (aquiline, spatulate, *retroussé*) were represented; there were full-lipped fishmouths, rosy girlish mouths, thin, straight, austere-looking mouths that appeared to have the labial tissue on the inside, out of sight, like a dun-colored bird with brilliant hidden plumage. Most of the monks had smooth shiny skulls, like amber blown-glass globes, but there were a few rugged, scabrous skulls with Pachycephalosaurus-like bumps and indentations which reminded me of the nun Mochizuki, whose cratered scalp I knew better than I knew my own.

As I scrubbed the ancient wooden corridors, I pondered the human habit of stereotyping character according to facial topography, and genetic happenstance. Take the "weak chin"; why should the absence of bone and cartilage reflect a lack of principle, or resolve? Why should narrow lips preclude a passionate nature? And why should inadvertent corneal motility—"shifty eyes"—connote some sleaziness of behavior, as well? Only (I concluded) because the power of prejudicial suggestion is so insidious, and so strong.

I mused also, as I raked leaves and scoured toilets, on the chromatics of Japanese skin. Where, I wondered, did the myth of the Japanese being a "yellow people" originate? Probably in the semi-literate journal entries of some color-blind foreign bigot with an ill-fitting codpiece and an advanced case of syphilis. The Japanese, black-belt masters of self-deprecation, readily embraced this myth, and I have known several young Japanese women with pale translucent skin who, every time we met, would place their milk-white arms next to mine and wail, "Oh, I'm so yellow!"

Japanese skin is not yellow; it is olive, or brown, or beige, or golden, or "the color of cherry blossoms." That phrase derives from *Hagakure*, a quirky 17th-century book of samurai ideals and etiquette; it was Yukio Mishima's favorite book, and he published an annotated version in the 1970s. "Men must be the color of cherry blossoms, even in death," *Hagakure* proclaims, and it goes on to suggest that if a samurai wakes up pale and hung-over he should discreetly apply a bit of rouge before going out to face the feudal world.

Chroma, hue, tint, shade, tincture. What color is a firefly in full mid-summer flame—silver, gold, platinum, the transparent star-color of light? During one break in the first evening's activities, I looked into the graveyard to the right of the guest-meditation area and saw what I thought was a flock of fireflies. I was thrilled, but then I discerned human figures, the dark shapes of monks with their moth-wing sleeves, connected to the flares. Oh, it's match-light, I thought. They're lighting incense to place on the graves of the old masters. ("About suffering they were never wrong ...") I was filled with joy at the thought of the young monks taking time to commune with their spiritual ancestors, to commemorate the sacred continuum of Zen.

On the second day, they concentrate on sounds ... The sound of one object striking another: the bell struck by the brass wand, the wooden fish struck by the padded mallet, the slumping shoulder struck by the jikijitsu's vigilant stick, the mesmerizing music of the chants, and always the subtle-textured sound of stillness, tempered by nature's subliminal continuo: birds and bugs and frogs and dogs and fish and wind and rain.

One evening toward the end of the week, the customary silence in the dining room was broken when we were served a special treat: hand-rolled udon noodles in a rich shiitake-mushroom sauce, garnished with sliced leeks and crushed daikon and toasted sesame seeds. In Japan, it is an egregious breach of etiquette not to slurp your noodles (and the custom has been extended, curiously, to Western-style coffee and tea), so for that brief half-hour the hall resounded with the robust sounds of sluicing broth and noodles being vacuumed into eager monastic mouths. I did my timid best to contribute to the din, but high-chair cultural conditioning dies hard, and my noodle-slurping style was cramped by the id-deep awareness that such noisy, joyous consumption of food violated at least one of the basic tenets of my childhood bible, *Manners Can Be Fun.*

On several occasions I thought I heard the disturbing sound of someone, out of sight, roughing up the shy, hapless, moon-faced monk Jun-san, who looked, that entire week, as if he might be about to cry. Ironically, the cynical young monks who were merely serving time in the Sodo in deference to parental pressure were easily able to twist their legs into the prescribed pretzel-shape, while Jun-san, who was seriously committed to a life of monasticism, apparently found it impossible to force his thick, bowed turnip-legs into the lotus position. Every day I noticed new additions to the galaxy of welts and bruises on his arms and legs. I knew that "constructive hazing" and physical remonstration were part of the Zen tradition; I knew too that there could be another explanation for the sounds, and the bruises. Had I glimpsed the dark side of Zen? I didn't dare ask anyone, and I wasn't sure I wanted to know.

And of course there were the exotic, ever-intriguing sounds of sanzen: the crash of crockery, the confrontational "Kwatz!," the assault with a lively weapon. Forget about silent applause; what is the sound of one hand slapping? Finally, stretching the parameters, there was the sound of my alarm clock (the same green alarm clock that interrupted my devadasi dream) going off every morning at three a.m.; every morning, that is, except one. On the fourth day of the Sesshin, I opened my eyes and noticed an unexpected line of light under the sliding doors of my room. I reached for my clock and was shocked to see that it said 8:30. I was five hours late! In a panic, I got dressed, fed the kittens (the Cat Auntie was out of town, and I hadn't had time to find them another home), put them under the kotatsu to keep warm, and rushed over to the Sodo.

As I walked down the empty hall toward the Zendo, I was consumed with the classic late-for-school, tardy-for-work, missed-the-bus anxiety. I had so wanted to do everything right, to be an unobtrusive and harmonious presence. And now, because I was too scatterbrained to pull out the alarm button on a simple two-button clock, I would be revealed as a sleep-dulled slugabed masquerading as a devotee of discipline. Perhaps I'll even be barred from attending the rest of the Sesshin, I thought, and the sick dread rose from my entrails and filled my throat with bile.

Toku-san's door was ajar, and as I passed I heard him say my name in a severe, magisterial tone of voice. "Hai," I said, and I knelt on the floor outside, trembling with shame and apprehension.

"Come in," he ordered, and I scooted into the room, still on my knees.

"Please, please forgive me," I said. "I was careless, and I overslept. Please punish me as you see fit." Toku-san sat with his arms folded across his chest, watching me impassively. His eyes were serious, and the twinkle was nowhere in sight.

"What do you think would be an appropriate punishment?" he asked.

"I don't know," I said. "Maybe no food for a day, or cleaning out the latrines for the rest of the week. I'm so sorry, and so ashamed." I placed my forehead on the mat, and when I cautiously raised my eyes after a few importunate minutes, I was astonished to see that Toku-san was smiling, and the benevolent shine had returned to his eyes.

"I'm not going to punish you," he said. "I think you've taken care of that already. Everyone's entitled to one mistake; just don't let it happen again." I couldn't tell if his final remark was meant in jest, but I wasn't going to take any chances. That evening after leaving the Sodo at nine p.m. I went to the shopping street and bought an auxiliary alarm clock, with an even more clamorous ring than the one I already had, and every night for the remainder of the Sesshin, I checked the knobs and buttons of both clocks at least three times before going to sleep.

On the third day, they concentrate on smells ... The fragrance of landscape: a vine of tiny white-blooming flowers in the garden, the fecund green smell of moss after a rain, fallen-leaf bonfires at dusk in the already smoky light. Earthy, archaic food aromas: grain and fungus, fermented curd and sour miso, seaweed and spinach, garlic and ginger and sesame, shiso and soy and salt. The sweet golden smell of fresh perspiration on a monk who had been digging a tree-hole in the back garden, his light gray work-jacket calligraphed with streaks and arcs of sweat.

Incongruous smells: the fetid worldly odor of hair-grease on a layman-guest one night, the cloying smell of bubble gum hidden in the pockets of a troop of Boy Scouts who came to sit (giggling and restless, whispering "Harro" as they filed past my seat) one afternoon. A startling whiff of whiskey on the breath of a magazine reporter, sent to interview the Boy Scouts about their brush with Zen. He stopped to talk to me as I was doing one of my less menial work jobs: pasting rice-paper patches on all the torn shoji screens. "It must be very difficult for you, living this monastic life every day," the reporter said. He had chapped lips and hangover-bags under his eyes, and he looked as if he could use another drink.

"Not at all," I said. "Once you get the rules and the rituals straight, it's easy. No decisions, no choices, nothing to plan. It's ever so much harder to live on your own."

Incense, of course: camphor and sandalwood, mandrake and myrrh. If the virgin's 3-D dreams of rapturous copulation spring from the collective unconscious, perhaps there is also a communal storehouse of sensory recollection. How else to explain the intoxicating intimacy of incense, the wishful Druid flashbacks, the strange sudden vision of Bubastis, the cat-goddess? "Good, thick, strong, stupefying incense smoke" (Browning) doesn't merely scent the air; it enchants it.

And at the same time every evening, there was the faint smell of smoke from the dark graveyard. It wasn't until the third or fourth day that I realized that the monks weren't piously lighting joss sticks for the old masters' graves, at all; they were sneaking a quick forbidden cigarette in the shadows of the mossy tombstones. That was one of my first inklings that monks were as frail and human as I was, and that being perfect desire-free beings was a struggle for them, too. I was shocked by the worldly truth about the foxfires in the graveyard, those will-o'-the-wisps of light, and I relinquished my wishful fantasies of fireflies and filial piety with reluctance, and regret.

On the fourth day, they concentrate on tastes ... Physiological fact aside, I believe the human taste buds are directly connected to the brain. Memory works in close collusion with the nostalgic palate, and that is why we often remember the chocolate mousse more clearly than the conversation. I can still taste that Sesshin in my mind; those simple country meals are among my favorite gastronomic memories, and whenever I return to Japan, one of my first acts is to follow my mnemonic tongue to a restaurant serving *shojin ryori*: vegetarian fare modeled on the temple food of Zen.

Every morning after zazen, while it was still dark, we were served the same salty, watery, delicious gruel. One day in mid-week there was a variation: thin translucent slices of green apple, with satiny chartreuse ribbons of peel, floating in the pale, granular murk. The sweetness, the sapidity, the sheer surprise; as I ate my first and second bowls of apple-spiced gruel, I realized the truth of one of the Buddha's basic teachings: that there can be more satisfaction in simplicity than in sophistication.

To someone who is accustomed to a Grand Hotel breakfast of liquorish soufflés, elaborate pastries, lurid compotes, and the flayed flesh of pig and cow and salmon, all washed down with sugary, stimulating drinks, rice gruel would probably seem like prisoner's fare, and the addition of a few slices of apple would hardly offset the agony of croissant-deprivation. But I felt very fortunate to have apples in my gruel, and even more fortunate to be able to appreciate them, and it occurred to me that I might end up learning more about life, and about living, in the dining room of the Sodo than in the meditation hall.

On some nights, after evening meditation, there were snacks donated by parishioners. The first night's treat was a chilled banana, so profoundly delicious that I thought for a moment I had experienced the epicurean equivalent of satori. On another night, I was given a poignant Occidental sandwich of cucumber and mayonnaise on soggy white bread, and once there was a sweet, warm, seedy tangerine, like a small ripe sun.

On the fifth day, they concentrate on sensations ... "In pain there is progress," I whispered to Jun-san as he limped by carrying a wooden bucket. He cocked his head, and winced. "No," he said. "In pain there is pain."

I wasn't walking too well myself; by the fifth day, I had developed permanent leg-cramps from so much sitting, and large lavender lotus-bruises had appeared on my thighs. My shoulders felt tight all the time, and I had grown bold enough to request the therapeutic whack of the jikijitsu's stick, once or twice a day. *The peculiar intimacy of beneficent violence*, I wrote, and it seemed aeons ago that I had feared the keisaku-patrol, or held my breath as they passed.

The pain was not exclusively physical; I was constantly amazed by the variety of mental experiences which the seemingly simple activity of zazen could yield. Sometimes there was a pleasant floating sensation, a benign sense of disembodied being which, I fancied, resembled astral projection, or a sentient coma. But there were some terrifying sessions, too, when my rambling mind, through a sort of passive auto-psychotherapy, would dredge up regretful, guilty memories (the kindness not done, the love not voiced, the gift refused) and I would blink back to reality at the end of forty minutes feeling singed and vivisected, as if my psyche had been held captive in a waffle iron. Sometimes, after a particularly harrowing trip through past faults and follies, I even shed a few tears, hastily camouflaged with synthetic hay-fever sneezes.

On the sixth day, they concentrate on keen intuitive power ... Once the initial etiquette-gaffes were behind me, I began to enjoy the Sesshin immensely. Sensory and intellectual stimuli aside, I liked having every activity planned for me, being a part of such an intriguing group, and spending almost every waking moment inside the walls of my beloved Sodo. The only major disappointment was that I had not been given a koan, nor was I permitted to speak with the roshi. I found it hard to apply intuitive power to my self-assigned koan (I was still gnawing on the catfish in the gourd) when everyone went shuffling off to sanzen, with Jun-san limping far behind in magnificent suffering. I felt left out, shunned, and avidly curious, and I would comfort myself with outlandish sanzen-fantasies involving Shinto cow-masks and absurd bilingual puns on the word "mu."

Even today I have no clear idea what goes on in a sanzen session; it is, for me, one of the last great mysteries of life. I may never know, for no monk, even an embittered Zen dropout, will ever discuss his koan, or his experiences with the roshi. I have often wondered, but have never dared to ask, whether any frustrated monk has ever tried to feign comprehension of his koan by taking the old stories as a model and behaving with the reckless assertiveness that historical Zen seems to condone, and reward. I did realize, as a result of my farfetched fantasies, that part of my fascination with sanzen was that it reminded me of the old Greek myths in which some omniscient, intimidating intellect, often in grotesque demonic-female form, waylays a hapless traveler and poses a seemingly unanswerable riddle.

On the seventh day, they concentrate on "Ahhhhh ..." When I first asked permission to participate in O-Zesshin, Toku-san had said, "You're welcome to work and eat and meditate with us, but you'll have to go back to Kaiko-in to sleep, of course."

"Of course," I said, but as the Sesshin-week progressed I became increasingly curious about what I was missing by leaving every evening at nine, just after the extended meditation session.

On the next-to-last night, I found out. "Can you stay a bit longer?" Zo-san asked when I was slipping on my shoes in the genkan.

"Absolutely," I said, wondering if I might have forgotten to clean one of the latrines. But Zo-san simply led me to the garden and said, "Just pick a spot, and sit." I looked around in amazement, for the moonlit temple garden was full of meditating monks. There were monks on the ground, monks on the rocks, even a monk or two in the trees. Nu-san appeared to be floating on a cloud of moss, like a big-eared Bodhisattva, and the bruised, bedeviled Jun-san was perched on a flat rock in the middle of the pond, looking like a large, pale, disenchanted frog.

I assumed the lotus position on the nearest unclaimed surface, a rough, squarish boulder, but I found it impossible to concentrate on the perplexing metaphysics of the catfish and the gourd. The setting was too picturesque, the moon too bright, the garden too fragrant, the frogs too loud. I thought instead about the essential essence, the gateless gate, the weightless weight: the somatic seventh-sense awareness of interlaced existence that was evoked as well by the Beatles, in their psychedelic-Sufi period, as by any alchemist or philosopher: *I am you as you are me as you are he and we are all together* ...

When it was over and Zo-san asked me how I had enjoyed my first alfresco zazen session, I just said "*Kaeru*," a word which can mean either "I'm going home" or "The frogs," and he smiled as if he understood exactly what I meant.

* * *

Every day during the noontime break, and again at five p.m., I used to race home to feed my three tiny ginger kittens. On the final day of the Sesshin, just as I was about to leave on my daily errand, Nu-san called me into his office. He handed me an ink painting of a single iris blossom, and explained that it was a gift from the roshi, "because he admires you." Why in the world would an eminent Zen master admire *me*? I thought, but I swallowed those words and accepted the painting with gratitude, and wonderment.

Just then the bell signaling the beginning of the next zazen session rang, and I realized that I wouldn't be able to run home and return in time. Oh well, I thought, I'll go on the next break.

We meditated, we raked leaves, we chanted, we sat some more. Finally, it was time for the five p.m. interlude, and I headed home to feed the kittens. As I passed Toku-san's room I noticed that the door was open, and then I heard a voice say, "Come in and have some tea." They were all there, the senior luminaries of the Sodo: Toku-san, Zo-san, Také-san, Nu-san, Den-san, Mon-san, Zan-san, all smiling and glowing and saying, "Dozo." These were the people I idolized and adored; how could I say no? The cats will be all right, I told myself as I joined the monks around the table. I'll feed them the minute I get home tonight, and I'll never ever neglect them again.

As I left the Sodo at nine p.m. I realized how much I was going to miss the ceremonial, predictable, ever-surprising progression of a Sesshin-day at the Sodo. At the moment, though, I was feeling completely euphoric. I had strived, I had survived, I had endured the pain, I had savored the pleasure, I had learned how to cleave to the shape of things, and no matter what happened, I would always have the memory of a week of ritual and mystery and medieval images. The supraliminal shock of satori had not struck, but I felt more acute and more aware, and very pleased with my progress.

My rice-paper parasol was exactly where I remembered having left it that dark, damp, early morning, on the right side of the genkan. Proudly, I picked up the umbrella and headed out the door, but when I emerged into the white-graveled courtyard the full moon was shining as brightly as a gold-leaf goddess, and the sky was perfectly clear.

HUNGRY GHOSTS

For every evil under the sun
There is a remedy, or there is none
If there be one, seek till you find it
If there be none, never mind it.

Mother Goose

—KYOTO

"Hi, kitties," I said cheerfully as I slid open the door. "*Tadaima*—I'm home!" The gratifying resolution of O-Zesshin had left me feeling energized, elated, and quite pleased with myself, but right away I noticed something odd. The windowless room was usually cool and dark and sarcophagal, but today it was uncomfortably warm and the floor was suffused with an orange glow, an almost caldera-like light. Oh, it's just the kotatsu, I thought. But it shouldn't be so hot, or so bright.

I lifted the quilt that covered the heat-table and slid out the box, and for a moment I thought there had been a surrealistic substitution: I had left three furry little kittens and had returned to find what appeared to be a trio of large baked prawns. Then I noticed that the control on the kotatsu-heater was pointing at High, not Low. All at once I understood the heartbreaking, horrific, irremediable thing that had happened, and I screamed, softly, and then began to cry.

The next thing I remember clearly is being out in the garden with Yukio, long after midnight. (I had telephoned him in Tokyo, and he caught the last bullet train to Kyoto.) We built a bonfire of dry grass and branches, and we were chanting the Hannya Shingyo while the tiny rice paper–wrapped bodies of Kachina, Kabuki, and Kiranosuke went up in smoke. Yukio was perfect: strong and wise and supportive, and (this was essential) completely asexual and unromantic in his gestures toward me.

"I'm a murderess, a butcher, an agent of death," I said after the pyre had dwindled to a heap of tragic ashes. "I don't deserve to live." We were sitting on a large rock waiting for the funeral incense we had stuck in the embers to burn down so we could bury the cat-cinders under a maple tree in the corner of the garden. The three undulant wisps of smoke that rose from the fat bundles of incense looked like ghosts, and I began to sob again.

"Don't be so hard on yourself," Yukio said, holding out his handkerchief. It was red-and-black paisley, a quintessential gaucho's bandanna. "Accidents happen, you know; you were careless, that's all, not evil. Humans are an imperfect species, and all we can ever hope to do is to learn from our mistakes."

"But if I had just double-checked the kotatsu before I left, or come home at noon like I was supposed to, or even at five o'clock. And all the time I was congratulating myself on my progress and my popularity, those poor little babies were slowly cooking to death. No, I wasn't just careless and absent-minded; I was vain, and self-absorbed, and unforgivably irresponsible."

"Look," Yukio said sternly, "those kittens were very young, dangerously young; they might have died even in a vet's care. And they certainly would have died in the bushes if you hadn't brought them home. At least you gave them a week of love, and milk, and a nice warm place … oops, sorry." We buried the ashes in silence, and laid some fresh chives Yukio had brought on the communal grave. "I couldn't find any catnip at this hour," he said, and I felt as if my physical heart had just been ripped in two. Yukio offered a few more rational, comforting comments, but everything he said just made me cry harder, so he finally gave up and went home. I was glad to see him leave; I wanted to be left alone with my soul-shattering grief, my gargantuan guilt, my stone-in-the-stomach feeling of intense self-loathing.

The next couple of days passed in a fog. At one point I remember asking Mondo, the cynic, how an enlightened practitioner of Zen would handle such a situation. "They wouldn't handle it at all," he said breezily. "They would have just left the cats to die in the bushes." Over and over, I flogged myself mentally for what I should have, could have, might have done to prevent the tragedy. The joys and agonies of

Sesshin were forgotten; indeed, my quest for spiritual self-improvement now seemed like a sordid joke, a narcissistic exercise in omphaloskepsis, a shamefully conceited, self-centered, dilettantish lark.

I could barely bring myself to write in my journal. Instead of being a repository of poetic images, it now became a vehicle for self-condemnation. "Evil woman," "demon of death," "morally bankrupt," "subhuman slime": those were some of the more charitable names I called myself. The first day I stayed in my room, mechanically writing kanji in a gridded practice-book, and sometimes I would look down and see that I had been doodling instead, drawing litters of cartoonish, smiling, jaunty-whiskered cats. I didn't eat or drink anything all day, and when the Oku-san appeared at my room sometime after dark with a tray of fragrant miso soup and roasted mochi I mumbled that I wasn't feeling well.

The next day I wakened to the realization that while it might be my prerogative to wallow in grief and regret for the rest of my life, I had no right, particularly in such close living quarters, to inflict my gloom and suffering on others. I still felt utterly devastated, though, and I was certain that I would never laugh again, much less attempt a joke or witticism myself. I was also certain that I would never again experience feelings of romantic love or desire. Indeed, it occurred to me with a negative-epiphany chill that the cat tragedy was my retribution for having mixed the two mysteries, sex and Zen. I should never have tried to juggle romantic pleasure with purity of mind and spirit, I thought, and now I was being punished for having recklessly juxtaposed my dueling selves—the potential courtesan and the partly-nun—without allowing time for a psychic costume change.

During those dark post-mortem days, I remembered something a macrobiotic weaver named Ariel had said to me once as we sat in a colorful Cambridge kitchen picking over green-enameled colanders full of pinto beans. Incidentally, when I complimented Ariel on her name, she confessed that she had changed it, unofficially, from Angela. I had suspected as much, for those were the days of rampant reinvention of self, when Ginnie became Gudrun, Calvin became Caliban, Cheryl became Scheherezade, and Gerald Greenberg became Gwyddno Garanhair. I should admit, in candor, that one day in 1965 I tacked a hand-made name card which read "Basilica Baudelaire" on the door of my Central Square apartment. An hour later I sheepishly removed the card, and reverted to my own unglamorous name.

"You have to dig yourself before you can dig anyone else," Ariel-*née*-Angela told me that day, while the organic short-grain brown rice simmered in a huge cast-iron kettle. "That's the Delphic Motto." The Delphic motto I had always heard was "Know Thyself," but I gave Ariel the benefit of the doubt. Perhaps her oracle held court in Delphi, Indiana, not in ancient Greece. At any rate, I now saw the wisdom of that updated oracular pronouncement, and I found it hard to imagine that I would be able to dig myself—absent-minded docent of the dark side, cat-killer, Shiva with a blue dress on—ever again.

Heartbreak and nausea go hand in clammy hand, and on the second day, I wasn't sure I was ever going to feel like eating again, either. But I was haunted by the look of hurt and bewilderment on the Okusan's sweet face when I had refused the soup and mochi the day before, so I decided that while I would continue to fast, I would not refuse any unsolicited offers of food. It was, I reasoned, more important not to hurt other people's feelings than to cling to a rigid course of self-abnegation. This was the origin of what I came to call the *isoro danjiki*, the freeloader fast, although freeloader is a somewhat misleading term in this context since it implies deliberate sponging or leechiness.

The truth was, I was secretly hoping that no one would offer me anything to eat or drink all day, for I wanted to suffer for my crime. But it didn't work out that way. First there was a knock on my door; it was Inaka Hakamune, off to school in his paramilitary uniform of scratchy black wool with gold buttons, dropping off my share (he said sweetly) of his latest haul from home: a miniature bag of glutinous rice and an absolutely convincing trompe l'oeil egg made from colored agar-agar and confectionary bean-paste. Not the most bizarre breakfast I've ever had, I thought as I cooked the sticky rice and sliced the ersatz egg. But definitely close.

Although I didn't feel like dancing, or being social, or seeing my reflection in a full-length mirror, I dragged myself to my weekly Bharata Natyam lesson. I performed the steps and sang the cadence-chants by rote, without feeling, but Vasanthamala didn't seem to notice. On our break, after a discussion of past lives (hers) and present problems (mine), I asked the ritual question, "So, when will I be allowed to start dancing with bells?" then waited morosely for the inevitable answer: "When you are ready."

To my surprise, Vasanthamala said, "Today." She reached into her mirrored bag and pulled out a set of silver bells attached to red ankle-tie ribbons. "Put on your bells, my dear, and let's dance," she said, and this time I leaped about with verve, and gratitude. "Until next week, then," Vasanthamala said at the end of the lesson. "I'll be here with bells on," I said, and I smiled for the first time in days.

* * *

I hadn't been home for more than two minutes when there was a knock on my door. It was the Okusan, bearing an amazing feast: miso soup with toasted mochi; steamed daikon-radish slices garnished with shiso leaves; sesame-rice balls wrapped in seaweed, with tiny tart *umeboshi* plums hidden inside; a deep-fried tofu-and-vegetable cake; takuan pickles; and a pot of *kukocha* tea, brewed from wild grasses.

"Did you like anything in particular?" the Okusan asked when I returned the tray.

"I liked everything in particular," I said, and the Okusan looked pleased.

"By the way," she said, "Madoka Dekiboshi called and asked me to remind you that she's expecting you around seven."

"Expecting me where?" I started to say, and then I remembered. About a month before, Madoka Dekiboshi (an ex-geisha turned oil painter who was a friend of the Okusan's and, according to neighborhood gossip, the mistress of my company-president pupil, Mr. Shakudo) had invited me to come to dinner on this date, and of course I had forgotten. Much as I liked both Madoka and Mr. Shakudo, I was disappointed by the timing; the freeloader fast was supposed to be a rigorous form of penance, and instead it was turning out to be an epicurean bacchanal.

Madoka Dekiboshi lived just around the corner from Kaiko-in, in a small wooden cottage set in a garden filled with roses. Mr. Shakudo was already there when I arrived, and while Madoka labored in the kitchen, singing softly to herself, the Shacho and I worked on the speech he would be giving at the end of the summer to a delegation from the United Nations which was going to visit his factory. Everyone, including Madoka, addressed Mr. Shakudo as Shacho-san, which means "Company President." It is a term of great prestige and respect in Japan, even if your "corporation" has only one employee, and that is you.

We had been working on the speech for months, and both the prose and Shakudo Shacho's delivery had become quite polished. Now he was beginning to worry about extemporaneous questions from his English-speaking audience. "What if they ask me something and I don't understand?" he fretted. "Oh my God—what if they want to use the lavatory?" After he had mastered the English-language directions to his factory's restroom ("Down the hall, first door on the left"), we took a break.

"I'm very proud of Madoka," said Mr. Shakudo. With typical restraint, he referred to her as Dekiboshi-san. "She has worked very hard at her painting, and she has just been offered a one-woman show at a big department store, in early September. I wish you could come; it's on the day of the United Nations visit, so you could help me, too." I explained about my ship's departure date, and the Shacho looked so downcast that I quickly changed the subject.

"What's that?" I asked, pointing to a tiny miniature shrine.

"That's a shrine to Benten, goddess of beauty, and of the arts," said Mr. Shakudo. "Madoka loves the old Shinto rituals; she prays every day, and she often takes plates of rice and beans to the Inari shrine, for the fox-messengers of the gods."

The Shacho picked up a *Japan Times*, and I went to ask Madoka if she needed help. "Always!" she laughed, and while we peeled long, warty cucumbers and grated foamy *tororo* (mountain potato) we talked about her alliance with Shakudo Shacho. "We've been together for a very long time," Madoka said when I remarked on their almost tele-pathic rapport. "We thought of getting married when his wife passed away, but we decided that it would be more romantic, and more practi-cal, to maintain two separate households. Fortunately I was able to save some money when I was a geisha, and now my paintings are beginning to sell, so I'm financially independent, and it just works out better this way for us. Everyone is scandalized, of course," she added with a sly smile, "but that's their problem, isn't it?" I felt great admiration for this strong, kind, talented woman, and I felt something else, too: a stirring of proto-feminist (or proto-humanist) indignation that a pair of indepen-dent, resourceful people, who also happened to be a loving but non-married couple, had been labeled for life by their narrow-minded contemporaries—including, no doubt, great many married but non-loving couples—as "a company president and his mistress."

We ate at a low table, around a vase of plush-petaled American

Beauty roses. The menu was completely vegetarian, imaginatively conceived, exquisitely prepared, and artistically presented; symphonic, sophisticated combinations of miso, tofu, rice, beans, vegetables, herbs, spices, and pickles, served on an assortment of rose-patterned plates and dishes. The crockery, like the faces of the monks at the Sodo, came in an assortment of shapes: round, square, oval, rectangular, even octagonal. I was reminded of an unattributed *senryu* poem I had seen in an anthology: "European food—/ Every blasted plate/ Is round!"

At the end, when I was expecting at most a cup of tea, Madoka turned off the lights and emerged from the kitchen carrying a lavishly decorated cake, vanilla with buttercream frosting and piped-on roses, lit with pink and yellow birthday candles. "Today is a special day for geisha," she said. "We usually celebrate with a rice-flour *kotobuki* cake, but I thought you would prefer something more familiar."

I don't deserve such kindness, I thought, but I just said, "I've never seen such a beautiful cake."

* * *

Life went on; I attended to my studies and responsibilities, feigned cheerfulness for the usual stream of visitors, and ate what I was offered: mostly tea, sweets, senbei, and an occasional tangerine. On the fourth day, I began to feed myself again, for I realized that the relief from my continuing misery lay not in the masochistic comfort of punishment but in the difficult process of growth. On that same day, I went out and bought a lightbulb; the overhead bulb had burned out on the night the kittens died, and I had played along with that sledgehammer symbolism by living without electric light for several days. I spent a lot of time trying to figure out the lessons to be learned from the tragedy, but all I came up with was "Be careful; Be conscious; Be diligent, Be perfect."

"Gomen kudasai," called a male voice at the door one afternoon. It was Saku-san, the husky, appealing monk from the North country. My heart leaped, for I hoped he might be bringing more cats, but it turned out that he had come to invite me to go for a walk. This was a first, and ordinarily I would have been thrilled, but at the time I was more interested in cats and redemption than in romance, or friendship. We walked beside the glittering green river, and Saku-san told me about his home village, and the pretty little temple he would inherit when his father retired. After a while he said, "Would you like something to drink?"

"Sure," I said. I couldn't help thinking that this was the closest I had ever come to having a date with a monk, and that all things being equal (which they emphatically were not) I wouldn't have had any trouble at all falling in love with this gentle, magnificent-looking young man. Saku-san emerged from a nearby store with two bottles of *ramune*, an odd carbonated beverage which tastes a bit like bubble gum and comes in curvilinear blue or green glass bottles stoppered with a glass marble that drops into the bottle's hollow torso when the storekeeper disengages it with a special opener. The empty bottles make excellent flower vases, or maracas.

"Shall we sit on the riverbank?" I said, and Saku-san looked suddenly distressed.

"Please forgive me," he said, "but I just realized that it wouldn't look good for a novice unsui to be seen drinking in public with a woman. In fact, I probably shouldn't even be walking around with you." I concealed the opened bottles in my satchel, and we started back toward Zenzenji. I offered to keep a respectable three-pace distance, but Saku-san insisted on walking side by side. He was dressed in his loose calf-length blue koromo, and I was wearing a long blue skirt and dark blue jersey, and I couldn't help thinking that we made a splendid-looking couple.

We ended up drinking the tepid ramune, somewhat anticlimactically, back in the courtyard of Kaiko-in. "I was wondering—" Saku-san said, and just then Mondo-san called me inside to answer a long-distance telephone call. When I returned to the front garden Saku-san was gone, but there was a slightly crumpled daisy (which he must have had hidden in his sleeve) stuck in my empty ramune bottle.

That was the last time Saku-san and I were ever alone together, and I was touched that he had risked his reputation by taking a walk with me in public. With most of the monks I felt that the dynamics were: Enlightened Beings (them) tolerating a struggling one-celled organism (me). With Saku-san I was certain, from the yearning way he sometimes looked at me, that there was an element of subjunctive boy-meets-girl in our casual friendship: a sense of what might have been, if things had been different. But they weren't; he was a propriety-conscious monk, training to take over his father's country temple, and I was a female foreigner in love, with problematic simultaneity, with the Zenzenji Sodo, with the glorious Yukio Yanagida, and (whenever I happened to see him) with an elegant enigma named Fuji Mugen.

With Zan-san, the involuntary co-star of my embarrassing, unforget-table Sesshin-dream, I felt a different sort of imbalance; "Devadasi meets Bodhisattva," I called it. I felt that the dream-monk saw me as Woman, perhaps even as Temptation, and there were times (like the day when he passed me on the slope and said, simply, "Ah, it's you!") when I felt he might be wishing he were free to be man instead of paragon. The odd thing was, I wasn't really attracted to Zan-san in my waking state, but the casting director of the subconscious mind makes some strange decisions.

One wet gray mid-morning, the Okusan knocked on my door. "Please come to a tea party," she said. I followed her through the low-roofed narrow halls of the living quarters of Kaiko-in, through the kitchen, and into the Obaasan's room. I had never been in that room before, and I was enchanted by the many-layered view: the moonstoned eaves, the lush rained-on garden, the dragon-tiled roof of the temple at the top of the hill, the soft ochre-green hills beyond.

On the low lacquer table was a rusty-glazed Bizen-ware vase contain-ing a ruffly lavender morning glory, and as we sat sipping our tea the Okusan said, "That flower reminds me of you, do you know why?" The first remark that sprang to mind was a self-deprecating joke ("Because it climbs the wall, and wilts before noon?") but I forced myself to give a more gracious, thoughtful answer. "Um, is it because of the poem about the bucket stolen by a morning glory?"

"Exactly," said the Okusan. "To me, that poem sums up your charac-ter perfectly."

"Thank you," I said, for it was a very nice compliment indeed.

The morning-glory haiku was written by a woman poet named Kagano Chiojo, and it is often cited in books about Zen as an example of a metaphysical moment of truth, of what D. T. Suzuki calls "mutual seeing." The inspiration: a poet went to her well one morning and found the bucket entangled with a morning glory in full, dewy bloom. Not wanting to disturb the flower, she went to borrow water from a neighbor. The poem (in Suzuki's straightforward translation) goes like this: "Oh, morning glory!/Bucket taken captive/I beg for water." Suzuki discussed the poem in terms like "bifurcation of subject-object" and "discrimina-tive understanding," but I saw it more simply: as a captivating nature-mystic vignette, and an illustration of the values I hoped to live by.

It was a lovely tea party, but while the Obaasan was as pleasant and serene and beautiful as ever, I couldn't help noticing that she seemed to have shrunk since our last meeting. She looked very fragile and tired, but still she kept up a spirited conversation, talking about flowers and poetry and the way Kyoto used to be before the cars and smokestacks and buses began to pollute the historic air, before ugly concrete towers disrupted the architectonic rhythm of the shrine-and-temple skyline.

The Okusan had outdone herself once again, with *Abekawa mochi* (soft rice-cakes coated with sweetened soy flour, the color of caramels), roasted lute-shaped squash glazed with white miso, and dense, rich-tasting tofu made from sesame seeds. Just as we were scraping our plates, the Osho-san came in, dressed in his rumpled blue salaryman's suit, with a corporate pin on the lapel, where there could have been a rose. "Tadaima," he said, "I'm home," and we responded with the customary response: "Okaeri nasai" ("Welcome home"). I thought then, as I often had, about the Japanese ritualization of quotidian comings and goings, givings and partakings, and how it creates a stable, comfortable, graceful framework for the rampant unpredictability of life.

"I came home early because there's a ceremony today," the Osho-san said, before vanishing behind a sliding door. A few minutes later he appeared in his priest's guise, wearing a splendid robe of peridot satin embossed with a pinwheel pattern and edged in silver brocade. The Osho-san had a few minutes to spare before the ceremony, so he sat down, drank a cup of tea, and told a poignant story: "I was orphaned when I was a boy," he said, "and from then on I lived at the Sodo, but I went off to school every day like everyone else. I never felt particularly aware of how unconventional my home life was, except at lunchtime. But then the other kids would unpack their metal boxes full of rice and fish and pickles, and all I had was a couple of stalks of hollow bamboo filled with rice gruel, and a little jug of tea."

* * *

Around the corner from Kaiko-in there was a fruit stand selling pale-fleshed melons and tangerines and summer berries in rough-woven wooden baskets. One day I put a basket of strawberries out on the verandah to ripen, and forgot all about them. The next day when I went to retrieve the basket, I saw that the berries had been turned into impromptu jam by the summer sun.

That night, I dreamed of a strange intricate garden full of abandoned kittens. I carried nine ginger-striped cats home in a box, but then I accidentally left the box in the sun for an entire day. When I finally looked in the box the cats had melted, and nothing remained except a pale-orange puddle of semiliquid DNA, the apricot jam of life. It should have been a nightmare, but it wasn't, and for some reason I awakened feeling full of hope.

Ironically, where before I had dreaded finding more cats, I now became obsessed with the desire to save every thrown-away cat in the universe, or at least in the neighborhood. I combed the grounds of Zenzenji two or three times a day, peering under every bush and pursuing every muffled peep and squeak, but the source of the sound always turned out to be a low-nesting pigeon, or a rusty bicycle wheel. Zenzenji had evidently become a cat-free zone, so I expanded my search to nearby pockets of greenery: the snake-goddess shrine; the shrine with the bronze boar-statue; the red-gated fox shrine; and the temple of the water lilies, whose crew-cut priest drove a lily-white Mercedes. But there were no cats anywhere, and although my sense of humor and desire for romance had begun to assert themselves again, I was still haunted by cat-ghosts, and by a feeling of secret desolation.

One early evening I was trudging dejectedly up the Sodo slope, with the bamboo basket which I had hoped to fill with abandoned kittens hanging empty from my hand. As I passed the Sodo, I noticed a sweet, spicy, vaguely familiar smell in the air. They're burning leaves, I thought, and I felt a pang of envy for the ritual, the clear-cut goals, the insularity, the fellowship of the monastic life. Then, with a shock, I recognized the aroma: it was piñon incense.

My heart, which had been running on empty, suddenly filled to the halfway-mark with happiness, and gratitude: Zo-san hadn't thrown away my Southwestern incense, after all! For a moment I was transported back to the supernaturally starry night-skies of Sedona and Santa Fe: vast blue-black backdrops for the cool platinum moon, with long wisps of cloud-smoke trailing across the sky like rattlesnake ghosts, or the shawl of a long-dead dancer. But wait, I thought; surely one little box of piñon incense couldn't generate such an intense billow of fragrance? I passed the Sodo, breathing deeply with every step, and walked up the path leading to the walled sub-temple where Eisai once lived.

I had discovered one day in the early, voyeuristic stages of my infatuation with the Sodo that if I stood on a large ornamental rock at the top of the hill I could look directly into the monastery garden. What I saw now as I teetered on that spying-rock was a row of incense braziers, placed at intervals along the open hall and on the back porch of the Zendo: the part of the monastery that was closest to Kaiko-in, and to my room. This was a highly unusual configuration, and I realized, as my joy-gauge edged upward toward F, that the mass burning of piñon incense must be a conscious act of kindness, intended to cheer me up. When I thanked Zo-san later, he said, "Oh, everyone loves your incense. It makes us feel like cowboys camping out in the desert!"

Another thing the sibylline Ariel said to me in that steamy macrobiotic kitchen on Garden Street (after confiding that she had just met her true love, a carpenter named Timocles—né Tim—in the organic-produce department of a natural foods store on Newbury Street) was, "You should never go looking for love; when the time is right, love will always find you." I had already confirmed the verity of that country-and-western maxim, several times over, but it was in Kyoto that I first became aware of its corollary: "You should never go looking for cats, either."

One day I was practicing the devadasi stomp on a flat stone walkway in the secret garden, when I heard a burst of crying-animal sounds. The flurry of plaintive squeals was so brief that I thought it might have been my wishful imagination, but when I headed for home I heard the sound again, and then I spotted the source: a litter of five kittens huddled under a shiny-leafed bush, mewing and lurching blindly around and, most pitiful of all, nuzzling one another with their little succubus-mouths, searching for their mother, and her milk. I gathered my long skirt into an upside-down parachute, and placed the tiny kittens inside. Two were gray and white, and the other three, uncannily, were ginger-striped replicas of Kabuki, Kachina, and Kiranosuke. I took the quivering kittens home and cleaned them up, made them a cozy bed, ran out to buy some milk, and fed them one by one until they fell asleep. I decided to call them all Neko-chan, or Kitty; it seemed like a good compromise between anonymity and over-attachment.

It isn't often that you get a second chance, a Take Two, an opportunity, as Rilke put it, "to make good from afar the forgotten gesture"; and if you can make good from a-near, so much the better. I put the cats under the table, stuck my loudest-ticking alarm clock in their box to simulate a mother cat's heartbeat, turned the kotatsu on Low, scotch-taped the control in place just to be safe, said a prayer of gratitude to every god I could think of, and turned out the light.

BUT NEVER JAM TODAY

What should we think of dogs' monasteries,
hermit cats, vegetarian tigers?

Cyril Connolly
The Unquiet Grave

—KYOTO

"Fall down eight times, get up seven. No, wait! It's the other way around!" Toku-san laughed at my silly mistake, and I laughed too. We were sitting on the back verandah of the Sodo, overlooking the vegetable garden and the doghouses, talking about the resiliency of the human spirit as embodied in the unfloorable Daruma-doll, and (I thought to myself) in my own recent recovery of emotional equilibrium after the devastating loss of the three little kittens. "Well, I'd better go," I said. I had been there for nearly an hour, basking in the midsummer sun and watching the garden grow: deep purple eggplant, lacy-topped carrots, ruby-veined chard (a vegetarian vampire's dream). I would have liked to stay, quite literally, forever, but since that was not an option I didn't want to risk wearing out my welcome.

"Don't go just yet," said Toku-san. "We're about to have some tea." I knew that afternoon tea was not a regular part of the Sodo's day, but I figured that someone must have given the monastery some sweets—a not infrequent occurrence. I myself had delivered a large box of spongy maple-leaf-wrapped rice cakes filled with bean-paste several weeks before on May 5, Boy's Day. That holiday is celebrated with particular fervor in a country which places such primal store on its male lineage; the season is marked by the exhilarating sight of scallopy-scaled green and orange and red cloth carp flying from the thatched roofs of farm-

houses and the bleak balconies of condominiums, one carp for every son
in the family, and by the consumption of the maple-leaf treats which I
brought to the Sodo. My reasoning, I explained to a startled Zo-san as I
handed him the box, was that all men, including monks, are boys at
heart.

Now it was June, and the carp had all been taken down and stored
away for the following year. (Girls have their official Day in Japan, too,
on April 3, but it may be another generation or two before every female
is allowed to have her *day*.) Jun-san, the shy young monk who had so
much trouble with the lotus position, limped out of the kitchen carrying
a tray containing several cups of tea; Zo-san and Nu-san joined us on
the verandah, and then Den-san and Mon-san (who were not just co-jiki-
jitsu but best friends as well) straggled in.

As we sat sipping our tea, Jun-san returned with a large cardboard
box. Inside were two layers of individually-wrapped *jamupan* (*pan* is the
Japanese word for bread, borrowed from the Portuguese, and *jam* is an
unaltered English loan-word). Jamupan is an Occidental-style confection, but I have never encountered it outside of Japan. It consists of
sweet, dense, eggy bread wrapped around a large glob of seedy, sugary
strawberry jam. I had tried the rolls once before, and, to borrow a phrase
from Alice, while I am quite fond of jam (or at least of ginger mar
malade), I do not care for jamupan.

Toku-san was holding out a plastic-wrapped jam roll, smiling and saying "Dozo." There are so many things I should have said, so many things
I could have done. I could have taken the roll and eaten it, just to be
polite. I could have taken the bun and nibbled at the edges, then carried
the rest home to share, discreetly, with the pigeons. Or I could have
pleaded a full stomach, and asked if I might have one for later.

What I did do was truly awful, and boorish, and gauche. I said, "No,
thank you, I'm trying to cut down on my intake of sugar." *O grim, insuf-
ferable wench, O self-righteous drudge, O ungrateful guest with the social
skills of a slug!* (That isn't what Toku-san said to me, although he may
have been thinking something similar; it's a direct quote from my diary,
written later that day. Now that I read those lines again, they sound a bit
like off-grade St.-John Perse.) Toku-san just said mildly, "Oh, I didn't
know that," and then he unwrapped the bun I had refused and tossed it
to Shiro, who ate it in one socially-mellifluent bite.

After that a pall seemed to fall over the previously cheery gathering;

the monks talked among themselves, but not to me, and I thought I saw some bemused glances passing behind my back. Awkwardly, I took my leave; when I said "Gochisosama deshita" (the set-phrase, uttered after any repast, meaning "It was an honorable feast") the words sounded hollow and mocking. No one seemed to notice my departure; Zo-san raised a languid golden hand, Toku-san, who was deep in conversation with Nu-san, nodded vaguely, and even Shiro chose not to accompany me to the gate as he usually did.

On the way out, I met Jun-san, the perpetually injured monk who had served the snack. "I feel terrible," I told him. "I didn't eat the jamu-pan, and now I'm afraid I hurt everyone's feelings."

"Oh dear," he said solicitously, "you don't like jamupan?"

"Well, it's just that I've been eating too much sugar these days, and I decided to cut down," I said. It was the truth, but it was also a lie, for if the snack in question had been something I liked (a piece of cinnamon mochi, or a Bendicks Bittermint) I would have jumped on it like a blue-jay on a sunflower seed.

"Oh dear," Jun-san repeated. "I wish I had known. Toku-san sent me to the market especially to buy jamupan; he thought you would like it because it would remind you of America. It is an American delicacy, isn't it?"

Then it was my turn to moan. "Oh dear," I said. "Oh dear, oh dear, oh dear."

The jamupan disaster, with all its microcosmic implications, was good for another bout of depression, despair and self-loathing. I avoided the Sodo, and if I saw a bonfire at one gate, I took a different route, for I had learned that where there was smoke, there were monks.

One day, I developed a craving for kappa-maki, so I walked to the nearest sushi shop and ordered two rolls. I watched with salivatory antic-ipation as the *itamae-san* spread the vinegary rice on the greenish-black seaweed, painted a bright stripe of chartreuse wasabi (horseradish), placed several matchstick-sized pieces of cucumber down the center of the stripe, sprinkled a thin layer of toasted sesame seeds over the top, and then rolled the mixture in a miniature bamboo screen and cut it into bite-sized pieces. (Those sushi-rolling screens always reminded me of the reed-blinds the women in *The Tale of Genji* languished behind while waiting for a visit from some elegant, inappropriate lover.)

The sushi maker placed my order in a small box of balsa wood, along with a tiny fish-shaped container of soy sauce and a generous handful of pickled ginger, accepted my payment of a hundred yen, and sent me off with a cheery "Oki ni!" (Kansai dialect for "thank you"). I hadn't had sushi in ages, and I could hardly wait to get home and dig in. I started to head back by my usual route, but I saw smoke near the gate, and not wanting to meet any of the monks before whom I had disgraced myself, I took an alternate path.

As I walked through the gate by the lower playground, I saw that the monochromatic old man was at home. He was sitting cross-legged atop his pile of rags and bags, dressed in a brown kimono and matching beret, smoking a cigarette stub in a yellowed ivory holder, and looking uncannily like a literary aristocrat *en déshabillé*. "Good evening, young miss," he said, in a dignified manner. "Thank you again for the delicious banana." I was touched that he had remembered, and I wondered what he would be having for dinner on this humid summer evening.

I walked on, past an inscrutable locked pavilion with tall curved windows, and then I stopped and looked back. The homeless man had climbed down off his perch and was shambling toward the public restroom at the edge of the playground. Impulsively, I ran back to the gate and put my box of sushi under a package of Seven Stars cigarettes (as I had suspected, the pack was filled with salvaged butts), and then I ran away again. I continued running through the grounds, feeling very happy and virtuous, and as I barreled around the corner before the Sodo slope, I almost collided with Toku-san.

"Hooo!" he said, in his usual good-humored way. "Where are you going in such a hurry?"

"Just home," I said.

"And where have you been?"

"To the sushi shop."

"Oh, was it good?"

"Well, I didn't exactly eat it," I said, and then I explained what had just happened. I remember thinking that my altruism toward the old vagabond might somehow neutralize my thoughtless refusal of the jamupan, but all Toku-san said was, "That old man would probably prefer *maguro* (tuna) sushi! I doubt if he's a vegetarian."

"That reminds me," I said. I apologized for my behavior at the tea party, then added, "I've decided that I will begin eating sugar again, at least when it's offered to me. And especially when it's offered by

someone I really think the world of, and would never want to offend."
Toku-san nodded thoughtfully, and then he said goodnight. I never had
the slightest idea what he was thinking; I found his remarks and his
silences to be equally cryptic, but I felt that I had taken a step toward
making amends.

When I got home and slid open the door to my room, it took several
seconds to make sense of the scene I saw before me. The five kittens
were running around, covered with what looked like wet plaster, and
there were bits of the same ivory-colored plaster all over the floor. I
glanced at the ceiling, but it was intact. Then I saw the empty dish in
my cooking-alcove and remembered that it had contained a block of
fresh tofu. I began to laugh. "I guess you kids are ready for solid food," I
said, and then, still laughing, I cleaned up all the high-protein pawprints,
bathed and fed the kittens, and put them in their box for a nap. That
was when I noticed the gift-wrapped package on my table, amid the
clutter of books and papers and art supplies.

The box contained a small ceramic statue of Bodhidharma
(Daruma), the size of my thumb, with perfectly-rendered "sacred fool"
features, wearing a saffron-colored robe. A tiny card was enclosed: "To
Deborah," it read, "from your hedonistic friend, Clementine Josephine
Holcomb." It took me a moment to realize that the gift was from C. J.; I
wondered why she had signed her full name, which she had always
refused to tell me, and I also wondered why she disliked that name so
much. I thought it had a languid, genteel Southern ring, but perhaps
she had grown tired of the inevitable "Oh my darling" jokes.

I was touched by C. J.'s thoughtful gift, and I also felt a little guilty. I
hadn't seen her for over a month; at first because I hadn't wanted to
share my unhappiness over the kittens, and later because I just didn't
feel like hanging out at Popeye or going to rock concerts or being con-
fronted with the tripartite personification of the pursuit of worldly plea-
sures. I was still torn between asceticism and desire, and my meetings
with C. J., who evidently felt no such ambivalence, always seemed to
intensify the confusion. After a while C. J. had stopped calling and dropping by, and our last conversation had ended with her saying, "Well, just
give a holler if you ever want to do something wicked and frivolous."

I suddenly realized what a good friend C. J. was, and the differences
in interests and attitude that had seemed so important now struck me as
petty and trivial. I rushed out to the nearest public telephone, which

happened to be at the coffee shop where Toozie had first met Muni Nigamomo, the "Om Mani Padme Hung" monk. I dialed C. J.'s number, and Ramon answered. We chatted for a moment, and I thought he sounded unusually cool, or chagrined. "May I speak to C. J. ?" I said.

"She's gone," said Ramon.

"Oh, then could you please ask her to call me tonight? I'll be home all evening."

"No, I mean she's *gone*, back to North America."

"What are you talking about? She came by today and left a present for me."

"Well, I guess she was on her way to the airport."

"I don't understand," I said.

"You and also me," said Ramon, and it occurred to me then that he might have been sincerely, monogamously in love with C. J.

"Well, is she coming back?"

"Maybe on her honeymoon," Ramon said bitterly, and then, slowly and painfully, like a sea tortoise laying its eggs, he excreted the distressing details. C. J.'s old boyfriend from Fort Worth had come all the way to Japan just to propose to her, and she had been so overwhelmed that she had accepted, and they had gone home together.

"What was his name?" I asked. Ramon hesitated, and I heard him sigh.

"I think maybe Trevor Asthma," he said. "No, Asmus. Trevor Asmus."

"And"—I knew it was tactless and superficial, but I couldn't resist— "what did he look like?"

"I don't know," Ramon said glumly. "Like a cinema star, maybe, or a professional soccer player. Yellow hair and a pretty face and a large neck, like a cow, and very many muscles. Too many, I think, for my opinion."

"I have an idea," I said. "Don't go anywhere." I ran to the open market and bought the makings of okonomiyaki, and then I hopped on my bicycle and rode to Cherry Blossom Lane. The big house felt very empty without C. J.'s effervescent, binding presence, and Ramon and Arasuke seemed stunned and bewildered, like two small boys who have just had their tricycles stolen. I made amateurish but edible vegetable okonomiyaki, while the men drank large quantities of Sapporo beer. It was obvious that they were feeling hurt, and betrayed, and deprived of the woman they both loved, and they seemed intent on holding a romantic wake. This made for a lugubrious, introspective evening, and by the time I finished cleaning up the kitchen, the two jilted lovers had passed the synthetic-cheer stage of intoxication and were wallowing in maudlin self-pity. I tiptoed out without saying goodbye, and rode home under the stars.

* * *

The next day I taught English conversation for five hours straight; the high point was when I overheard little Chika-chan say, "Sometimes Deborah-sensei seems a little bit like a foreigner to me," and Kiko-chan replied gravely, "No, I'm absolutely certain she's Japanese."

Afterwards I went to the Zen library to see if they had any books about Daruma. They didn't, but as I was reading a primer on Zen I came across a passage that caught my eye. "*An important part of life in the monastery is the performance of secret good deeds. The benefit of the practice of* inji-gyo *(secret virtue) derives from the satisfaction of the deed itself, and from doing it in secret, not out of the desire to impress others.*" So that was it: I had committed acts of kindness and generosity, but I had negated the virtue by bragging about my actions to others. I had, as T. S. Eliot put it, been doing "the right thing for the wrong reason."

Most of the monks had gone home for summer break, so I had been practicing daily zazen out in the back garden of Kaiko-in, chanting the Hannya Shingyo and using a long stick of dark-green incense to measure a session. Sometimes Mondo or Saba-san sat with me; sometimes I sat alone, with a purring kitten on my lap. (The earth keeps some vibration going/There in your heart, and that is you ...) I missed the Zendo, but even when I heard the sounds that indicated the monks had resumed their usual routine, I felt awkward about showing up uninvited. I was elated when the Okusan gave me a basket of fruit to take to Zo-san one day, and I timed my visit so that I might be invited to stay for zazen.

There was a strangely unmonastic Chinese-restaurant smell coming from the Sodo kitchen; I noticed it as soon as I walked in the back door. Také-san was standing over the stove, shaking a pan full of strips of beef speckled with garlic and ginger while two younger monks looked on, salivating visibly. "Meat!" I said, unable to conceal my surprise.

"For the dog," one of the young monks said hastily, and I thought of the famous priest who accepted meat for the metaphorical dog in his belly.

Just then Zo-san came in; I handed him the fruit, then asked if I was too late for zazen. "There's no zazen tonight," he said. "The roshi is out of town. But you're welcome to go and sit in the Zendo by yourself." While the roshi's away, the monks will play, I thought as I walked down the zigzag hall. I hadn't realized how long that hall was until I had to clean it from end to end during Sesshin with a damp rag the size of a lace handkerchief.

It took longer than usual to calm myself down that day, for I was thrilled to have the place to myself. After a few minutes of jumbled free-association I managed to attain a state of suspended thought. I concentrated, out of habit, on the catfish-in-a-gourd riddle; I was sick of the koan, but I still loved the image. After a while I heard a buzzing sound at my ear. I thought at first that it was some faraway urban sound-effect, and then I realized it was a mosquito. I felt it sting my bare shoulder and a moment later I had an overpowering urge to scratch, but I concentrated even harder, and after that I didn't hear or feel the mosquito at all.

Much later, I became aware of a presence in the door. I opened my eyes and there was Zo-san. "It's been two hours," he said. "Your legs will fall off, like Daruma-san."

"Oh!" I said. "I didn't realize it had been so long." Zo-san smiled, his radiant sweet-souled smile, and then he went away.

I felt oddly detached, as if I were watching myself from above; I was dizzy, and when I tried to stand up I discovered that my feet were asleep. I hobbled around in agony, walking off the cramp, and then I stepped into the blue-violet light of the doorway and saw that both my arms were covered with hive-like bumps crowned with tiny rubies of blood, where the sanguinary insects had feasted on my flesh. This was an uncanny echo of a story I had read the day before in some musty old Zen book, about a single-minded monk who meditated while the mosquitoes "gorged to satiety" on his unconscious flesh. When the monk finally emerged from his meditation-trance, his body was covered with bubbles of blood, and he resembled a giant peeled pomegranate.

My first impulse was to walk out through the kitchen wearing my blood-rubies like a badge. Then I remembered the principle of secret virtue, so I dipped my handkerchief in the basin outside and carefully wiped away all the evidence. No one was around when I left the Sodo, but I thought I heard the sound of female laughter from within the labyrinth of thin-walled rooms, and I couldn't help wondering what other rules might be relaxed when the roshi was out of town.

I walked out through the terracotta courtyard, and as I passed the doghouse I saw that Shiro was asleep inside, with only his foxy snout poking out. I noticed, too, that his dish contained ordinary mud-colored kibbles. This confirmed my suspicion that the meat on the stove hadn't been for the dog, at all. But was it really any of my business, and did it really make a difference in the cosmological scheme of things? I answered both questions with an unhesitating No, and I felt that I had learned more from that brief colloquy with myself than from my two hours of blood-letting meditation.

In those days I used to give a lot of thought to the philosophy of eating; not in the Brillat-Savarin sense of *gourmandiserie*, but rather in moralistic terms. Having eliminated animals from my diet, I began to fret about the plants. I read the disturbing phrase "vegetable scream" somewhere, and I began to worry that picking a bean from the vine or a cherry from the tree might cause the plucked object to experience pain and even sorrow. Perhaps, I thought, the only truly harmless menu would consist of those fruits and vegetables and grains which had dropped to earth of their own accord. Since I was living in the middle of Kyoto at the time, my path was not exactly littered with free-falling manna, and I soon amended the "do absolutely no harm" doctrine to "do as little harm as possible."

Once, when I first came to stay at Kaiko-in, the Okusan cooked a batch of rice mixed with minuscule fish, each one about the size of a fingernail paring. She brought me a dish of the rice, and after she had left I stared in horror at the horde of tiny bodies. I was hungry, but I couldn't bring myself to eat the dead fish, so I carefully picked them all out. The process reminded me of one of those fairy tales in which the heroine is given some impossible task (count all the grains in a bushel of millet, before dawn) and is assisted by some friends from the insect kingdom. No ants or termites showed up to help me with my fairy-tale task, but by the time I was finished the bowl of rice contained only a few suspicious black specks—eyes, perhaps, or microscopic fishhearts.

I wrapped the deleted fish in a tissue and ate the rice, and when I returned the empty bowl to the kitchen the Okusan said, "Oh, good, you ate every bit! Would you like seconds?"

Three months later, I had begun to see that a hundred tiny fish were just a few drops of water under the digestive bridge. I almost hoped the Okusan would bring me another bowl of fishy rice, so I could eat it, miniature corpses and all, in front of everyone. In retrospect, one of the most valuable lessons I learned during my stay at Zenzenji was that it is egocentric folly to attach a greater value to your gastronomic idiosyncrasies than to the feelings of other people, even if they unwittingly offer you something that has not been approved for passage through your sigmoid flexure. As my attitude toward eating became less rigid, I found it increasingly difficult to tolerate the self-absorbed dietary zealots who spent the majority of their time worrying about the purity of their cloacal chambers. I was ashamed to recall that I, too, at the nadir of my digestive egomania, had once chosen to disappoint someone who had baked me a plate of sugar cookies rather than risk polluting my pristine macrobiotic system with a few grains of glucose and a speck or two of unfertilized "chicken embryo."

One day, after a long bicycle ride to the west side of Kyoto in search of gold-flake paint, I wandered into a little grocery store looking for a snack to sustain me till I got home. There were boxes of coconut wafers, bags of rice crackers, bananas, and net bags filled with tangerines. I felt hungry enough to eat them all, and more. I had just about settled on a bag of shiso-speckled senbei, a plastic jug of tea, and a juggler's stack of mandarin oranges, when something in the display case caught my eye. "What are those?" I asked rhetorically, but I already knew.

"Jamupan," said the elderly man behind the counter. "Just like you eat in America!" He had long yellowish-white hair, the color of antique piano keys, and he wore a white strap T-shirt, for the heat.

"Why, so they are," I said, feigning small-world surprise. "I'll take four, please."

"Would you like something to drink? The jamupan are a trifle dry," the old man said as he wrapped my package (pink paper, hospital corners, hairy green string).

"No, that's all right," I said. The drier the better, I thought grimly.

I rode my bicycle onto the grounds of a nearby temple and found a sunny hillock overlooking a green-glazed duck pond. I chanted the appropriate mealtime chants and put a larger-than-necessary piece of the eggy yellow bread aside for the hungry ghosts. The strawberry filling reminded me of my melted-cats dream, but I was paying for a different sin today.

The buns weren't nearly as bad as I had expected; with a large mug of tea, they would have made a tolerable snack. Four was too many for anyone to choke down at one sitting, though, but that was the point. I was happy to exchange my nagging regret for a stitch in the stomach, for as any serious self-abnegator knows, penance is the Pepto Bismol of the soul.

On the way up the hill to Kaiko-in I met Toku-san, out walking the dog. "Where have you been?" he asked.

"To the other side of town," I said.

"And what did you do?" I was tempted to pour out the self-aggrandizing tale of my penitential tea-less snack, but then I remembered the lesson I had learned. Inji-gyo, I reminded myself: secret virtue.

"Oh, nothing much," I said.

Toku-san smiled, that wise, wry sapient smile. "Let's go, Shiro," he said, and they went.

GOOSEFLESH
ABBEY REVISITED

I, you know, am partly nun
Often drawn to ceremonies
Of escape . . .
                    (Kyoto, 1970)

—KYOTO

The public bath house had a long narrow mirror along one wall, above the hot and cold water taps. I used to wonder about the purpose of that mirror, for when I sat on one of the little wooden stools and rinsed the soap from my body with brassbound-cedar bucketfuls of water (the required pre-immersion ritual) all I could see reflected was my embarrassingly opulent Occidental torso. Eventually I realized that while the mirror was at sternum-level for me, it was at eye level for the Japanese women who patronized the bathhouse. I saw them peering into it as they washed; occasionally, a woman would lather her entire face and shave, like a man, for Japanese standards of beauty do not celebrate gently-waving fields of female facial hair. Still, I couldn't help seeing the reflection of my decapitated naked body as a metaphor for the way too many men perceive too many women: as headless, brainless torsos, objectified odalisques of lust.

There's something about a visiting a public bath that fosters reflection in the mind, as well as in the mirror. Surely there is a tale, in some old mulberry-paper book, of a struggling Zen acolyte who found satori in a steamy bath: hot water as midwife of insight. The Japanese love the bath-womb, and I wouldn't be surprised to hear that there is a sect somewhere practicing *onzen* (the Zen of heat) at a deep-mountain *onsen* (hot spring).

On this particular summer evening, as I languished in the bath in preparation for my long-awaited and much-considered reunion with Yukio, I wasn't thinking about the human male as satyr, or the human female as object of purely carnal interest. Instead, I was wondering how virgins used to be prepared for sacrifice. I imagined that they were bathed in flower-filled tubs by ladies-in-waiting murmuring madrigals, then anointed with essence of gardenia, made slightly drunk with blackberry wine, dressed in rainbows of woven silk, and led off to the torchlit altar to meet the beast of darkness.

As I performed my own version of this ritual with Ivory soap, seaweed shampoo, and a disposable razor, I couldn't help thinking that it should have been more ceremonial and more august. Of course, the parallel wasn't really accurate at all, for not only was Yukio the antithesis of the Beast, offering him my virginity was not a sacrifice at all. The true sacrifice, now that I was absolutely certain of the depth of my love and the purity of my desire, would have been to remain celibate a moment longer.

It seemed paradoxical and perfect that I had spent this, the designated last day of my life as a virgin, consorting with nuns. One day the previous week, as I was sitting at the back of the bus with my accordion-pleated sutra book unfurled in front of my face, I heard my name and looked up to see two shiny-scalped women in gray robes standing in front of me. One was Mochizuki, the senior nun whose head I had shaved; the other was the lily-like Yuriko.

Yuriko simply bowed and murmured "It's been a while," but Mochizuki reproached me rather loudly for not having returned to visit the nunnery, and before I got off the bus she extracted a promise that I would stop by on a certain day, at a certain time. Yuriko seemed more solemn than ever, and I thought I detected an odd look in her eyes (supplication? sorrow? desperation?). Once again I found myself speculating about why she had become a nun, and once again I concluded that she had been lacerated by love.

On the specified day, at the appointed time, I rode the red bicycle through the geisha alleys, along the streetcar tracks, and up the hill to Mumyo-in. I felt none of the sentimental-homecoming emotion that a return to Zenzenji, after even the briefest absence, always stirred in me. Rather, I felt an unpleasant tightening in my lungs as the old stranger-in-a-strange-nunnery anxieties resurfaced. The moment I slid open the door, it hit me: that indefinably oppressive odor of metaphysical mildew and philosophic funk. I longed to run away, but a promise was a promise.

"Gomen kudasai," I called out, and after a moment a petite young student-nun came to the genkan. She seemed pleased to see me, and my mood immediately lightened. The young nun led me into the dowdy Western-style sitting room and brought me a cup of weak, tepid, straw-colored tea.

"I came to see the abbess, and Mochizuki, and Yuriko," I said. "Oh dear," said the young nun. "Mochizuki-sensei is out, and the abbess is in Tokyo, and Yuriko—well, Yuriko is gone."

"Gone?" I echoed.

"Yes, one morning she wasn't at prayers, or at breakfast, and when I asked Mochizuki-sensei she said that Yuriko was gone, and that we should forget about her." Aha, I thought, romantic intrigue. Perhaps the man who broke her heart had walked all the way from Tokyo on his knees, and they had eloped together. I pictured the man as a glamorous cross between Yukio and Arasuke, with a sensitive face and a raffish topknot.

"Mochizuki-sensei will be back soon, and she said that I should entertain you, if you don't mind my boring company," said the nun, wrinkling her tiny nose. "Would you like to see where we live?" The young nun, whose name was Chieko, stashed the flowers I had brought in a wooden bucket (mauve clematis, purple coneflowers, and metallic-blue globe thistles, purchased from the neighborhood florist-philosopher). Then she led me through a labyrinth of dark, windowless wood corridors, out into a large tree-lined courtyard, and through the door of an ugly new ferroconcrete building.

"This is my room," she said, opening a door at the end of the hall. I was speechless. I had expected an austere tatami room, with blank walls and a single vase containing a summer wildflower. What I saw was more like a fifties-movie concept of an American teenage-girl's room, with pink-coverleted beds piled high with stuffed animals, and walls plastered with posters of archaic American rock and roll singers: Frankie Avalon, James Darren, Fabulous Fabian. They had all been popular when I was in junior high, but even then we had laughed at their prefabricated personae, their sanitized-Elvis pompadours, and their insipid, crypto-sexual songs.

The only hint that this was a room in the dormitory of a training school for nuns was the small altar on top of a bookcase crammed with comic books, women's magazines, and 45-rpm records. There was a figurine of the Buddha seated on a brocade doll-cushion, an incense holder, a bell, and a miniature book of sutras. In front of the Buddha were several offerings: a tangerine, a half-empty plastic bag of dried squid, and a box of "milk caramels" with a picture of Benten (the most lubricious goddess in the Shinto pantheon) on the front.

I pointed at the bag of squid. "I thought the Buddha was a vegetarian," I said, with a smile. Chieko blushed, and I realized then that she must have been nibbling the snacks herself; hence the opened package, and the depleted contents. When I turned around I accidentally knocked the container of candy off the shelf, and when I picked up the box I noticed that it, too, was nearly empty. "Like taking candy from the Buddha," I said. Once again Chieko blushed, and I wished that I had kept my jokes to myself. The trouble with impromptu wit, I realized for the thousandth time, is that it is so often at odds with simple kindness.

As we were leaving, Chieko's roommate, Izue, came back from the bath, dressed in a pink nylon robe and matching fluffy slippers. I chose to interpret this incongruous sight—an Oriental face with a shaved head above a classic pajama-party costume—as another disturbing bit of evidence that the Pure Land sect was at the opposite end of the spectrum of taste, aesthetics, and discipline from Zen.

On the path through the courtyard, we met Mochizuki. "Come, let's take a walk," she said to me, and Chieko looked relieved. We strolled through a nearby park, under blossoming tulip trees, past statues of generals on horseback and cages of peacocks. It was a perfect summer day, and the park was full of people; several times I overheard the muttered phrase "gaijin to *ama*" ("a foreigner and a nun") and it occurred to me that we were both curiosities, misfits, marginal players in this conformist, male-centered society of Insiders Only.

We stopped to eat at an alfresco noodle restaurant with a painterly view of the green and golden park and the archival city beyond. There were only two things on the menu, and they were out of one of them, so we both ordered "deluxe *ramen*," by default. When the bowls arrived I was horrified to see that the noodles were covered with a greasy pointillist layer of meat-broth, and garnished with lurid slices of red-edged *char siu* pork.

Mochizuki had insisted on treating me, so my new rule of giving the other person's feelings precedence over my dietary preferences was in effect. Gingerly, I extracted the noodles from the coagulating broth, being careful to leave the revolting bits of pork in the bottom of the bowl. While we ate, Mochizuki was lecturing me on the superiority of the Pure Land sect to Zen (she insisted, absurdly, that Zen was snobbish, lax, and corrupted) so I was amused to notice when we stood up to leave that my ostensibly herbivorous companion had devoured every drop of the meaty broth, and every shred of processed pork.

I couldn't resist letting her know I had noticed. "Did you enjoy the noodles?" I asked.

"They were all right," she said.

"I didn't recognize that brown vegetable with the red edges," I said slyly, and Mochizuki gave me a dirty look.

"That was pork," she said.

"So how do you rationalize eating the flesh of a pig?" I asked.

"I was so caught up in our conversation that I didn't even notice what I was eating," said Mochizuki. "Food is just fuel for the body, and the body is just the carapace of the soul."

"Maitta wa," I sighed, which in this context might be translated as "Touché," or "You got me."

As we walked back through the park to Mumyo in, arguing all the way, I knew that I would never see Mochizuki again—at least not voluntarily. All we had in common was a bit of shared Gothic history, and it was not a chapter I wished to recall. She seemed to find our constant clash of opinions stimulating, but I just found it wearisome. Besides, I was afraid that she might be planning to ask me to shave her head again. "By the way," I said when we reached the gate where I had left my bicycle, "what happened to Yuriko?"

"She left," said Mochizuki, in a tone which made it clear that it was none of my business. "I can't tell you any more than that." I suspected she was punishing me for giving her a hard time about the pork, so I let the matter drop. As I was leaving Mochizuki surprised me by saying that she had enjoyed our excursion and asking if I could stop by again before I left Kyoto.

"I'll try," I said, but I knew I wouldn't.

On the way home, my heart swelling as it always did at the prospect of being inside the walls of Zenzenji again, I thought about Yuriko. What did her lover think of her shaved head? Would she cover it with a wig until the hair grew out, or would she wear outrageous wide-brimmed hats? The Lily Child in love; it was a happy thought.

* * *

On the way up the Sodo slope I met Zo-san, returning from the market with a basket full of green beans. We stood outside the tunnel-gate, chatting comfortably about Ingen, the Zen monk who supposedly brought green beans to Japan from China. "Speaking of food, I hear you've been fasting," Zo-san said, "and I just want you to know that as long as the Zenzenji Sodo exists you never need to go hungry. We'll always be happy to feed you."

The phrase "go hungry" brought to mind images of starving children (and adults), and I suddenly saw my voluntary fasting as repellently self-indulgent and spiritually bourgeois. Before I could put this negapiphany into words, Zo-san channeled the conversation in a surprisingly intimate direction. "For the first two or three years after I entered the Sodo I was tense," he said, "but now my heart is full." He used the word "muga-muchu," defined by my ever-lyrical Kenkyusha dictionary as "the ecstasy of self-effacement." I said that I was concerned about finding the balance between being too ascetic and too worldly, and Zo-san said, "So was the Buddha! Just do what seems right for you, and you'll be fine."

That's easy for you to say, I thought; you're a perfectly luminescent Enlightened Being. What I said, alas, was: "May I ask you a question about Zen?"

"I don't know anything, but you're welcome to ask," said Zo-san, and even though I knew it would probably spoil the moment, I plunged ahead with one of my typical tortuous two-part queries. "What do you think Suzuki means by the phrase 'moral virility'? Is that in opposition to moral femininity, whatever that might be?"

There was a brief silence while Zo-san looked at me with his shining amber eyes. This is it, I thought: he's finally going to share one of the secrets of Zen. And that's exactly what he did; he handed me the vegetable basket and said, "Come and help me shuck these beans."

* * *

Later that day, somewhere between the blue hills and the green river, I stepped through a lichen-frosted bamboo gate. Genji Masamune, the son of a famous tea master and Fuji Mugen's best friend, had called to invite me to visit him at home, and I had happily accepted the invitation. "This house is three hundred years old," Genji was saying as we walked along the garden path between burgundy-leafed maples and yellow-green bamboo. "Of course, we've had to replace some of the plumbing." I laughed absently, for I was wondering what it must be like to have such a clearly-drawn family tree, to know that your ancestors walked up this same stone path on their way to practice the same spare, sophisticated ceremony of tea that now shapes your life and dictates your destiny.

I hoped that Genji wouldn't ask me where my forebears were three hundred years ago, for I would have had to confess that I wasn't too sure. Some were in Scotland, some in Bohemia, some in England, some in Ireland, while (according to family legend) others were gypsy outlaws, living on blood sausage and superstition in the Andalusian hills. I had heard talk about Cherokee blood, too, but I had too much respect for Native Americans to make that claim without substantiation. In an almost monoracial country like Japan it seemed untidy, somehow, to have such widely scattered antecedents, and I felt guilty about not knowing more about my eclectic genes and my garbled lineage. *It's half past the Apocalypse,* I wrote that evening. *Do you know where your ancestors are?*

We passed an elderly gardener with a bamboo rake, standing in the miniature garden by the detached teahouse, and I was reminded of the Japanese saying: "A tea master's garden should be as narrow as a cat's forehead." The old man nodded respectfully to Genji and addressed him as "Young Master." There was a small pile of leaves at the man's feet, but some remained strewn on the path he had just raked. I had read somewhere that leaving a few symbolic fallen leaves on a garden path was part of the Zen/tea aesthetic; but, I thought, what if I hadn't happened to assimilate that bit of information? Would I have made some crass remark about the gardener's competence, or his need for corrective lenses? My self-congratulatory glow faded as I realized that for every faux pas thus avoided, there must have been twenty others committed, unwittingly, through clumsiness and ignorance. What you don't know can't hurt you, I reassured myself, but what really concerned me, the entire time I was in Japan, was that what I didn't know might hurt someone else.

As expected, the house was unspeakably elegant: subtle, elemental, harmonious in every detail. Bamboo, in all its protean gold-and-amber adaptability (latticed ceilings, fluted walls, woven baskets) was everywhere, along with fine dark wood, hand-made mulberry paper, and smooth, matte plaster the color of café au lait. I was no connoisseur of Japanese art, but I could sense that the scrolls and furniture and ceramic pieces were rare and valuable works, each with its own history and pedigree and poetic associations. I knew that my hosts would serve tea before too long, and I remember thinking: if the main house is this sublime, what must the *teahouse* be like?

Sure enough, seconds later Genji said, "Follow me, we're going to have something to drink." This has to be the ultimate tea party, I thought as I bounced along behind him in anticipation. To my surprise, Genji led me not to the freestanding teahouse we had passed in the garden, but rather up three stairs and through a Western-style door with a shiny brass knob. "Please wait here for a moment," he said. "I'll be right back."

I sat down and looked around in amazement. My first thought was that if extra-galactic decorators had tried to reconstruct a typical American living room based on photographs from *Home Beautiful* magazines from the 1950s, they might have come up with something like this. The room was a short rectangle, with one stagey-looking lace-curtained window; it was furnished with two large chairs and a cumbersome couch, covered in black naugahyde and overlaid with multiple layers of antimacassars, petit-point doilies, clan-plaid wool shawls, and gold-fringed satin banners bearing the surrealistic inscription, "Rotary Club of Royal Oak, Michigan." The coffee table was covered with boomerang-patterned pink and gray Formica; on top of it stood a mammoth white-warted bud vase, and in the vase was a maintenance-free bouquet of yellow paper roses which could only have fooled the most myopic eye.

The walls were hung with the sort of oil-painting atrocities sold by the inch at discount-furniture warehouses; there was a dead-trout-with-banana still life, a gaudy gap-toothed clown, and a drab, desultory seascape. There was no fireplace, just a disembodied mantel wrought from ornate pre-molded plaster, hovering beneath a gold-veined mirror. On either end of the mock mantelpiece were two large glass jars; one

contained foil wrapped Hershey's Kisses, the other M&M's in most of
the physiological primary colors. Between these hypoglycemic book-
ends was a nightmarish parade of doodads, gewgaws, and knick-knacks:
a blue glass moose, a verdigris-encrusted model of the Eiffel Tower, a
miniature Statue of Liberty in the same moldy metallic green. In the
center of the mantel, like the high priest (or priestess) of this temple of
kitsch, stood a startling apparition: a naked, androgynous kewpie doll
with troll-like features and ankle-length platinum hair.

It was (and is) not uncommon for affluent Japanese houses to
include one grotesque "Western-style" room; like this one, most of them
bore no resemblance to any room I had ever seen, anywhere. I was trying to figure out how people with such a highly-refined sense of aesthetics could allow something so hideous to be a part of their lives, when I
heard the doorknob turn. Quickly, I replaced my look of consternation
with a welcoming smile.

Genji Masamune entered the room, followed by three generations of
stately women in spectacularly tasteful kimono: his grandmother, his
mother, and his sister. The sister, who had Genji's thick, dramatic eyebrows, bore a tray containing a floral-patterned teapot, five matching
teacups, and a plate heaped high with the fancy krumkakes and rolled
cookies that are sold, in octagonal tins, at the best department stores.

Genji's sister poured the tea, and I saw that it wasn't tea at all, but
hot chocolate. I thought of G. K. Chesterton's "vulgar beast," and
smiled; and then I realized, with a feeling of sheepishness and shame,
that all these Western appurtenances (like the Sodo's heartbreaking
jamupan) were for my benefit, and my comfort. Obviously the
Masamunes thought I would feel more at ease in the oasis of bad taste
that some interior designer had fobbed off on them as the apogee of
Occidental authenticity, than in their ancestral teahouse. "This is
exceptionally delicious cocoa," I said, and everyone looked relieved, and
pleased.

* * *

I hadn't seen Yukio for several weeks, and we had arranged to meet that
evening at nine o'clock. "I have something to tell you," he had said on the
telephone. "I have something to tell you, too," I'd replied. I assumed that
his news would relate to the difficulty, for an astonishingly passionate

man, of being in love with a virgin, and I had decided to preempt his announcement with one of my own: "I'm ready to explore the midnight mysteries, and I want you to be my guide."

I lingered too long at the bathhouse, and I had to rush home to change my clothes. It was a warm summer night, but I put on my long-sleeved full-skirted purple jersey dress because I remembered that the beautiful, brutish Kuri had remarked that no virgin should be allowed to wear such a sexy dress in public. When Yukio appeared at my door I was pleased to see that he had dressed up, too. He was wearing a summer suit of ecru linen, a tan-and-green striped shirt with a white collar, and a forest-green necktie, the color of the trees at Takao.

I had never seen Yukio looking so conservative, so dapper, so North-ern-hemisphere, and much as I liked his return-of-the-prodigal-gaucho look, I found this other side of his fashion personality very appealing. He had grown a beard and moustache since I had last seen him; the whiskers gave him a dashing samurai-desperado air, but I wondered later if he had grown them for the same reason that hit men wear sun-glasses at night.

Yukio didn't seem to be in a very cheerful mood, and he avoided making eye contact with me. I thought I knew why: he was nervous about telling me that I wasn't fulfilling his corporeal needs. "Listen," he began, but I interrupted.

"Let me go first," I said, and I launched into my semi-prepared speech, all about Fate and trust and timing. I expected some strong reaction after the line about the midnight mysteries: a kiss, a hug, a whoop of joy. But I was unprepared for the look of sorrow on Yukio's face when he finally raised his eyes to meet mine, and I was shocked to see tears rolling down his cheeks. He shouldn't be *that* moved, I thought, and then it hit me, like a sucker punch to the spleen: I had read the situation all wrong, and Yukio's news was not what I had thought.

"This is the hardest thing I've ever had to say or do in my life," Yukio was saying. "And your sweet, flattering offer has made it twice as hard. I can't tell you how tempted I am to just take you away somewhere and spend the night making incredible love, but that would just make things worse, and I would still hate myself as much (and probably love you more) in the morning."

I felt sick. "What are you talking about?" I asked, but even as I spoke, I knew. Sure enough, my jilted-woman's intuition was correct; it was a classic story of doomed romance, straight from a television "home drama." Evidently Yukio's mother had found out about our blossoming relationship, and had given him an ultimatum. He was never to see or communicate with me again; if he violated this agreement she would withdraw all financial support, forever, and cut him out of the will.

"If I wanted to be anything but a doctor I'd tell her to go straight to hell," Yukio said, staring down at the floor. "But vet school is so expensive, and if I had to work my way through it would take forever, and then setting up a practice costs a fortune, and I've always wanted to raise my children here in Kyoto, in the house where I grew up. You can't imagine how terrible I feel; I really do love you, and there is nothing I would rather do than travel the world with you, or even live together forever on some idyllic island, but I'm a prisoner of my ambition, and my heritage, and my dreams. And, I suppose, of my cowardice, too."

As I listened to Yukio's tortured monologue it suddenly occurred to me that he had not gotten dressed up for my benefit, either to love me or to leave me. He had another appointment that night. I could guess where he was going; there was a limited number of scenarios, and my natural suspiciousness reduced the number to one. "You don't want to be late for your o-miai (marriage meeting)," I said, and Yukio's Patagonian-sunset blush told me that I had guessed correctly. "God," he said, and the anguish in his voice was a small, selfish comfort. "You know me so well."

"Actually," I said, "I think I know your mother better than I know you, although I've never met her. It's so transparent: she wants you to marry well and properly, but not too soon, so she'll introduce you to a smart, beautiful, socially appropriate girl who also wants to wait a while, and then she'll pray that you will keep each other wholesomely occupied until the time is right for marriage." I knew I was talking too much, but that's what always happened when I was ambushed by cruel reality; I developed defensive logorrhea.

"If it weren't for my mother, do you think we could be friends, or at least maintain courteous relations?" Yukio asked.

"No," I said. Being friends would be too painful, and in the context of lost love, "courteous" is just "cold" in a three-piece suit. Casting about for an organic metaphor to show that while my emotions were devastated, my mind was still working, I remembered the unfortunate virgins and their sacrificial wine. "The blackberry vine doesn't bear, um, turnips, you know," I said, hoping the words would make more sense in Japanese than in English.

Evidently they did, for Yukio looked relieved and said, "I know exactly what you mean. Anyway, I love you too much to ever be your friend. Now close your eyes; I want to give you something to remember me by." I thought the memento would be a bittersweet kiss, but it turned out to be something more useful and, I suspected, much more difficult to part with: his precious, funky, putty-colored gaucho hat.

Yukio went off to his marriage meeting, and I went to bed alone, feeling ashamed and abandoned and chilled to the foolish bone. This is how it begins, I thought as I fell into a fitful sleep: the glaciation of the human heart. I had several erotic, supernatural dreams that night, about men I had never met; for some reason those strange dreams cheered me up, and the next morning I woke up feeling that it wasn't completely tragic to be a virgin still—in body, if not in imagination. At least Yukio had the decency to dump me before we made love, I thought, but I was still so angry with him that I had to hide his hat in the back of the futon closet, out of sight.

On a whim, I climbed on a bus and rode into the deep green countryside, to look at a Zen nunnery Mon-san had told me about. Maybe I should live in a nunnery for a year, after all, I thought as the bus rambled past old daimyo mansions and rice storehouses and sweet-potato farms. My stab at being a liberated lover of men had been a humiliating, heartbreaking failure; perhaps that was a sign, a stroke of cosmic career counseling.

The nunnery was located at the end of a country road. It was very small compared with the Sodo; just three one-story buildings with tile roofs and bell-windows, connected by open-air hallways and surrounded by a thick greenish-yellow grove of bamboo. There was a high wall around the compound, but the gate stood open. "Tombo-in" ("Dragonfly Temple"), said the antique wooden sign. Just inside the gate a young nun was sweeping the stone walkway. She didn't look unlike the nuns at Mumyo-in—the same shaved head and gray homespun kimono—but her aura was very different: humorous, radiant, contented, and calm.

The lack of surprise with which she greeted me (an unexpected foreigner in an ankle-length Mexican pinafore of ivory cotton embroidered with sunflowers) seemed to be another piece of evidence of the Zen nun's enlightenment. I asked her if it would be possible to walk around the compound ("Alas, no," she said) or if a foreigner might be permitted to live in the nunnery for a year ("Alas, no," again). "Well, then, thank you," I said dejectedly. I felt very alone, and excluded: a sacrificial virgin manquée who couldn't even get her size-eight foot in the door of a nunnery.

I pretended to walk off down the road, but what I really did was to climb the steps diagonally across from the nunnery, which led to a run-down country shrine. There was an altar with a few broken porcelain foxes, and a fly-covered plate of red beans with rice (supposedly a favorite fox-treat), and, as I had hoped, there was an unobstructed view of the Tombo-in compound. I was not accustomed to being turned away from the objects of my dragonfly-attention, and the rebuff had merely intensified my curiosity.

I sat down on an odd platypus-shaped rock and for the next two hours, I spied on the nunnery. There was an open-sided corridor which bridged the garden and connected two of the buildings, and most of the action took place on this raised runway that reminded me of the *hanamichi* ramp to the kabuki stage. I saw gray-clad nuns carrying buckets, nuns carrying tea-trays, nuns carrying baskets of vegetables. In the garden, one white-kerchiefed woman was mulching the exposed roots of a flamingo-pink azalea, while two others raked leaves.

The scene and the ambience were so reminiscent of the Sodo that I felt a great wave of longing to be a part of that orderly, predictable, uncomplicated life. I pictured myself planting lupines, pickling turnips, sharing tea and riddles with the wise Zen abbess. By the end of the second hour, I had made a decision: I would return to Tombo-in in a year or so, and sit in front of the gate, with my head bowed over my Bohemian baggage, until they agreed to let me in. Then I would stay for at least a year, to prove to myself that it was truly monasticism I loved, and not just monks, and mystery, and atmosphere. And yes, I would even let them shave my head.

In the meantime, in preparation, I decided to create my own secular nunnery, a personal, portable, self-contained Sodo. I would be a celibate, vegetarian, nonmaterialistic nature-mystic; I would practice forgiveness, ego-transcendence, secret virtue, and *dohzen*—the Zen of movement, wherein any sort of concentrated motion, dancing or gardening or martial arts, is thought to contribute to the pursuit of enlightenment. I had been very happy to discover this concept at the Zen library, for much as I loved the ritual and the aura of zazen, I was beginning to think that I, with my tendency toward foot-cramps, was not cut out for a lifetime locked in the lotus position. I might, I thought, even give my nunnery-without-walls a name: Our Lady of Perpetual Bewilderment, perhaps, or the Morning-Glory Cloister.

I stood up and stretched my legs, and before I started down the steps of the shrine I took one last look at the nunnery where I now felt certain I would live someday. "Oh my God," I said out loud. Gliding along the polished wood corridor was a tall, slender nun in a gray kimono. I recognized the gait, and the grace, and the gamine face: it was Yuriko. "Oh my God," I said again. So that was it: she had defected to the more challenging realm of self-salvation. No wonder no one at Mumyo-in would tell me where she had gone; they considered her a traitor.

Yuriko vanished behind a shoji screen and a moment later she reappeared with her arms full of bright orange day-lilies. Even from a distance, I could tell that her sorrow had been replaced by solace, and that her heart was full at last. The Lily Child in love with Zen; it was the happiest thought I had had all day.

ZENZENJI
BY ZODIACAL LIGHT

The decadent song of cicadas
The crick of the cricket in love
The buzz of the bees
In the honeydrip trees
The Sanskrit sky above
(Kyoto, 1970)

—KYOTO

As the purple-robed priest passed me on the Sodo slope, he gave me his usual look of incredulity, or alarm. I couldn't help seeing myself as I must have appeared to him: a tall foreigner with long loose hair, dressed in an indigo jersey and a blue silk skirt (subtly patched, like a monk's koromo), clacking along in wooden geta with red velvet straps, carrying a round serving tray of glossy scarlet lacquer. I was on the way to return the borrowed tray to the Sodo, at the Okusan's behest. I loved those errands, for everyone adored the Maedas, and when I entered the monastery as their emissary I felt that my presence took on a legitimacy and a dignity it lacked when I passed through the gates as merely myself: my wondering, worrying, always-hungry-for-something self.

I may never see him again, I thought as the long-lobed priest brushed by me with a curt nod, leaving a faint scent of cryptomeria sachet. I could picture his wife packing the starflower-colored ceremonial robe away after each use, scattering little silken bags (red, or purple, or turquoise, tied with gold and silver cords) of the intoxicating essence-of-cryptomeria among the lustrous folds. The sachet-bags (*nioi-bukuro*) were sold in a shop in Gion; I had bought several for myself and for gifts, and I liked to wander in whenever I got the chance, just to take a whiff.

"Welcome to olfactory Nirvana," I used to say to first-time visitors to Kyoto, as I led them into the dark, fragrant shop. "This is the smell of a medieval courtesan's bedroom, of a priest's secret storeroom, of an old geisha's memories." It amazed me that such a potent and paradisiacal aroma could be produced from mere wood chips. I thought the trees must have come from some enchanted forest: perhaps from the supernatural woods on Mount Kurama, the legendary roost of the red-faced goblins.

There was still a week until my departure for Tokyo, but already every outing, every encounter, every little ritual had taken on the bittersweet patina of parting. Even an unprecedented, novel occurrence—a First—was also, potentially, a Last. My last bouquet of purple balloonflowers, I would think. My last mound of jade-green sugar beans. My last trip to the library, my last visit to the marketplace, my last lunch here, my last supper there ...

"My last bowl of zaru-soba," I said to the proprietor of the Daruma Noodle Shop. That wasn't really the name of the place, but it should have been, for the proprietor was not only a collector of scrolls, statues, and other depictions of the patriarch of Zen, he was a live ringer for the old cosmic curmudgeon: domed, hairless head, intricately-sculpted Hindu nose, exophthalmic eyes. I sometimes fantasized that the gypsy I had met by the river might be the noodle-man's separated-at-birth twin, but I kept that farfetched thought to myself.

"I'm going to miss you; you're a loyal customer," the proprietor said, as he rolled out a floury circle of buckwheat-flour dough from which to cut the narrow noodles for my soba. Not that loyal, I thought guiltily. My first choice for lunch had been the hole-in-the-temple-wall restaurant, but it had disappeared again.

* * *

"This may be our last chance for a tea party," the Okusan said, later that day. "My mother is feeling better today, so we'll have it in her room." The Obaasan, hair combed into a low chignon, dressed in a heather-colored silk kimono that smelled faintly of cryptomeria sachet, was sitting up at the black lacquer table, looking alert but shockingly thin; her bedding had been folded up and stowed away, and I was touched to think that these preparations had been made for my benefit.

In the center of the table there was a gray crackle-glazed vase containing a single vermilion poppy with a granular, sentient-looking black center. I had only seen the much smaller yellow-orange California poppies, and I was captivated by the glamorous bloom. "What is this?" I asked, reaching out to touch a crenulated-taffeta petal.

"*Papaver orientale*," said the Obaasan. "*Keshi*, in Japanese. I like it because it's so bold, and so bright; it reminds me of a flame, or an asteroid." She explained that in order to keep the flowers from wilting you had to sear the bottom of their stems over a flame.

"Moths to the flame," I said automatically.

The Obaasan smiled. "Flames to the flame," she said, and just then the Okusan arrived with a tray of tea and caramelized-chestnut cakes. All day the images of that gathering resonated in my mind, and even now, whenever I come across the words *Papaver orientale* in a garden book or a seed catalog, I feel as if I am back in that pleasant, tranquil room, gazing up the vaporous valley, sipping tea with two of the loveliest women I have ever known.

* * *

"Well, my dear, this is our final session," Vasanthamala said as we did some double-jointed yogic stretches prior to strapping on our bells (*our* bells!) and climbing up on the stage. "You've made a great deal of progress, and I shall miss our lessons. I hope we'll meet again someday."

"Maybe in another incarnation," I said, and Vasanthamala shot me a quick narrow-eyed look, as if I might be making fun of her belief in the transmigration of souls.

"Perhaps," she said warily.

As we stamped our feet and chanted "Te jun ta ha te jun ta ta, te a te te a te te a te te a te ..." I couldn't help wondering what Vasanthamala's next incarnation would be. She seemed to be a principled, thoughtful, creative person, so perhaps she would be promoted to some higher life form: a dolphin, or a hummingbird, or a giant panda. After the lesson we drank glossy rose-petal tea, just as we had at our first meeting. Vasanthamala raised her white porcelain cup in a toast, then said exactly what

I was thinking: "We've come full circle, haven't we?"

"Yes," I said giddily. "From tea to shining tea."

* * *

"I can't believe you're deserting us," Nashiko said. "Nor I," said Shakudo Shacho. "Nor I!" "Nor I!" piped Chika-chan and Kiko-chan. We were speaking Japanese, for the benefit of the children, while we drank Uji-tea and feasted on the treats everyone had brought: sticky sweets and salty senbei and expensive out-of-season fruit. We had decided, in lieu of individual last-lessons, to have a mass *sobetsu-kai* (parting party), and as I looked around at the animated faces, I had a sudden vision of myself, gray-haired and bespectacled, still teaching illogical English-conversation idioms to a doddering Mr. Shakudo, to an elegant middle aged Nashiko, and to two charming young matrons (Chika-chan and Kiko-chan, all grown up) with two darling kokeshi-doll daughters of their own.

There would, I thought, be a certain satisfaction and symmetry in living in the same place all your life, practicing secret virtue and knowing that your funeral would be well-attended by people who remembered you when your hair was the color of the sun, and not of the clouds.

I thought about the elderly neighborhood merchants, the sellers of seaweed and incense and soybeans: the endearing personifications of the Japanese work ethic in its purest form. Most of them would probably die in the cluttered room-behind-the shop where they were born, without ever visiting the other god's-tear islands of the Japanese archipelago. What if I were reborn, with my taste for travel, into a family that ran a tiny, barely-profitable stationery store, one of those shops with green glass apothecary jars filled with primary-colored pencils and cuddly-animal erasers? Would I docilely take over the shop, counting out the tinny one-yen pieces into the customers' cupped-mudra hands until I died, or would I somehow manage to escape?

"Oh, Miss Teacher!" Nashiko said, waving her hand in front of my reverie-glazed eyes. "You promised we could play a game in English."

"All right," I said, trying to think of something the little girls would be able to participate in, and comprehend. "This is an original American invention, a little something we call 'Scissors, Paper, Rock.'" No one challenged me on this bit of tongue-in-cheek cultural plagiarism, so I finally had to explain that I was joking. (I don't know if they were being respectfully polite, for a teacher of anything is revered to the point of absurdity in Japan, or whether they thought it was just a coincidence that the same game existed in both countries.) We played several other games—Button, Button; the Name Game; Musical Zabuton—and it was antic and hilarious. The children beat everyone else handily, and I gave them little prizes: bunny-shaped erasers from the neighborhood stationery store, and a shiny copper American penny apiece.

* * *

Later that afternoon, on my way home from a final visit to Fushimi Inari, my favorite fox-shrine, I met Fuji Mugen coming up the slope. I hadn't seen him for weeks, not since I had been left at the sacrificial altar by Yukio and had decided to become a free-lance nun. Mugen looked me up and down (I was wearing my mattress-cover skirt) and said derisively, "You've been in Japan too long."

"Well, I'll be gone soon enough," I said cheerily, for I was in an incurably good mood. "In the meantime, would you like to go for a walk with me, maybe up to that hilltop temple?" I realized with alarm that dragon-fly-nun vows notwithstanding, I still found Mugen distressingly attractive.

"I'm busy," Mugen said coldly. "And I'm sure you have someone else to meet." I had no idea what he was talking about, and before I could ask for an explanation, he was gone. It was a disagreeable and bewildering encounter, and I was haunted by the unfriendly remark: "You've been in Japan too long." Was that an indictment of my eccentric costume, or of my entire being?

When I got back to Kaiko-in I noticed an unfamiliar pair of sneakers in the genkan, and I thought one of the Maeda boys must have a guest. But when I slid open my door and caught a whiff of M5 ("Men's Fashion-Toiletry for Civilized Hairstyle"), I knew that the caller was mine. Ah, I thought (for I was in my *fin de séjour* mood), the last unexpected, uninvited, but not entirely unwelcome guest.

Totsuo Takatori was sitting at the low table, playing with my current crop of cats, two yellow-eyed black-and-white beauties named Montsuki and Motherwell. (I had gotten reckless again, naming cats I couldn't keep.) "Hi," he said. "I had some free time and I decided to jump on the train and surprise you."

"You certainly succeeded," I said. "But you look so different!" Totsuo had grown a thin beard and moustache since our last meeting and I was reminded, painfully, of Yukio's bandito-transformation.

"Where are you staying?" I asked.

"At an inn around the corner," said Totsuo. "You'd like it—every room comes with its own resident cat. Mine is a calico with a short tail, like a rabbit!"

That evening we went out for okonomiyaki; we had a tiny tatami-room to ourselves, and we lingered there for hours. I sipped a bizarre soft drink called "Orange Crash," which tasted like undiluted citric acid sweetened with sucrose, while Totsuo tossed off mug after mug of *chuhai*, a potent alcoholic drink made from potatoes and garnished with mandala-slices of lemon. He was in rare form that night: singing bawdy folk songs from his native Kagoshima, reciting "The Love Song of J. Alfred Prufrock" in Japanese, doing a spot-on imitation of Joe Cocker in spasmodic concert, and saying disquietingly complimentary things about me. Every few minutes he would pause to work on a colored-pencil sketch of a futuristic cityscape of rubaiyat towers and turquoise topiary, his oil slick of black hair flopping over his eyes, tongue protruding from one side of his mouth in child-like concentration.

As I watched him draw, I thought about the mysteries of romantic chemistry. Totsuo was bright, funny, artistic, and undeniably good-looking, but for some reason I had never been able to think of him as anything but a friend. Perhaps it was his moodiness (for he could be suddenly cruel and aloof); maybe it was the difference in values (he was a cynic, a miser, and an arrogant atheist); it could even have been the noxious brilliantine. Just as I was congratulating myself on having managed to convert a potentially terminal disparity of romantic interest into an entertaining friendship, Totsuo looked up, his lower lip carousel-striped with red and turquoise colored pencil, and said, "Let's go back to my inn and spend the night together."

* * *

The next morning we hopped on a wooden funicular train with green velvet seats and polished-brass luggage racks, and rode through farmland and forest to the end of the line: Kurama-yama, one of Japan's most magical small mountains, legendary home of the long-nosed red-faced goblins known as *tengu*. Kurama was one of my favorite haunts; the melding of natural beauty (deep woods, celestial vistas) with deliciously complex mythology (snake-women, tiger-gods, flying pyromaniacs) always left me feeling exalted and inspired. Totsuo, it turned out, was not only an atheist but a mythophobe as well.

"Don't you believe in tengu?" I asked, as we trudged up the thousand-step stone staircase to the vermilion temple. "I believe in money, and alcohol, and art, and love," said Totsuo.

I glared at him. "Two out of four isn't bad," I said.

"Oh yeah?" he retorted. "Which two?" In retrospect, I should have realized that the moody, pragmatic Totsuo was not an ideal companion for a fanciful pilgrimage. On this day he alternated between surly silence and cryptic sarcasm, obviously intent on punishing me for having declined (very politely) to spend the previous night with him at his inn.

By mid-afternoon I was thoroughly fed up with Totsuo's churlish company. "I have an idea: let's walk back to Kyoto," I said disingenuously as we approached the open-air station. It was at least five miles, maybe even ten, and I was certain that Totsuo would opt to take the train, thus giving me some time to myself.

"That's a terrific idea," he growled, with a degree of hypocrisy that made my self-serving proposal seem utterly sincere. "Just let me get some cigarettes."

So we walked back to Kyoto, following the mutable liquid boulevard of the Kamo River. Mostly we traipsed along in silence, but Totsuo occasionally stopped to light a match or strike a pose—arms akimbo, beautiful cold face wreathed in smoke from the cigarette in his old-fashioned pewter holder—and lob an insult in my direction. (I remember "You're no fun," and "You'll probably die a desiccated spinster.") I was lost in my own rueful thoughts when Totsuo suddenly pointed at the hazy skyline and said, "Look, there's Kyoto Tower; we made it. Let's take a taxi the rest of the way. I'll even pay for it."

"No," I said stubbornly, "we've come this far, and it won't be an adventure if we don't walk every step of the way."

"Fine," snapped Totsuo. "*You* have an adventure. I'm going to take a cab, and when you get back, I'll be gone." And so he was, to my great relief. I didn't learn anything new about the boy/girl gavotte from that horrendous outing, but that was the day when I first began to understand the vertical wisdom of traveling alone.

* * *

More finality: my last visit to the post-medieval mansion of Gordon
Coyne. When I arrived, Gordon was busy showing his wares to a bevy of
well-dressed American antique collectors, so he led me into a sunny
room full of art supplies and said, "I know you won't mind entertaining
yourself for a while." Mind? I was in dilettante heaven, surrounded by
reams of colored paper, racks of bamboo brushes, and the intoxicating
smells of oil paint, turpentine, acrylic glaze and toxic fixative. I found a
roll of rough, thirsty black paper and a fat badger-hair brush and a jar of
gold paint, and I began to copy sutras from my kyo-hon onto the paper,
in amateurish but ecstatic calligraphy. It was such a transporting activity
that Gordon had to call my name three times before I looked up. "The
girl with the golden arms," he said, laughing, and I ran to the kitchen to
wash off my inadvertent gilded tattoos.

Ayame Tanbo had made an elegant afternoon tea, with raisin-stud-
ded scones and strawberries in cream and Scottish stem-ginger biscuits
and Darjeeling tea, brewed from aromatic leaves and served in Ch'ing-
dynasty cups patterned with short-robed, long-whiskered sages. "How
would you ever live without Ayame?" I asked, when she had left the
room.

"I wouldn't," Gordon replied. "I have the garbage, and she has the
garbage pail."

Afterwards, with a goosebump-producing recording of *Carmina
Burana* playing in the background, Gordon told my fortune. "Hmmm,"
he said, peering at the soggy clot of tea leaves in the bottom of my cup.
"I see you becoming a herbalist." He squinted and shook the cup. "Or
perhaps a hermit."

"Maybe I'll end up living alone with a garden full of basil and
spearmint and lemon balm," I said, not unprophetically. While Gordon
placed a call to a *tansu* collector in Dunedin, New Zealand, I headed for
the bathroom. There was sandalwood incense burning in an antique
brazier with heart-shaped holes, and on the counter a book was lying
open, with these lines underlined in navy-blue ink: *And through thick
woods one finds a stream astray/So secret that the very sky seems small/I
think I will not hang myself today.* G. K. Chesterton again; always a
source of great quotations, though I was still puzzled by the apparent
bigotry of the phrase "Tea, *although* an Oriental." I jotted the secret-

stream quote down in my journal, to be used as a mood restorative some day when I wasn't feeling quite so chosen, or so cheerful.

Before I left Kyoto, the Okusan had asked me what time I expected to be back. This was unusual, for she had never inquired about my plans before. "I don't know exactly," I said.

"Well," said the Okusan, "do you think you could be here by seven o'clock? I want to show you something."

"Of course," I said, but I was mystified. What did she want to show me on such a precise timetable? An eclipse? A comet? A night-blooming cereus?

I was planning to catch the six o'clock train in order to be at Kaiko-in by seven, but just as I was about to embark on the long walk to Ashiya station, Auden Fujinami, Gordon Coyne's repatriated–nisei business partner, showed up with an American couple in tow. Auden made the introductions in the genkan, and when they heard that I lived in a temple, the new arrivals said, "Oh, please tell us about it before you go!" I looked pleadingly at Auden and he said, "Don't worry, I'll drive you to the station in plenty of time to make your train."

Would I have stayed if the American man's face had not been so beautiful, and so familiar? (He had had a major role in one of the most popular musicals in Broadway/Hollywood history.) It was a sensuous, stoical, Aegean-samurai face, sandwiched between an anvil-shaped haircut and an inhumanly lithe, smooth-muscled body. His companion was a long-haired, long-legged dancer with the kind of shockingly lovely features that cause even the most inventive writers to spout clichés without shame: doe-eyes, raven tresses, rosebud-lips, alabaster skin. What impressed me most about the handsome couple, though, was not their extraordinary physical charisma but their almost awestruck curiosity about what they called my "exotic lifestyle," as if the bright lights of Broadway were some parochial outpost.

"Sorry I can't give you a lift, but my palanquin's in the shop," Gordon joked as Auden and I rushed off to the station. I had gotten caught up in the conversation, and had neglected to watch the time. We sped through the narrow alleys in Auden's blue Peugeot, but his performance-driving was in vain; I missed the six o'clock train by a good ten minutes. The next train was at six-thirty, and even though I spent my whole week's wages on a cab from Kyoto Station I was still almost half an hour late. Oh dear, I thought, what if the Okusan needed me for something important right at seven o'clock? She has always been so kind and generous to me, and she's never asked me for anything before; how could I have been so irresponsible?

I burst through the gate and into the genkan, calling out, "I'm home; sorry to be so late!" Even after my eyes had adjusted to the dim light, it took my brain a moment to make sense of the unusual scene before me. The big peacock-doored room at the far end of the wide tatami-hall was open, and sitting there, seraphic in the seance-light from a forest of votive candles, were some of my favorite people in the world: all of the Maedas (except for the Obaasan, who had gone to sleep early), Toku-san and Zo-san ("representing the Sodo"), Madoka Dekiboshi, Mr. Shakudo, Inaka Hakamune. The faces turned in my direction, like a bed of heliocentric marguerites stretching toward a phantom sun, and then I saw the platters and dishes of food and realized that this was a surprise party, for me.

"You're incredibly tardy," said Mondo. "We were about to start without you!" I apologized again and then explained what had happened, and since everyone (including the monks) had seen the film version of the famous musical, I was soon forgiven. The table was set with the Okusan's best china and lacquerware, and the serving dishes were filled with my favorite foods.

There was rice with green peas; miso soup with elfin squares of tofu, tiny button mushrooms, and shiso leaves; deep-fried bean-curd-and-vegetable croquettes from the tofu-man; oden (boiled potatoes, eggs, shiitake mushrooms, and bow-tie konbu seaweed, anointed with pungent Chinese mustard); cucumber-and-sesame sushi-rolls; crisp, lacy tempura of sweet potatoes, carrots, string beans, and wheel-shaped lotus roots; and a secondary-color rainbow of pickled cabbage, eggplant, and turnips. It was the most considerate, carefully thought-out menu I had ever seen, and I realized that every time the Okusan had brought me a snack and then asked solicitously, "Did you like that?" it was all leading up to this touching farewell feast.

"I didn't deserve this at all," I said at the end, as we were sitting around sipping green tea and crunching translucent crescents of nashi (Japanese pear).

"That's for sure," said Mondo, and everyone laughed.

* * *

My passage to America had already been arranged; the Slovenian freighter was scheduled to depart from Yokohama on the day after summer school ended in Tokyo, so there wouldn't be time to return to Kyoto to say goodbye. I was looking for closure, for conclusions, for easy epiphanies, for the *reductio ad absurdum*, or *de profundis*: "I went to Japan to get away from Zen, but Fate found me a room in a temple, and I fell in love with the Sodo, and this is what I learned ..." I had an image of how my days at Zenzenji should end: with a great flowering forth of love and understanding and resolution, a sort of emotional satori. I envisioned a gathering in the kitchen of the Sodo with everyone milling around, whispering farewells and benedictions and cosmic truths, and then I imagined Mugen appearing in the door, luminous and demonic, to escort me to my midnight train.

But it didn't happen like that at all. For one thing, the train I had decided to take left at noon; for another, no one seemed to want to cooperate in my quest for a symmetrical conclusion. "You'll be back," the monks said offhandedly, as if they knew more about my itinerary than I did.

"I'll say so long, but not goodbye," Toku-san said on my next-to-last day, as he stood silhouetted in the gateless gate with the rosy-mauve sunset behind him. (I had just returned from Kobe, where I had found Montsuki and Motherwell—my Last Kittens—a home on a freighter bound for Piran.) "That's fine," I said. "I'm planning to come back in a year, to live at Tombo-in."

"Don't waste your time in a nunnery," said Toku-san. "Women can't become Buddhas, anyway. Why don't you come back with a husband instead?"

Only the women of Kaiko-in seemed to realize that I was going far away, for a long time. The Okusan (apologizing in her soft voice for the humbleness of the gift) gave me two lovely notebooks covered with hand-made paper and decorated with her delicate twelfth-century calligraphy. "The Obaasan has a present for you, too," she said, and she led the way to the room where we had such lively, unforgettable tea parties.

The Obaasan was lying under her gray silk futon, looking even frailer and more diminished than the last time I had seen her. "Please plant these in America," she said, and she handed me two packets of seeds: morning glories and Oriental poppies. I thanked her and said that I was looking forward to seeing her again when I returned to Japan. The

Obaasan smiled wearily, closed her eyes, and shook her head, and then the Okusan signaled that it was time to leave.

"Is the Obaasan sick?" I whispered as we tiptoed, single file, down the narrow hall.

"No," said the Okusan. "I think she's just very, very tired."

* * *

Finally, the night before I left, the last zazen session. I hadn't expected them to retire my burgundy zabuton, but I was a little disappointed that no one seemed to know or care that I was leaving. I was so filled with emotion at the thought of saying farewell to Zenzenji that I found it impossible to concentrate; I kept flicking my eyelids up to sneak a peek at the mesmerizing scene of meditating monks before me. Later that evening, I wrote: *If memory were strong enough I think I would travel halfway around the world just to experience the overwhelming clarity, calm, and joyful familiarity of sitting in the Zendo in the diaphanous blackberry-dark. Such a beautiful, pure, never-to-be-fathomed world, and I am honored to have been allowed to teeter clumsily on its periphery for this bittersweet sip of time.*

Den-san was the jikijitsu on duty; he must have sensed the fragmentation of my thoughts, for halfway through the session he loomed in front of me. In response to my request, he struck me on both shoulders with particular force, and I was especially grateful. When the lights went on I sat blinking, reluctant to get up and leave, and then suddenly Toku-san was standing before me, holding a basket. "*Pan,*" he growled. "Bread."

I reached out and took one of the gold-glazed rolls, said "Itadaki-masu," and bit into it, and there it was: a taste, at least, of the symbolic summation I was seeking. The roll was filled with strawberry preserves: jamupan! Was it coincidence, or did Toku-san plan that last-night snack as a circular completion, sweet sticky redemption for one of my gaudiest gaffes? Either way, I think the jamupan cycle may have taught me something about how to bend without breaking, particularly in relation to principles of diet. As my old friend Ursula used to say: "*Je plie, mais je ne me romps pas.* But boy, do I *plie!*"

The last dawn, the last dusk, the last frog-sutras, the last tofu-concerto, the last ripe persimmon left for the old man under the gate, the last scattering of seeds for the temple birds. Finally, the last glimpse of Zenzenji, looking back through the ancient gate as I set off to catch the train to Tokyo. The Maedas had gone out somewhere, but Mondo walked me to the corner, said a gruff "Later," and then sauntered back toward Kaiko-in.

As I passed Madoka Dekiboshi's house she came bustling out, elegant as always, but with her hands, face, and smock daubed with bits of paint in the colors of late-summer roses: carmine, apricot, ivory. "Here," she said, pressing a brocade-wrapped amulet into my hand. "I bought this at the shrine this morning, and I prayed for you to have a safe trip, and a happy life."

"Thank you for everything," I said, and we started to bow to each other, then Madoka said, "This is silly," and she gave me a quick linseed-scented hug.

I was carrying two suitcases, and I had mailed a boxful of gifts. "You don't have much baggage," Madoka said. I laughed at the inadvertent metaphor. "Most of my baggage is invisible," I said, and I had a sudden wishful vision of myself sailing back to America with both hands filled with bright rings of insight and completion, like that early-spring procession of yellow-hatted children on Cherry Blossom Lane.

Around the corner I crossed paths with three monks in begging garb: short black robes, straw sandals, faces hidden under big mountain-mushroom hats. One by one, as they passed, they said "Hooo," in a sort of three-part round. I recognized them by their dear, familiar voices, and by the shape of their sturdy calves: Den-san, Mon-san, Saku-san. They were on takuhatsu, so they couldn't stop to chat, but I didn't mind, for I had never been very good at goodbyes.

When I glanced over my shoulder at the retreating monks I saw that Saku-san, in sweet violation of monastic etiquette, was looking back at me with his hat tilted up above his broad, beautiful, smiling face. He tipped his hat, I waved, and then he vanished around the corner. I hailed an orange taxi and headed for the train station, musing about doomed love, fateful coincidence, and the peculiar perpendicularity of parting.

A PIECE OF CAKE

You be good, and I'll be as good as I can.
Rufus Perryman, Jr.

—KYOTO

Another law to live by: School always starts on a Monday, except when it doesn't. There was a long line at the Kyoto Station ticket window, and as I shuffled along with the crowd I remembered that there was some unopened mail in my bag. A couple of letters from family, a couple of postcards from friends, and a letter from Sophia University. I scanned it, expecting some dull message about unpaid library fines. *Due to a delay in renovations, summer session classes will begin on Wednesday, instead of on Monday as originally scheduled ...*

Wait a minute, I thought, stepping out of line. That means I can spend the weekend in Kyoto! I was breathing heavily at this revelation, the way someone who is madly in love begins to hyperventilate at the mere thought of seeing the beloved again. Laden with luggage, I went into a little coffee shop, ordered a hot lemonade and a vegetable sandwich, and reviewed my options.

1) Go to Tokyo as planned, and spend the extra time seeing friends and finding somewhere to stay.

2) Grab the nearest taxi and rush back to the place I adored. You can't go *om* again, I told myself sternly. (I had been waiting for years to use that joke.) *Oh yeah?* said my ever-defiant self. *Just watch me.*

* * *

Entering the incense-scented genkan of Kaiko-in, I felt as much a stranger as I had that day in early spring when Karen first called out

"Gomen kudasai" and Toozie thundered "Welcome to Hotel Satori!" "I'm back," I called out in a timid voice, feeling suddenly sheepish at having turned all the fine farewells into an anticlimax. Oh no, I thought, this wasn't the right thing to do at all. No one seemed to be at home, so I turned and walked through the tiny front garden—"no larger than the forehead of a cat"—hoping to return to the station unnoticed. I had done it again: gotten greedy for experience, and ruined the symmetry of the moment.

"Deborah-san! I knew you'd be back. Were the trains all full?" It was Toku-san, on the way back to the Sodo with Shiro frisking at his heels. *Perfect symmetry*, I thought. *This is more like it.*

"Um, yes, more or less," I said craftily, cloaking my deception in the useful ambiguity of the Japanese language.

"Good," he said, "then you can come sit with us again tonight. It's the last time we'll do zazen for a week, so it's now or never." I went back into Kaiko-in, deposited my baggage, and went for a walk around the temple grounds. Even as I gazed around at the beloved tableaus—children playing on the swings, white-kerchiefed monks burning leaves in a far corner, pigeons in the eaves, the old man asleep in his temple of rags—I felt, along with an affection that nearly took my breath away, a sense that it was time for me to move on to other places, and to do other things.

"Deborah-san!" It was Zo-san, coming back from the market with his bamboo basket. There was a white cloth over the top, so I couldn't see what he had bought. "I knew you'd come back," he said, his broad face breaking into that irresistible illuminated smile.

"I guess everybody knew except me," I said, and we both laughed at that for an inordinately long time.

"I believe that the ultimate aim of Zen is laughter," Zo-san said, and then he walked away. A few hundred yards along the path he turned to look back at me, and I saw that he was still laughing.

On the way back to Kaiko-in to change into a longer skirt, I saw an unfamiliar blue-robed monk standing by the signboard that said "The Gateless Barrier." He looked different from the unsui of Zenzenji, somehow, and then I realized it was because he was wearing sunglasses.

"Who are you?" he asked abruptly, in what sounded to me like Tohoku dialect.

"My name is Deborah, but—" I said, and before I could spew forth the appropriate pleasantries the strange monk interrupted.

"Oh, I've heard of you," he said. "Stray cats and Indian dancing, right?" "Right," I said, amused by the reduction-to-essence of my sojourn at Zenzenji.

"So what did you learn in your time at Zenzenji?" the monk asked, holding out a bag of green-tea-flavored hard candies. I took one and thought for a moment while the bittersweet tea-taste engulfed my taste buds. "I suppose I learned to keep on learning," I said slowly.

It wasn't a very glamorous answer, but even now, I think it's the truth. For while enlightenment may begin with a flashbulb-pop of revelation, conscientious being is a slow and often clumsy waltz (two steps forward, one step back; skip, slide, stumble, splat): the dance of life, lessons for a lifetime. Don't be a racist, don't be a bigot, share your wealth, be kind, be conscious, be honest, work hard, play harmlessly, beware of being enslaved by the pursuit of pleasure, be compassionate toward your fellow creatures (marauding slugs and flying roaches may require extra effort); vote, walk, read, conserve (remember the cabbage leaf); practice secret virtue whenever you get the chance.

The monk nodded, neither impressed nor unimpressed, and then he said "See you later," gave a nonchalant wave, and started down the hill. I thought of calling after him, "Wait! What did you think about what I just said?" but it seemed like a good time to start exercising some restraint, so I just watched his indigo-clad back recede down the slope, and listened to the mythopoeic clop of his clogs on the cobblestones. *Deus ex unsui*, I thought, but I felt curiously happy, and whole.

When I entered the Zendo twenty minutes later, I knew that the procession of penultimates and surprise reprieves was at an end; this truly was the last time I would ever climb onto the reddish-purple zabuton in that long room with its doors framing garden and graveyard. It was the last time I would look into the meditation hall and see thirty familiar faces, all intriguing, many beloved, all struggling (in varying degrees) to live by ancient rules in a modern, muddled world. I took in the gleaming heads, the glowing faces, the parchment-colored light through bell-shaped windows, the incense, the chanting, the bells. For once I wasn't thinking ahead, or behind; I was focused on the present moment like a hummingbird on a fuchsia blossom, and the moment was like nectar: clear and sweet and evanescent.

Reveling in my new clarity of mind, I began to meditate. Not on a koan, for I had concluded that the pre-natal face and the claustrophobic catfish in the impregnable gourd didn't have much to do with me. I thought instead about the gates of Zenzenji. Passing through them a year ago had changed my life forever, and leaving them behind would surely do the same. I thought about horizontal versus vertical knowledge, and about the gateless gate of Zen, and I realized that after all this time, Zen Buddhism was still as exotic and inscrutable to me as ever.

I remembered a phrase I had read somewhere, attributed to Flannery O'Connor: "She has the facts, but not the phosphorescence." What better metaphor for the attempted study of Zen by analytical Western minds? In my case, I suspected that what would stay with me was the phosphorescence, and not the facts. And that was as it should be, in the prickly, paradoxical tradition of the Zen sect, with its simple mysteries, mind-bending riddles, and exquisite aesthetics.

As I was leaving, walking along that zigzag corridor for the last time, the door to Toku-san's room slid open. "Enter," he grunted, and I entered. Toku-san, Zo-san, and Nu-san were sitting around the low table. In front of each of them was a small, opened single-serving bottle of milk, exactly like the bottles I had seen at the gate and been so scandalized by, back in my rigid-ideologue days. I had learned, somewhere along the way, that milk was not a forbidden substance, after all. In fact, the Buddha himself was supposed to have become enlightened while drinking a glass of milk, and it was in celebration of this that the senior monks traditionally shared a drink of milk at the end of a sesshin. But this wasn't sesshin-time, just an ordinary weekday session of zazen.

There was a fourth, unopened bottle at the remaining place at the table. "Sit," said Toku-san, and I sat. All eyes (brown eyes, green eyes, amber eyes) were on me as I fumbled with the blue foil seal on the fourth bottle. It had been nearly two years since I had yielded to the "cow's milk is food for young cows" argument and had eliminated dairy products from my regular diet. I picked up the bottle and one by one the three monks reached across the table and clinked their bottles against mine. "Cheers," said Toku-san, and that seemed to be the signal for everyone to drink the milk in one long gulp.

"That was delicious," I said, as I looked around at the smiling milk-moustached faces of the monks, and then I smiled too.

I still visualize that scene sometimes, and wonder what the subtitle should be. "How to bend, not break"? "Another completed circle"? "The

milk of human kindness"? Or, simply, "Mu"? Not bad, but I think Toku-
san provided the perfect caption for that comical microcosmic tableau
when he said "Kanpai!"

The next day passed in a festive blur, and then, once again, it was my
last full night in Kyoto. I had a reservation on the Sunday evening slow
train to Tokyo, and this time there would be no reprieve. Several friends
had come by during the day, but by six o'clock everyone had left, the
Maedas had gone out, and I was left feeling gregarious, sentimental, and
superfluous. That's what happens when you say goodbye and then
return, I told myself; you lose your place in the flow of things. I thought
of going over to the Sodo, but I felt I had used up all my coupons for
intruding on the life of the monastery. So I just went out for a solitary
walk, my final stroll through the enchanted landscape of a temple at twilight.

On the way back up the slope where so much had happened, I met
Fuji Mugen. He glowered at me and then asked, in the brusquest possible way, "Where are you going?"

"To America," I said dramatically.

"Right this minute?" he said.

"No, not until tomorrow evening."

"And where's your handsome veterinarian?"

"Probably with his fiancée," I said.

Mugen's whole demeanor changed, and I realized that he had been
jealous of Yukio. "In that case, come along with me," Mugen said, using
a friendlier verb-form and a more inviting tone of voice, and I went
without argument.

It was strange; I hadn't thought about Fuji Mugen that often during
the summer—maybe once a day, at most—but the moment I saw him I
felt the same strong attraction, the same fluid rapport, the same sense of
fateful connection as before. He took me to a long, narrow, blue-lit bar
around the corner from Zenzenji, a place I had never noticed, which
was owned by a former geisha. The stunning proprietress and her customers (all male) talked about me as if I weren't there, addressing cen-
sus-questions about my age, height, and nationality to Mugen. I thought
his answers sounded a bit proprietary, but I didn't mind.

Before I could say "I don't drink," a cup of warm saké had appeared
before me, and I took a token sip. My first thought was "This is delicious"; my second was "This doesn't taste all that strong"; my third

thought was "How can I be dizzy already?" and my fourth thought was: "Now I remember why I used to sneak out the window and drink beer with the bad boys when I was seventeen!" As I sipped my second and third cups of mildly sweet saké, I suddenly remembered that I had given up alcohol for the same reason I had postponed my entry into the sexual arena; I was afraid I might have the potential for liking it too much.

I hadn't been inebriated in years, and I noticed that as my gestures became grander and my speech more daring, my mood became less and less monastic. I felt giddy and reckless and blissfully detached; it was like astral projection with a touch of vertigo. "Saké is like liquid moonstones; that's why it's the official drink of the gods," I told Mugen, and he smiled, that demonic, angelic, all-knowing smile. I looked around the artistically-decorated bar and realized that everyone was beautiful, and everything was perfect. There was nothing in the universe I didn't understand, and no one I didn't love. *Maybe this is satori*, I thought. *No wonder Japanese people drink so much!*

A moment later, while reaching for yet another tokkuri of liquid moonstones, I knocked over my water glass. "Oops," I giggled, and Mugen stood up. "We'd better go," he said. "You know the old saying: 'On the first cup, the man drinks the saké; on the second cup, the saké drinks the saké; but on the third cup, the saké drinks the man.' Or in this case, the woman."

We got into a taxi, and I didn't ask where we were going, or why. All my values and inhibitions and behavioral ideals were suspended, and I felt more like a courtesan than a nun. I leaned against Mugen's sturdy shoulder and closed my eyes and watched my consciousness spin like a pinwheel, or a Tibetan fish-mandala. Mugen smelled of saké and smoke and the ubiquitous bosky sachet, and his presence affected me like some potent poem-inducing elixir of poppies. At one point, apropos of nothing, he spoke into the dizzy silence. "I'm strange," he said, "and I don't even understand myself."

After a long ride the taxi stopped at Arashiyama (Storm Mountain), a place of waterfalls and pole-boats and famous temples; during the day it was thronged with sightseers, but at night it was eerily deserted, and perhaps that is why Mugen paid a small fortune in cab fare to take me there. After we tumbled out of the taxi Mugen guided me gently along a dark, narrow path above a broad river, his hand on my nerveless elbow, talking about something: the importance of pure water in the tea ceremony, perhaps. I was busy with my own vertiginous runaway train of thought: I wouldn't mind having this man's child, I was thinking. I could raise it on my own, then return twenty years later and introduce it to its father. With luck, the child would have my height, and Mugen's eyes.

As I stumbled along I suddenly saw the opening of a novel on the blank screen of my mind. *Everything had changed, but nothing was different. The crumbling saffron wall was still saffron, still crumbling; the pigeons chanted the same susurrant sutras in the ancient pines; the same bells rang, the same wooden blocks were struck with the same antique mallets, the same incense perfumed the still, urban air. A bonfire was burning at the bottom of the Sodo slope, and my heart quickened as we approached, for the group of white-kerchiefed monks standing around, faces exotically underlit by the flames, looked so familiar, and so dear. But when we came abreast of them, and felt the warmth from the fire, and smelled the autumnal aroma of cypress-smoke, I saw that they were all strangers. They looked at us with mild interest—a tall Caucasian woman and her extremely tall son, a twenty-year-old with caramel-colored hair and Oriental eyes—and then they turned back to their fire.*

"Over here!" said Mugen, shattering my reverie. It had started to rain, and we took shelter in the shadows beside a tarp-covered bandstand. "The next time we meet, we'll probably both be married to other people," he said reflectively.

"In that case," I said, "tonight is our last chance to do this with a clear conscience." I leaned down and gave Mugen a brief exploratory kiss, and he responded with such velocity, ferocity, and force that I was stunned. A moment later I was lying on the bandstand, with a light rain falling through the overhanging trees, and Mugen was above me in straight-arm push-up position, looking down at my face and saying, "I've always known this was meant to happen ..."

* * *

When we got back to Zenzenji it was very late, and the big gate to Kaiko-in was closed. The smaller side-door was held closed by a metal weight suspended from the inside doorjamb by a heavy wire; it could be forced open, but the process made a horrible ghouls-dragging-chains noise that would have wakened everyone in the neighborhood. Feeling like a degenerate delinquent and an ill-mannered guest, I climbed over the wall, dropped down on the inside, and tiptoed through the loamy-smelling garden, past the glimmering morning-glories, blossoms demurely folded, waiting for the sun. After all the agony and ambivalence and meditation, I was thinking, does it come down to this: sneaking into the cloister after a wild night out with a worldly mock-monk?

Maybe it was the lingering spell of the saké, but I still felt more delighted than debased, more alive than ashamed. Besides, sly elliptical implications aside, I had returned from Storm Mountain with my virginity intact. Mugen had surprised and impressed me by saying, after a singularly passionate kiss or two, "I've never wanted to do anything so much, but I couldn't face my ancestors if I took advantage of an intoxicated gaijin." It may have been self-delusion, but I even thought that the monks —several of whom had expressed concern over my unmarried condition—would be happy to know that I had spent my last night in Kyoto being silly and amorous, not sitting solitary zazen like a sexless old frog.

I'll never drink again, I vowed the next morning as I steamed my eyelids open with a damp washcloth. I'll never ... I was on the verge of renewing my vow of celibacy when I was struck by a major morning-after revelation. Romantic love and sexual desire were the big guns in Nature's arsenal of species-propagating weapons; everyone knew that. But it occurred to me that perhaps the reason I was reluctant to give up the courtship-company of men was because I was meant to become a mother (among other things), and to pass on the genes of my forebears—some semi-famous, some infamous, all quite interesting—to a new generation. Or maybe Vasanthamala was right; maybe I really had been a temple harlot in another life, and I was working off my courtesan-karma in slow, easy stages.

Fanciful rationalizations aside, I realized that while becoming a nun might be a noble and brave thing for some people to do, for me it would be an act of cowardice, a ceremony of escape. My One Road was clear: to try to live in the world in a harmless, constructive, cheerful manner, and to make the hard daily decisions about what to believe, how to behave, who to love; to strive to struggle correctly while walking the ontological tightrope between the wanton sensualism of the devadasi and the lonely asceticism of the anchorite. After all, the Buddha found the Middle Way only after first trying the extremes of promiscuity, gluttony, drunkenness, vanity, and materialism; and, at the other pole, self-denial, self-abnegation, even self-torture.

As for Zen, I didn't regret a minute of the time—the exhilarating, excruciating time—I had spent in the Zendo, but I realized now that any enlightenment I might ever attain would come from living, from making mistakes, from thinking things through, just as the most valuable lessons I had learned in Kyoto about how to be a less-flawed mortal mammal took place outside the meditation hall. Perhaps, in attempting to fit my relentlessly rational Occidental mind into an elusive, intuitive Oriental discipline, I had been like one of the ugly stepsisters in Cinderella, trying to cram her size 10D battleship-foot into the narrow gondola of a 4AA glass slipper. No matter how intently I meditated, I was never completely able to transcend my analytical "Western lobe"; and in the end, I wasn't completely sure I wanted to.

Would my last-day conclusions have been different if I had practiced zazen the night before, instead of getting tipsy and reckless and rained-on with my all-time favorite well-dressed madman? I'll never know, and one thing my bedazzled dalliance with Zen taught me, albeit by osmosis, is that a wise navigator doesn't fret over the phantom path of might-have-been.

It rained all day on my last day in Kyoto, from dawn till dusk and on into the evening: an entire, seamless day of zodiacal light. Toku-san had poked his head into my room in the morning and said, "Don't forget to come over and say goodbye before you go," and now it was time. I felt very relaxed as I ducked through the low door beside the gate, for my perpetual nervousness had vanished when my love for Zenzenji was transmuted from covetous, needful desire into loving admiration and gratitude, and when I realized that it was not my fate to be a nun, or a female monk, or even a life-long practitioner of zazen.

There was a cluster of monks standing in the dim-lit kitchen, shaved heads shining, dressed in black; I wanted to hug them all, for a bow seemed insufficient to express how much they meant to me, but I knew such contact would be inappropriate. To my surprise, they offered their rough hands one by one for a Western-style shake. I was pleased to notice that their clasps were warm and strong, for many Japanese shake hands with considerably less firmness and sincerity than a Golden Retriever.

The final farewell was exactly as I had fantasized it should be for my first, false departure: everyone milling around and talking at once, saying everything except "Goodbye forever." Toku-san said, "Come back

on your honeymoon," and handed me a package which contained a
priest's ivory-ringed surplice. "You can wear this on Halloween," he said,
with a grin. Mon-san handed me a three-leafed clover and stared into
my eyes for a long moment, to make sure I got the message. Den-san
said, "When you get to Arizona, climb a red mountain and play
'Kurokami' and think of me!"

Do-san stood off to one side, looking slightly less fearsome than
usual, and once, when I accidentally caught his eye, he put his hands
together and bowed very low, like a member of the House of Commons
presenting a writ to the bewigged Home Secretary. Zan-san shot me a
humorous raised-eyebrow look, then disappeared into the night under
one of those beautiful bamboo umbrellas. Ryu-san, the Motown Monk,
said, "Please say hello to Percy Sledge and Aretha Franklin, if you happen to see them," then added in a whisper, "Only five months, nine
days, three hours, and forty-seven seconds to serve!"

Jun-san limped up and said, "Please stay well," and I replied, "You
too," though perhaps "Get well" would have been more appropriate in
his case. Saku-san said, "Uh, uh, the thrown-away cats are going to miss
you, and, uh ..." and I responded, boldly, "I'm going to miss you, too."

"It's all a dream," Zo-san said, "but it's the only dream we have."
Then he added, still in Japanese, "The next time I see you I promise I
will speak only English!" Také-san said, "Please introduce me to your
child someday!" and then Nu-san called me over and murmured something truly profound in my ear. At that moment I looked up and there
in the doorway stood Mugen, my laudanum lover, my lizard king,
dressed in a silvery silk kimono, looking very elegant and extremely jealous.

Later, at the station, he said, "What did Nu-san whisper to you?"

"Just the secret of the universe."

"Oh, good, I thought it was something important."

"Do you mean something personal?"

"Yes."

The slow train to Tokyo had plush seats the color of mustard greens,
and luggage racks of brass-studded oak. I climbed on the train, stashed
my bags above an empty seat, and returned to the open door. Mugen
was standing on the platform. "Well," I said, as I felt the train beginning
to stir beneath my feet. What to say, and how to say it?

Mugen solved the problem for me. "Ai shite'ru yo," he said. "I love you. I've wanted to say that for over a year, and I hope you understand why I had to wait until it was too late."

"I do understand," I said, "and I love you too."

I thought that exchanging declarations of doomed and hopeless love was a perfect ending, but there was more. Mugen took hold of my hand and stared at me with his limpid tea-colored eyes, and then he said, "If only you were Japanese, and you weren't quite so tall …"

"Then what?" I said, but of course I knew.

"Then we would be married, forever."

"Maybe in another life," I said, borrowing a bit of Vasanthamala's Hindu fatalism. Just then the train began to pick up speed, and our fingers were pulled apart. I looked back at the complex, charismatic man standing on the platform in his high geta and luminous ghost-kimono, fluttering a purple handkerchief, and I thought of a new variation on an old koan: What is the sound of one hand waving goodbye? As the train sped through the rainy night, past the swooping roofs and vermilion gates of twenty-five hundred temples and shrines (one of which I loved as my heart's own home) I could only marvel at the intriguing planet we live on, the endearing species to which we belong, and the amazing stories life writes for us to live.

* * *

Halfway to Tokyo, I awoke from a fitful sleep to find my train window filled with a glorious abalone dawn, pearlescent pink and blue with a river of silver along the horizon, like spilled mercury from the thermometers of a whole skyful of hypochondriacal gods. I stared blearily at the slowly-lightening sky, wishing I had paid the extra thousand yen for a sleeping cabin, and then I suddenly remembered what Nu-san had whispered in my ear in the Sodo kitchen amid all the valedictory handshakes and un-goodbyes. *"If you go to a birthday party,"* he said, *"be sure to eat a piece of cake."* All these eventful aeons later, I still find myself trying to live by those words of infinite wisdom: to keep an open mind, to try not to take myself too seriously, and not to be afraid to eat a little sugar, or have a little fun.

Japan's Modern Writers

BLACK RAIN

Masuji Ibuse
Translated by John Bester

Based on actual diaries and interviews with the survivors of
Hiroshima, a literary masterpiece about friends, neighbors, and a
city that suddenly ceased to be.

PB, ISBN 0-87011-364-X, 304 pages

CASTAWAYS Two Short Novels

Masuji Ibuse
Translated by David Aylward and Anthony Liman

The story of a castaway who travelled the world and returned to a
secluded island nation on the brink of westernization.

PB, ISBN 4-7700-1744-8, 160 pages

SALAMANDER AND OTHER STORIES

Masuji Ibuse
Translated by John Bester

An engaging collection of short stories ranging from biting satire to
wry lyricism. "A brilliance and humour which is frequently
memorable." —*Times Literary Supplement*

PB, ISBN 0-87011-458-1, 136 pages

WAVES Two Short Novels

Masuji Ibuse
Translated by David Aylward and Anthony Liman

A brilliant retelling of the 12th-century war between the Heike and
Genji clans. "Subtle ironies and unsentimental sympathy."
—*New Statesman*

PB, ISBN 4-7700-1745-6, 176 pages

LOU-LAN AND OTHER STORIES

Yasushi Inoue

Translated by James Araki and Edward Seidensticker
A series of tales about lost worlds and epic battles by one of Japan's
most popular writers.

PB, ISBN 0-87011-472-7, 164 pages

Japan's Modern Writers

TUN-HUANG A Novel
Yasushi Inoue
Translated by Jean Oda Moy

An intriguing explanation of one of the great mysteries of western China—how the sacred scrolls of the Sung dynasty were saved from the barbarian tribes of the Hsi-hsia.

PB, ISBN 0-87011-576-6, 216 pages

INTO A BLACK SUN
Takeshi Kaiko
Translated by Cecilia Segawa Seigle

"No other account of Vietnam has been so vivid, so intimate or so moral." —Edmund White, *The New York Times*

PB: ISBN 0-87011-609-6 224 pages, 110 x 182 mm

HOUSE OF SLEEPING BEAUTIES
And Other Stories
Yasunari Kawabata
Translated by Edward Seidensticker
Introduction by Yukio Mishima

Three short stories which center on a lonely protagonist and his peculiar eroticism. Kawabata explores the interplay of fantasy and reality at work on a mind in solitude.

PB, ISBN 0-87011-426-3, 152 pages

THE LAKE
Yasunari Kawabata
Translated by Reiko Tsukimura

By Japan's first nobel laureate for literature. "Seizes the reader's imagination from the first page." —*Village Voice*

PB, ISBN 0-87011-365-8, 168 pages

MONKEY BRAIN SUSHI   New Tastes in Japanese Fiction
Edited by Alfred Birnbaum

Fresh, irreverent, and post-Zen, an astounding collection of the brightest and boldest voices in contemporary Japanese fiction.

PB, ISBN 4-7700-1688-3, 312 pages

Japan's Modern Writers

RAIN IN THE WIND Four Stories
Saiichi Maruya
Translated by Dennis Keene

"A fascinating marriage of Borges and Nabokov with Japanese literary tradition." —*The Times Literary Supplement*

PB, ISBN 4-7700-1558-5, 240 pages

SINGULAR REBELLION A Novel
Saiichi Maruya
Translated by Dennis Keene

A quiet middle-aged businessman marries a young model, and her granny, fresh out of jail for murder, moves in with them.

PB, ISBN 0-87011-989-3, 420 pages

THE VOICE AND OTHER STORIES
Seicho Matsumoto
Translated by Adam Kabat

Six of the best detective stories from Japan's leading [late] mystery writer. An intriguing series of atmospheric mind benders.

PB, ISBN 4-7700-1949-1, 180 pages

ACTS OF WORSHIP Seven Stories by Yukio Mishima
Yukio Mishima
Translated by John Bester

Seven key stories spanning Mishima's entire career. "Beautifully translated... skillfully wrought." —*The Washington Post Book World*

PB, ISBN 0-87011-824-2, 224 pages

HARD-BOILED WONDERLAND AND THE END OF THE WORLD
Haruki Murakami
Translated by Alfred Birnbaum

An unnerving, fantastic tale of technological espionage, brainwave tampering, and the most lyrical sort of fear and loathing. "Breathtaking imagination and skill .... Sensational." —*Booklist*

PB, ISBN 4-7700-1893-2, 416 pages Paperback available in Japan only.

Japan's Modern Writers

SUN AND STEEL

Yukio Mishima
Translated by John Bester

Part autobiography and part reflection. "His literary testament."
—*The Times Literary Supplement*

PB, ISBN 0-87011-425-5, 108 pages

A WILD SHEEP CHASE   A Novel

Haruki Murakami
Translated by Alfred Birnbaum

"Haruki Murakami is a mythmaker for the millennium, a wiseacre wise man." —*The New York Times Book Review*

PB, ISBN 4-7700-1706-5, 312 pages

ALMOST TRANSPARENT BLUE

Ryu Murakami
Translated by Nancy Andrew

"A Japanese mix of *A Clockwork Orange* and *L'Etranger*."
—*Newsweek*

PB, ISBN 0-87011-469-7, 128 pages

H   A Hiroshima Novel

Makoto Oda
Translated by D.H. Whittaker

A surreal universe of people of varying racial and ethnic backgrounds struggle against the desecration of society and the environment symbolized by the first atomic bomb.

PB, ISBN 4-7700-1947-5, 218 pages

THE SILENT CRY

Kenzaburo Oe
Translated by John Bester

Awarded the 1994 Nobel Prize
"A major feat of the imagination." —*The Times*

PB, ISBN 0-87011-466-2, 288 pages